PIASA Books
are imprints of
the Polish Institute of Arts
and Sciences of America,
New York

Jan Lechoń in the library of his New York apartment.

Jan Lechoń

Evening on the Hudson
An Anthology of Jan Lechoń's American Writings

Selected, Introduced, and Annotated by:
Beata Dorosz

Translations by Various Hands

PIASA Books
NEW YORK
MMV

Jan Lechoń (Beata Dorosz, ed),
*Evening on the Hudson: An Anthology of Jan Lechoń's
American Writings*

ALL RIGHTS RESERVED: PIASA BOOKS
The Polish Institute of Arts and Sciences of America
208 East 30th St
New York, NY 10016
tel: (212) 686-4164
fax: (212) 545-1130
www.polishbooks.org

ISBN 0-940962-66-7

The cover designed by Mariusz Bargielski presents a fragment of a
larger work by the poet's friend Zdzisław Czermański, from the
collections of PIASA.

CONTENTS

On History and Politics

Jan Lechoń: Polish Poet — New Yorker with a Global Vision

INSTEAD OF A PREFACE
Beata Dorosz

The reader of this book may ask the question: for whom is it published? Who is the intended audience? It is addressed to those Americans who read at least one book by Czesław Miłosz. The picture of Polish literature and Poland in general cannot be complete if on the same shelf next to Miłosz's poetry we do not place a book by Jan Lechoń.

The history of the Polish experience with the Nobel Prize goes back to 1905 when it was awarded to Henryk Sienkiewicz for his outstanding achievement in the epic genre, and especially for the novel *QuoVadis*, which turned out to be an international best seller published and republished in many languages and filmed as a grand production in Hollywood in 1951.[1] Sienkiewicz's position can be described as that of an author of one famous book known all over the world, and otherwise unknown outside of his own culture. This situation is reminiscent of another Slavic Nobel Prize winner from 1958, the Russian Boris Pasternak, whose novel *Doctor Zhivago* became a world-wide sensation and was filmed in the United States in 1965 by David Lean.[2] Almost twenty years after Sienkiewicz, in 1924, the Nobel Prize was granted to another Pole, Władysław Stanisław Reymont, for his extraordinary peasant epic entitled *Chłopi* [The Peasants]. This text, however, was so infused with Polish history and culture that in spite of the prize it never entered the international book market.

The next commensurate Polish success came only after many years when Czesław Miłosz received the Nobel Prize in

---

[1] Directed by Mervin Le Roy, with Deborah Kerr, Robert Taylor and Peter Ustinov.

[2] Starring Omar Sharif and Julie Christie.

1980. At that time he was better known in the United States as a poet and a professor at Berkeley than in his native country where all information about his scholarly and artistic activity in emigration circles was strictly controlled by the Communist censorship.

The Nobel Prize for Miłosz was very visible, also for political reasons, as it was awarded in the year when the Poles expressed a decisive "No" to the Communist régime and fought for their dignity by creating Solidarity under Lech Wałęsa's leadership. Solidarity was not only an independent trade union, but also a space of freedom, patriotism, morality, and honor untainted by the scars of political slavery. The bestowing of the Nobel Prize upon Miłosz in such a special moment was perceived by many Poles as a gesture of appreciation for Polish achievements, and Miłosz became the greatest political and literary celebrity of that time. However ...

In fact it is from this "however" the present book begins.

Once there was a Polish poet known as Jan Lechoń (in reality Leszek Serafinowicz) born in 1899 in Warsaw. He was an extremely talented child whose debut took place very early, when he was still at school. Lechoń's early career invites comparisons to the very young Mozart and the teenage Chopin, whose virtuoso performances and compositions inspired admiration and evoked passionate applause from their audiences. Similarly, the appearance of a teenage Lechoń in Polish literature gave rise to the legend that continues to this day. The poet spent the last fifteen years of his life in New York City. He died tragically, in taking his own life in 1956; in doing so, quite possibly denying himself a Nobel Prize. In other words, I boldly suggest — inasmuch as my statement may sound controversial to some readers — that Czesław Miłosz remained the only Nobel Prize candidate in Lechoń's absence. The prize should have gone to both of them.

What is the mystery of Lechoń's greatness?

A brilliant début: the collection of poems entitled *Karmazynowy poemat* [Crimson Poem] which came out in 1920, soon after Poland regained independence after years of partition. The poem contains only seven miniature masterpieces and manifests unusual contradictions in the poet's feelings: he was captivated by the Polish past and national tradition, yet at the same time he reacted against the pressures wrought by this same tradition. The poems express anxiety about whether Poland would be able to rise from the burden of its tragedies and come back to life. These anxieties resonated with the feelings of the majority of society, which recognized in the young author its new national poet (*wieszcz*).

Before long, together with Kazimierz Wierzyński, Antoni Słonimski, Julian Tuwim and Jarosław Iwaszkiewicz, Lechoń became one of the founders of a group of poets known as "Skamander." This was the most important literary group in inter-war Poland, which not only affected the development of Polish poetic discourse as such, but also significantly contributed to the perception of the social role of poetry in Poland. Its popularity has not declined up to this day, and the "Skamander" poets hold their acclaimed position in the Polish literary establishment; they do not live only as monuments and encyclopedia entries, but are still alive, sought after, and read by poetry lovers and ever new generations of readers.

Since then, Lechoń's name has been continually associated with his legend. Over the years many elements have contributed to this legend and I can at least indicate some of them, such as Skamander's aura and popularity, Lechoń's unusual debut, his active participation in the highest political, artistic, and social circles of inter-war Poland (the Second Republic), his diplomatic career in France in the 1930s, his extraordinary personality, the atmosphere of scandal surrounding him due to his suicide attempts and his notorious homosexuality. War migrations, his politically determined emigration to the United States, and his absence from the literary scene of Poland (the postwar régime's censorship controlled every piece of news about him) and finally his tragic death in New York further contributed to the Lechoń legend.

Lechoń entered the European scene as a diplomat in Paris in 1930 where he achieved great personal success due to his intelligence, imagination and social skills. He arrived in this world capital of culture and art without any knowledge of French, yet, paradoxically, after ten years left it as an art connoisseur befriended by the Parisian intellectual élite and high diplomatic circles. Gatherings in Lechoń's apartment brought together the most famous representatives of the world of literature, art, and politics, such as Louis Ferdinand Céline, Jean Cocteau, Daniel Halévy, Serge Lifar, Misia Sert, and Paul Valéry. Indeed, his unusual personality and striking intelligence were decisive in expanding the range of his social contacts and his creating his "salon persona."

The defeat of France by Nazi Germany and subsequent capitulation in 1940 were probably the most important breaking points in Lechoń's life. The decision to leave Paris, and later Europe, meant a real departure. Symbolically it signified a farewell to the life style and the system of norms engrained in European culture, which formed him and in the development of which he himself participated.

After a year spent in Brazil, in August 1941 Lechoń arrived in New York. He was emotionally and organizationally involved in the Polish cause, but despite his engagement in public matters, he continued to be primarily a poet. Lechoń's poetry was deeply rooted in the national tradition and culture, but at the same time it connected to general concerns and, on an emotional level, intimately responded to the experience of the human condition. It was erudite and evocative of great cultural and literary figures and artifacts relating to famous world authors and titles which functioned in the mind of a learned reader as metaphoric shortcuts producing specific intellectual and emotional associations. It only seemed simple, due to its traditional structure, while in reality Lechoń's poetic language was dense with meaning, full of images and visions that were sometimes sublime and full of pathos, yet at other times struck the reader with the simplicity of a folk song. It would be misleading to notice only the captivating monotonous rhythm of Lechoń's rhyme. His verse deeply resonates with complexity and universal and humanistic values.

When World War II ended and the hope of returning to a truly free Poland proved unattainable, Lechoń tried to find his place in the United States. It is surprising that even though poetry was his main means of expression, he only wrote two poems relating directly to the American chapter in his biography – *Bzy w Pensylwanii* [A Lilac-bush in Pennsylvania] and a moving hymn *Do Madonny nowojorskiej* [To Our Lady of New York]. In other poems created in New York (his so-called New York poems) New York is absent, as if the poet, overwhelmed by grief for his country and his growing nervous crisis, did not notice the city and failed to render it in poetic language.

His *Dziennik* [Journal] on the other hand, in which the poet wrote every day from the end of August 1949 until almost the very end of his life (the last entry is made a week before his death), is full of American reflections. It is probably his most important work relating to his New York period, an invaluable source of information about the poet himself, the people he knew, and the events he participated in during this time. If read from a thematic perspective, the *Journal* strikes the reader with its fragmentariness: it is full of impressions, disconnected notes, and observations. New York architecture sometimes captivates Lechoń with its beauty, yet at other times alienates and overwhelms him with its grandeur. The *Journal* is full of sublime descriptions of American nature. The reader is struck with the depth of Lechoń's psychological and sociological reflections on American life, and the scope of his insights on current political events, literature, and art. Paradoxically, even though Lechoń constantly lamented his inadequate knowledge of English, he was quite well read in American literature and especially admired William Faulkner and Ernest Hemingway. He maintained that it was American literature that held the leading position in the world. He pointed to its influence on European prose and stressed its "moral sanity," for instance, in comparison to degenerate and corrupt French literature. His knowledge of film, art, and American cinema in particular was phenomenal — something he gained during the American period in his life, since when he lived in Europe cinema was never so popular.

Paradoxically again, this European — by birth, education, life style, and the system of values he believed in — proved his thorough knowledge of the history of America, its current political and social life, and the people who played significant roles in that life. Lechoń was also an avid collector of all past and present traces of the Polish presence in America and noted all such "polonica" in his *Journal*. In this context too, he admired America, and perceived it as an astounding melting pot in which all immigrant minorities fused together and functioned well as one unified organism, while at the same time not losing anything from their cultural identities.

Thus reconciled with America's otherness, and realizing that a return to a free Poland was unrealistic, he gradually started treating the United States as his new fatherland, maintaining that "This is a wonderful country for laborers, and for artists (who after all are an infinitesimally small minority) it is the country of freedom. Is it therefore not the best of all the not-best worlds?" (*Journal*, May 19, 1950) And earlier he claimed: "I think that every free person who feels a bond with the world, belongs in the end to every country in which he lives; if he is able to really love his country, he'll find something to love in others. My third fatherland, for which I long greatly — was Brazil, and America, despite everything, is ever more becoming a fourth. All of this is said with the *caveat* that we all have but one fatherland" (*Journal*, May 3, 1950).

It was necessary for Lechoń to stay in America for a few more years to become fully immersed in every-day American life. He closely observed American socio-political and cultural reality and jotted down his reflections in an essay entitled *Aut Cesar aut nihil*, which was written slowly and with an effort between 1953-1954 to be published in London in 1955. (It came out in an American translation posthumously as *American Transformations* in 1957).

The essay was a specific statement of belief in American civilization written with the enthusiasm and tone of a neophyte. In a sense it represented a polemic voice, which juxtaposed the concept of Americanism as a healthy instinct to the morally and spiritually exhausted Europe (and especially France). Lechoń stressed that, contrary to the opinions of the European (and again, especially French) intellectuals who were paralyzed and fascinated by the energy of the Soviet communism, it was America that offered a source of vital energy able to revive humanity.

Aut Cesar aut nihil is a full manifestation of one person's belief in America's world mission. It is an expression of a mature, deep thinker whose world vision is grounded in the social contract between employees and employers and the American model of democracy that Lechoń understood very well without being an economist. The text is a public expression of Lechoń's "American dream."

In *Aut Cesar aut nihil* as well as in his *Journal* the poet was constructing his *Wetlanschauung*, which from our present perspective seems more accurate than the visions constructed by many famous politicians of his time. It was Lechoń who demanded the truth about the Katyń Forest massacre, and strived for the freedom of expression and the untrammeled exchange of ideas all over the world. He reacted against the thinking of many free world intellectuals who were inspired by the ideology emanating from Moscow. He loved France and French literature, yet he never forgave French intellectuals and artists their "flirting" with the Soviet régime, its writers and ideology. It was Lechoń who continually attacked Winston Churchill's treacherous agreements with the Soviets in Yalta and hoped that America, under Eisenhower's lead, would sooner or later renounce the Yalta agreements as a dishonest treaty. Believing in Eisenhower and a United Europe he sensed that American politicians, through their political maneuvering (but, if necessary, by the use of force) would be instrumental in abolishing both the Yalta agreement and the Iron Curtain that it erected on the continent.

And so it happened. . . but Lechoń never lived to see it. A great poet, a deep humanist, a political visionary and a witness to his epoch, this great Polish and American patriot — defeated by depression and the combination of adversarial circumstances — passed away at the age of 56. He died too early, far too early to be noticed beyond a narrow circle of his readers and, perhaps, honored by the Nobel Prize.

If the non-Polish readers of literature are familiar with Czesław Miłosz and Wisława Szymborska (Polish Nobel Prize winners in 1980 and 1996), but have not read Lechoń, they only know the proverbial one side of the coin. Miłosz and Szymborska did receive the Nobel Prize, but ... the real poet Jan Lechoń was writing until the end of his life.

— Translated by Krystyna Iłłakowicz

I. *Selected Poems*
in Polish and English Translation

„Bzy w Pensylwanii"

Przed domem uschły biały bez,
Ulica szarą zaszła mgłą.
Smutek bez sensu i bez łez.
. . . *You know, you know*. . .

Lokomotywy nocą gwizd
Gdy się w tej mgle powoli szło.
I szary dzień, i smutny list.
. . . *You know, you know*. . .

Potem pod ziemią węgiel wierć
I sennie w barze patrz we szkło.
Co dzień to samo. I już śmierć.
. . . *You know, you know*. . .

"A Lilac-bush in Pennsylvania"

The lilacs at the porch are sere.
Grey fog, grey houses in a row.
A sadness lacking sense and tears
. . . You know, you know. . .

At night, an engine toots and clatters
As through that fog the men trudge slow.
Grey are the days and sad the letters.
. . . You know, you know. . .

They drill and blast; with picks they pry
The coal from dank veins far below.
They brood on barstools. Then they die.
. . . You know, you know. . .

— C.S. Kraszewski

Wielkanoc

Droga, wierzbą sadzona wśród zielonej łąki,
Na której pierwsze jaskry żółcieją i mlecze.
Pośród wierzb po kamieniach wąska struga ciecze,
A pod niebem wysoko śpiewają skowronki.

Wśród tej łąki wilgotnej od porannej rosy,
Droga, którą co święto szli ludzie ze śpiewką,
Idzie sobie Pan Jezus wpółnagi i bosy
Z wielkanocną w przebitej dłoni chorągiewką.

Naprzeciw idzie chłopka. Ma kosy złociste,
Łowicka jej spódniczka i piękna zapaska.
Poznała Zbawiciela z świętego obrazka,
Upadła na kolana i krzyknęła: „Chryste!"

Bije głową o ziemię z serdeczną rozpaczą,
A Chrystus się pochylił nad klęczącym ciałem
I rzeknie: „Powiedz ludziom, niech więcej nie płaczą,
Dwa dni leżałem w grobie. I dziś zmartwychwstałem."

Easter

A meadow-path, winding among the willows,
Through early yellow kingcups and milkweeds.
A thin stream purls by rocks and willow-trees,
And high aloft resounds the trill of swallows.

Through this same meadow, dewy with the dawn,
On this road, that once echoed with the lay
Of churchgoers, barefoot, Jesus makes his way,
His Easter banner in His punctured palm.

A peasant girl, with golden braids, walks toward
Him, dressed in homespun splendour. When she sees
Him (just like her prayer-card!), down on her knees
She drops and calls out, "My God and my Lord!"

Prostrate, in heartfelt despair at the Vision,
She trembles there. Then, gently bending, Christ
Says, "Go and tell the people: Dry your eyes —
The tomb's two days are past. And I have risen."

— C.S. Kraszewski

***

To, w co tak trudno nam uwierzyć,
Kiedyś się przecież stanie jawą.
Więc pomyślałem: chciałbym leżeć
Tam, gdzie mój ojciec — pod Warszawą.

Niech ci ta myśl się nie wydaje
Ani małością ni znużeniem,
Z największym kocha upojeniem,
Kto się z miłością swą rozstaje.

I nagle widzisz: jest noc chmurna
I niebo polskie ponad nami,
I stary ogród. A w nim urna
Z naszego życia popiołami.

***

It may be hard to fathom now,
But I've seen stranger things come true.
I thought: I'd like to lay me down
In Warsaw, Father — next to you.

Think it not petty lassitude,
This thought, for I know all too well:
He tastes love's best beatitude
Who to his love can bid farewell.

And then — a dark night — you discern
Beneath the Polish stars aflash,
A garden, in which stands an urn,
Containing this our mortal ash.

— C.S. Kraszewski

***

Od żalu nie uciekniesz, nie ujdziesz goryczy,
I każda twa pociecha — to widmo przeszłości.
Ach! czegoż się spodziewa i na cóż to liczy
Każdy z nas, co na tyle patrzał nikczemności?

I tylkoś jest zdziwiony, że jeszcze cię wzrusza
To drzewo całe w kwiatach, różowy wschód słońca,
I żyjesz, aby twoja nieśmiertelna dusza
Co dane jej przecierpieć, cierpiała do końca.

Cóż z tego, że, coś kochał — przemija jak dymy,
Że po tych, co odchodzą, żal serce ci tłoczy.
My z starym Sofoklesem spokojnie patrzymy
Na ten widok, na który chciałbyś zamknąć oczy.

STANISŁAWOWI BALIŃSKIEMU

***

There's no escape from sorrow, bitterness;
And every consolation — but the ghost
Of a dead past. What good then are our hopes,
We witnesses of so much wickedness?

And still you are astonished that you can
Be moved at trees in bloom and dawn's rose glow —
That you live on, so your immortal soul
Will suffer, what it suffers, to the end.

So you have loved — away like smoke love flies;
Your heart brims sorrow for departed throngs.
But we, with old Sophocles, stoic, calm,
Gaze straight at that, at which you'd close your eyes.

TO STANISŁAW BALIŃSKI

— C.S. Kraszewski

Poniedziałek

Bije dwunasta. Zaczyna się dzień
Mego planety księżyca.
Wkoło ta sama co zawsze ulica,
Koło mnie codzienny mój cień.

Do domu idę w księżycowej smudze,
Ale to nie jest mój dom; ja wiem;
Bóg jak do Pawła powie do mnie:
„Twoje życie jest snem,
I ja cię z niego obudzę."

Monday

Twelve midnight. And I go to greet
The dawn of my planet, the moon.
Around me spreads the same old street;
Around I cast the same old gloom.

Through moonlit haze I reach my house —
My home, yet not my home. I seem
Like Paul, to hear God say to me:
"Thy life is but a dream,
One day, from it I will thee rouse."

— C.S. Kraszewski

Matka Boska Częstochowska

Matka Boska Częstochowska, ubrana perłami,
Cała w złocie i brylantach, modli się za nami.
Aniołowie podtrzymują Jej ciężką koronę
I Jej szaty, co jak noc są gwiazdami znaczone.
Ona klęczy i swe lice, gdzie są rany krwawe,
Obracając, gdzie my wszyscy, patrzy na Warszawę.
O Ty, której obraz widać w każdej polskiej chacie
I w kościele, i w sklepiku, i w pysznej komnacie,
W ręku tego, co umiera, nad kołyską dzieci,
I przed którą dniem i nocą wciąż się światło świeci.
Która perły masz od królów, złoto od rycerzy,
W którą wierzy nawet taki, który w nic nie wierzy,
Która widzisz z nas każdego cudnymi oczami,
Matko Boska Częstochowska, zmiłuj się nad nami!
Daj żołnierzom, którzy idą, śpiewając w szeregu,
Chłód i deszcze na pustyni, a ogień na śniegu,
Niechaj będą niewidzialni płynący w przestworzu
I do kraju niech dopłyną, którzy są na morzu.
Każdy ranny niechaj znajdzie opatrunek czysty
I od wszystkich zagubionych niechaj przyjdą listy.
I weź wszystkich, którzy cierpiąc patrzą w Twoją stronę,
Matko Boska Częstochowska, pod Twoją obronę.
Niechaj druty się rozluźnią, niechaj mury pękną,
Ponad Polską, błogosławiąc, podnieś rękę piękną
I od Twego łez pełnego, Królowo, spojrzenia
Niech ostatnia kaźń się wstrzyma, otworzą więzienia.
Niech się znajdą ci, co z dala rozdzieleni giną,
Matko Boska Częstochowska, za Twoją przyczyną.
Nieraz potop nas zalewał, krew się rzeką lała,
A wciąż klasztor w Częstochowie stoi jako skała.
I Tyś była też mieczami pogańskimi ranną,

Our Lady of Częstochowa

Our Lady of Częstochowa, all in pearls and gold,
Intercedes on our behalf as in the days of old.
Her eyes shine with deep compassion as She kneeleth down.
Outstretched hands of angels bear the burden of Her crown.
Her blue garment is like midnight marked with shimmering stars.
Full of grief, She turns to Warsaw Her dark face with scars.
She whose picture doth adorn our every Polish home,
Every cottage, every manor, every church's dome,
Hands of every dying person, cribs where infants play,
To Her knights have offered pearls and kings gold from fiefs.
In Her even he believes who holds no more beliefs.
With those eyes which have for centuries read our minds and souls,
Holy Virgin, look with pity on the plight of Poles!
Grant to soldiers, always singing when they march in rows,
Rain and coolness in the desert, fire on the snows.
Let those flying be unseen and let them safely land,
And let those who roam the oceans reach the ports as planned.
May each wound find a clean bandage to heal over fast;
May the letters from those missing reach their homes at last.
Bring those suffering a relief for which they dare not ask,
Our Lady of Częstochowa, 'tis a Mother's task!
Cause barbed wires to be cut and cause slave camps to fall.
Raise Thy fair hand over Poland blessing one and all.
Move to love and to compassion every one who hates.
Crush the cruel tools of torture, open prison gates.
For all those who had been exiled to the land afar
Show them roads that lead to homeland and a guiding star.
Our land was oft invaded, our blood ran in streams,
But Thy shrine at Częstochowa on the rock still gleams.

A wciąż świecisz ponad nami, Przenajświętsza Panno.
I wstajemy wciąż z popiołów, z pożarów, co płoną,
I Ty wszystkich nas powrócisz na Ojczyzny łono.
Jeszcze zagra, zagra hejnał na Mariackiej wieży,
Będą słyszeć Lwów i Wilno krok naszych żołnierzy.
Podniesiemy to, co legło w wojennej kurzawie,
Zbudujemy Zamek większy, piękniejszy w Warszawie.
I jak w złotych dniach dzieciństwa będziemy słuchali
Tego dzwonka sygnaturki, co Cię wiecznie chwali.

Thou wert also cut, Our Lady, by the pagan sword,
Yet Thou reignest still above us with Thy Son, Our Lord.
Thus we always rise from ashes, from fires untold,
And Thou also will return us to our country's fold.
Trumpeteer will sound the heynal through the tower's arch.
Once again will Lwów and Wilno hear our soldiers march.
We will raise up from the ruins which the war laid bare.
We will build a bigger castle in the Warsaw square,
And we once again will listen, as in childhood's days.
To the silvery bell at dawn which ringeth Thy praise.

Manon

Wśród burz, co już szaleją i co grożą z dali,
Kiedy wszystkie się siły rozprzęgły w naturze,
Ocalić można wszystko, jeśli się ocali
To, co nas robi ludźmi: nasze własne burze.

Więc patrzaj nieulękły, jak czyha zatrata
Na tyle miast wspaniałych i świat cały płonie
I nie łam rąk, gdy widzisz, że się łączą dłonie
I usta, niepamiętne ginącego świata.

Czy słyszysz? Gdy w gruz pada, co wznosiły wieki,
W Weronie pod bombami, w ogromnym płomieniu
Do Julii Capuletti Romeo Montecchi
Wśród nocy, utęskniony, woła po imieniu.

Szimeno! Której szarfa bohaterów wieńczy,
Jak nic cię nie zmieniły te wojny wciąż krwawsze!
O Fedro, Mario Stuart, o Beatriks Cenci!
Wśród świata, co się pali, cierpicie jak zawsze.

Więc ty, na nic nieczuła, zawsze nieostrożna,
Manon, której się serce co chwila odmienia,
Spójrz na mnie, ty, dla której jednego spojrzenia
Przebaczę, czego nigdy przebaczyć nie można!

Manon

When over Nature's forces chaos reigns,
Now or in the storm that threatens from afar,
We salvage everything if we retain
What makes us human: those storms that are ours.

So watch without fear as the whole world burns,
And doom over splendid cities unfolds
And don't wring your hands when you have learned
Of forgotten mouths in the dying world.

Do you hear? As what centuries have raised
Falls to rubble, in Verona Romeo
Calls out to Juliet, despite the blaze
And the bombs, "all night till it be morrow."

Chimène, you still weave your heroes sashes,
As if unchanged by our bloodier wars,
Beatrice Cenci, Phaedra, Mary Stuart!
You suffer still in our world burnt to ashes.

And you, insensitive, careless, driven
To change your heart with each passing day,
Look at me, Manon, and for that one gaze,
I'll forgive what can never be forgiven.

— Gerry Kapolka

Nokturn

Cóż ja jestem? Liść tylko, liść, co z drzewa leci.
Com czynił — wszystko było pisane na wodzie.
Liść jestem, co spadł z drzewa w dalekim ogrodzie,
Wiatr niesie go aleją, w której księżyc świeci.

Jednego pragnę dzisiaj: was, zimne powiewy!
Więc nieś mnie, wietrze chłodny, nie pytając, po co,
Pomiędzy stare ścieżki, zapomniane krzewy,
Które wszystkie rozpoznam i odnajdę nocą.

W ostatniej woni lata, w powiewie jesieni
Niech padnę pod strzaskany ganek kolumnowy,
By ujrzeć te, com widział, podniesione głowy
Wśród teraz pochylonych, zamyślonych cieni.

Uciszaj, srebrna nocy, całą ziemię śpiewną!
A ja padnę na trawę, wilgotną od rosy,
Lub będę muskał cicho niegdyś złote włosy,
Których dziś już koloru nie poznałbym pewno.

Nocturne

What am I? Just a leaf fallen from trees.
What have I done? It's all written on water.
Just a fallen leaf in a distant garden
Blown into a moonlit lane by the breeze.

Today, I long again for you, cool gusts!
So carry me, cold winds, but don't ask why,
Through the old paths and the forgotten brush,
Which I recognize and can find by night.

In the last waft of summer, as autumn starts,
'Neath the shattered portico let me drop,
That I may again see those who take heart
Among disheartened shades, so lost in thought.

Silence, silver night, the world's overture,
And I'll alight on grass wet with dew from the air,
Or I will stroke softly the once golden hair
Whose color I no longer can tell for sure.

— Gerry Kapolka

Mokotowska Piętnaście

Nad obce wielkie miasto zmrok zapada obcy,
Stoję w oknie i patrzę, jak wolno śnieg prószy.
Ach! było to tak dawno, kiedy, mali chłopcy,
Biegliśmy przez Warszawę, rozcierając uszy!

Po tylu odtąd latach czyż jestem tak inny?
Gdy wszystko leży w gruzach, mnie zdaje się tylko,
Że znowu się otworzy nasz pokój dziecinny
I powiem: "Ja stąd przecież wyszedłem przed chwilką."

To przecież moja Matka szyje ręką drobną,
I widzę pochylony cień Ojca na ścianie,
Co nocami odrabia robotę osobną,
Za którą dla nas wszystkich ma kupić ubranie.

Mokotowska 15

The snow falls slowly. High up, I stand here
And watch a strange dusk dim this great, strange town.
How long has it been, since we ran around
A snowy Warsaw, rubbing our cold ears!

After so many years, have I changed so?
And still it seems, though all lies in ruins
That I might walk through our childhood rooms
And say, "I just stepped out an hour ago."

See? There's my Mother, sewing things with those
Small hands of hers, and Dad's shade on the blind,
Hunched over, scratching out his overtime
From which he buys each one of us our clothes.

— C.S. Kraszewski

Wielki Piątek

Kobieta, której nie stać na kir i żałoby,
Lecz z której twarzy czytasz całą Mękę Pańską,
Jak senna w Wielki Piątek idzie Świętojańską
I dziecko wynędzniałe prowadzi na Groby.

I nagle zobaczyła: zamiast kwiatów — skała
I nie pachną hiacynty, nie widzi przybrania.
I wtedy ta kobieta kamienna zadrżała,
Że może po tej śmierci nie być zmartwychwstania.

Lecz oto dźwięk przecudny spłynął w ciszę głuchą
I z chóru lekko zstąpił anioł urodziwy,
I tej trupiej kobiecie powiedział na ucho:
„Im cud jest bardziej trudny, tym bardziej prawdziwy."

STANISŁAWIE KUSZELEWSKIEJ

Good Friday

A woman who can't afford her mourning clothes
But on whose face is all Christ's Passion written
On Good Friday plods down Świętojańska, smitten
With fatigue; by her side a haggard child goes.

Then, at the Tomb, she sees: not flowers but stone,
No hyacinths; nothing adorns the cave.
She shudders as her mind admits a groan
That after death one might not rise from the Grave.

But then into the dead silence a sound flows clear
And from the choir an angel slips into view
And whispers in that ghostly woman's ear:
"The more difficult the miracle, the more it is true."

TO STANISŁAWA KUSZELEWSKA

— Agnieszka Maria Gernand

Mędrca szkiełko

Trawy takiej zielonej, chmur tak czarnych nie ma,
Jeżeli na nie spojrzeć zwykłymi oczyma,
Ni świętych barokowych jak z pogiętej blachy,
Nie znajdziesz Berniniego płaczącej Teresy,
Jak łamie swoje ręce w mistyczne floresy,
I nigdy się nie chwiały jak z El Greca gmachy.

Nie było go: Adama cudnego bez winy,
Co wznosi dłoń bezwolną znad stropu Sykstyny,
Ni jeńców zapatrzonych w swoje boskie ciało.
A są tacy, co wątpią, czy w najpierwsze rano
Płynął nad nami starzec z brodą rozechwianą,
I mówią, że to wszystko samo tak się stało.

Wszystkoś mi wytłumaczył w tej wyższej algebrze,
Że Adam na Zatybrzu, dłoń podnosząc, żebrze,
Że domy stoją prosto z odwiecznego planu,
Że nie ma żadnych cudów, zmarły wszystkie święte.
Ale są jeszcze przecież rzeczy niepojęte
Jak zapach heliotropu i kolor szafranu.

ZOFII KOCHAŃSKIEJ

The Glass of the Sage

You will never see clouds so black in the skies,
Nor grass so green, looking with everyday eyes,
Nor bronze holy men 'neath baroque porticoes,
You won't find Bernini's ecstatic Theresa
With her arms covered under mystical creases,
And buildings don't lean like those of El Greco.

There was no magnificent, innocent Adam
Weakly raising his hand in that Sistine stratum,
Nor captives entranced by the body divine.
There are those who doubt that there ever appeared,
On that very first morning, a man with a beard
And they say that the sun has always shined.

You've explained it all with your higher algebra,
Roman Adam with hand outstretched, is a beggar,
Buildings are straight up and down in sensible
Plans, the saints are all dead, miracles never were,
But there still are some things incomprehensible,
Like heliotrope's fragrance and saffron's color.

TO ZOFIA KOCHAŃSKA

— Gerry Kapolka

Piosenka

Droga Warszawo mojej młodości,
W której się dla mnie zamykał świat!
Chcę choć na chwilę ujrzeć w ciemności
Dobrej przeszłości
Popiół i kwiat.

Zanim mnie owa ciemność pochłonie,
Twoich ogrodów chcę poczuć woń.
Niechaj Twych ulic wiatr mnie owionie,
Połóż Twe dłonie
Na moją skroń!

Jak kiedyś zapach bzowych gałązek
Wśród kropli rosy i słońca lśnień,
Tak inny z Tobą marzę dziś związek:
Starych Powązek
Głęboki cień.

Marzę, że Ty mi zamkniesz powieki,
Lecz choćbym z ciężkich nie wrócił prób,
Będę Ci wierny, wierny na wieki
Aż po daleki
Wygnańczy grób.

Song

Dear Warsaw of my youthful days!
My happy memory's whole cache!
Through the dark gloom I long to gaze
On times gone by — bays,
Bloom, and ash.

Erst I in death's deep darkness drown,
I yearn to scent Thy gardens' balm.
May Thy streets' winds o'erblow me now
And place Thy cool palm
On my brow!

As once the lilac bough's strong scent,
'Midst sunshine and the sparkling dew,
I beg of Thee new covenant:
Powązki's ancient
Shade, deep, true.

I dream Thou'lt close in death my eyes.
But if banishment is my doom,
My troth is Thine, and for all times
Unto this exile's
Lonely tomb.

— C.S. Kraszewski

Sąd Ostateczny

Szczytne cnoty, dla których gwarny świat nas chwali,
Czyny, których przykładem przyszłość ma się ćwiczyć
I nasz honor kamienny, i wola ze stali
Na Sądzie Ostatecznym nie będą się liczyć.

Odpadną z nas, pokryte przez tłumu oklaski,
Uczynki miłosierne, co sławę nam szerzą,
I tylko pozostaną te mroki i blaski,
O których nikt z nas nie wie, czy od nas zależą.

Wtedy wyda głąb nasza, nareszcie odkryta,
Grzech, który cię przeraża, cnotę, co cię wstydzi.
Gdy wokół szumi życie, nikt o nie nie pyta.
Tylko miłość w nie patrzy, tylko Bóg je widzi.

IRENIE WILEY

The Last Judgment

Noble virtues, the noisy world's ovations,
Our deeds meant to teach our daughters and sons,
Stony honor, steely determination
Won't matter at all when Judgment Day comes.

We will lose these — though by the crowds acclaimed —
Those good merciful deeds which bring us fame,
And only the dark and the bright will remain
For which we don't know if we are to blame.

Then will our depth, at last exposed, bring out
The sin that you fear, the virtue that shames you.
No one asks about them, when life hums about.
Only love looks at them, only God sees what's true.

To Irena Wiley

— Agnieszka Maria Gernand

Spowiedź wielkanocna

Czyż nie cud to, czyś jeszcze nie zdał sobie sprawy,
Że to Bóg ciebie wybrał, że On cię ocalił,
Żeś jak tylu nie zginął na murach Warszawy,
Nie rozszarpał cię granat i mur nie przywalił?

Żeś później nie utonął we krwi polskiej rzece,
Żeś nie szedł przez Europę o żebranym chlebie
I że cię ominęły Oświęcimia piece,
Choć tylu w nich zginęło? I lepszych od ciebie.

Żeś własnymi rękami dzieci swych nie chował,
Że ciała ci moskiewskie nie szarpały kleszcze?
Jak to? I za to wszystko Bogu-ś nie dziękował?
Jakże musisz weń wierzyć, że Go prosisz jeszcze!

Easter Confession

Isn't it a miracle, aren't you aware,
That it was God saved you from many a close call:
You didn't die in Warsaw like many others there,
Weren't killed by a grenade or crushed by a wall?

For you didn't drown in the stream of Polish blood,
Didn't wander throughout all Europe on begged bread,
And avoided the Auschwitz crematoria,
Though so many of your betters died there, instead?

For you didn't bury your babes with your own hands,
Escaped Moscow's tongs that at other bodies tore?
How can it be, then? You haven't thanked God for that?
How strong must be your faith in Him to ask for more!

— Agnieszka Maria Gernand

***

Chorału Bacha słyszę dźwięki,
Na niebo ciągną szare mgły
I wszystko mi już leci z ręki:
Miłość i rozkosz, prawda, sny.

I w którąkolwiek pójdę stronę,
Wszędzie jesienny chrzęści chrust.
A jeszcze nic nie załatwione
I nie odjęte nic od ust.

Patrz! Dzikiej róży krzak serdeczny
W wichurze zeschły traci liść.
Ach! I Sąd jeszcze Ostateczny,
Na który trzeba będzie iść.

I hear the sounds of Bach's chorale
As heavenward thread misty streams.
All things slip through my hands now, all
Delight, love, truth, and all my dreams.

Whichever way I choose to go
Brown, dead leaves crunch beneath my feet.
Still, nothing is decided, so
Much sweet and bitter yet to eat.

Look! The wild rose bush, once so gay
And red, now Autumn's rough winds rend.
Alas, and then there's Judgment Day,
To which all mortal things do tend.

— C.S. Kraszewski

Cytata

Na cóż laur ci pochlebczy i kuszące brawa?
Na cóż szumnej gawiedzi okłask wielokrotny?
Zwiędną, przebrzmią, umilkną. Ale twoja sprawa
Jeszcze nie jest skończona, poeto samotny.

W jedyną zbrojny słuszność jako rycerz w męstwo,
Idź pomiędzy aleje, gdzie w ubogich grobie
Leżą ci, co wierzyli w za grobem zwycięstwo,
A umarli, pobici i podobni tobie.

Jak oni, wzgardź wawrzynem z kusicielskiej dłoni:
Niech w wieniec twój się plotą róże wraz z cierniami,
Abyś kiedyś mógł śmiało powiedzieć jak oni:
„Żyłem z wami, cierpiałem i płakałem z wami."

Quote

What should you care for bravos, the caress
Of flattering hands, the fickle mob's applause?
They too grow silent. But your fight, your cause
Is not done yet, you Poet, you Loneliness.

Armour yourself in Right's chivalric thew
And walk among the humble ossuaries
Of those who fought through death to victories:
The pummeled, slaughtered, so akin to you.

Like them, spurn laurels that but tempt to pride;
Let thorns entwine the roses for your brow,
And as they said once, so boldly say you now:
"I've lived with you, I've suffered, and I've cried."

— C.S. Kraszewski

Hosanna

Nie w tym pierwsza chwała Panu,
Że mu dzwonią w Watykanu,
Że w Piotrowej bazylice
Pyszną ma stolicę.

I nie temu Pan odwdzięczy,
Co nad świętą księgą ślęczy,
I nie temu się pokaże
Matka Boska w tęczy.

Ale temu, który w trwodze
Widzi ciemność na swej drodze,
Temu wskaże srebrną gwiazdę,
Temu poda wodze.

Bo dopiero niebo pęka,
Kiedy wielki grzesznik klęka;
Wtedy radość wśród aniołów,
Wtedy Pańska ręka.

Hosanna

The Lord's best praised not by the songs
Pealed by Vatican carillons,
Nor by the splended baroque throne
'Neath Peter's dome.

Nor does the Lord too highly prize
The sacred bookworm's bloodshot eyes,
Nor shall rainbow-clad Mary come
To such a one.

But him who bears his heavy load
Of penance on his darkling road,
Him will the Lord lead from afar
By silver star.

When a great sinner weeps and kneels
Heaven itself rumbles and reels —
Angels amazed in rapture stand
And praise God's hand.

— C.S. Kraszewski

Poezja

Ogród, z którego jesień wszystkie zdarła wdzięki,
Drzew wierzchołki strzaskane, bielejące kości,
Marmurowy Apollo bez głowy i ręki
I podarte sztandary szumiące w ciemności.

Miłość, która jak wicher przez dusze przewiała,
Łzy piła, jak zwierz była, co krew naszą chłeptał,
Wiarołomne przysięgi, któreś mi szeptała,
Zaklęcia, w którem wierzył i sam je podeptał.

A nad ową otchłanią, gdzie się razem stacza
Zło i dobro i w trupiej rozkłada się pleśni,
Głos się wznosi, co wszystko wskrzesza i przebacza:
„Ach! musi umrzeć w życiu, co ma powstać w pieśni."

Poetry

A garden that autumn has robbed of all charms,
And shattered treetops, and whitening bones,
A marble Apollo without head or arms,
Tattered flags flapping in darkness, windblown.

In a storm through our souls, love drinks our tears,
Just like some animal lapping our blood,
The false vows you whispered into my ears,
The spells I believed in but trampled in mud.

But from that chasm of putrefaction,
Where the good and the bad tumble headlong,
A voice of forgiveness and resurrection
Cries out, "One must die to arise in song!"

— Gerry Kapolka

Ojców

Coś we mnie mówi ciągle: "Zbieraj wreszcie plony,
Rządź się w końcu mądrością, jużeś się wyszumiał."
Nie słucham tego głosu. Wciąż bardziej zdziwiony,
Żyję tylko tą myślą, żem nic nie zrozumiał.

I na dnie każdej prawdy widzę rzeczy ciemne,
I w każdej słyszę ciszy okrzyk nieprzebrzmiały.
Wszystko wciąż mi się zdaje wielkie i tajemne,
Jak pagórki Ojcowa, kiedy byłem mały.

JERZEMU KRZYWICKIEMU

Ojców

A voice in me says: "Reckon up your gains,
Take stock of wisdom now, you've had your fling."
But I don't listen. Ever more amazed
I live this thought: I haven't learned a thing.

Each truth I see is deep and tenebrous,
In every still I hear a stifled call.
And all things yet are grand, mysterious,
Like the hills of Ojców were, when I was small.

TO JERZY KRZYWICKI

— C.S. Kraszewski

VIDES UT ALTA STET...

O Tobie myślę, dzisiaj w ten czas bezrozumny
Wrzasków tłuszczy bezbożnej i pochlebców szumu,
Coś uszedł między mirty i białe kolumny
Od nadętych pyszałków i tępego tłumu.

I tylko co najlepszych wokół siebie zwołał
I licząc złote strofy i sącząc płyn złoty,
Wśród tylu burz i pokus wolnym zostać zdołał
I nie zrzekł się rozkoszy, nie zdradzając cnoty.

Więc chociaż wielkim klęskom muszę dotrwać wiernie
I choć mi nie przystoi rozstać się z żałobą,
W ten jeden letni wieczór chciałbym przy falernie
Na Soracte pod śniegiem — patrzeć razem z Tobą.

VIDES UT ALTA STET. . .

Amidst the hum of fawning parasites,
The shouts of the blockheaded mob, the rage
That fills this senseless and impious age,
I think of you, retiring from such blight

'Midst myrtle, marble, gathering around you
Only the best, for strophes gold and wine,
How you remained free in a slavish time,
And sacrificed nor pleasure nor virtue.

Thus, though it won't do to ignore these woes
And I must bear immense calamities,
On this one summer night, I'd gaze in peace
With you, and wine, at Soracte's cap of snows.

— C.S. Kraszewski

43

Oedipus Rex

Przypomniał mi się nagle, zasypany w piachu,
Sfinks stary, z którym przecież znamy się od dziecka.
I znowu pomyślałem, lecz teraz bez strachu:
Wszystko może się skończyć jak tragedia grecka.

Bo chociaż zawsze przy mnie rozbrzmiewa głos tkliwy
I stoi dom spokojny pod laurów ozdobą,
Sfinks stary mi powiedział: "Nie będziesz szczęśliwy
I musisz wszystko rzucić, ażeby być sobą."

Pod niebem dotąd czystym, co nagle się mroczy,
Nie skazany przez Boga, nie wyzuty z ziemi,
Rozsądziłem sam siebie i jak Edyp oczy,
Wyrywam z siebie serce rękami własnemi.

Oedipus Rex

The old sphinx I've known since my childhood years,
Suddenly, covered in sand, comes to me,
And again I think, but now without fear,
That all might end like a Greek tragedy.

For though loving voices always surround me,
And in a peaceful, laurel strewn house I dwell,
The old sphinx told me, "You'll never be happy,
You must reject everything to be yourself."

And so under once clear but now cloudy skies,
Neither banished by God nor exiled from land,
I judge myself, and like Oedipus' eyes,
I tear out my heart with my own hand.

— Gerry Kapolka

Erynie

Wiedziałem, o Erynie, że kiedyś przyjdziecie,
Lecz myślałem, że takie jak wiedźmy w *Makbecie,*
Spodziewałem się gromów, wichrów dzikich świstu,
A tutaj nagle z kartki zapomnianej listu,
W kapeluszach z wstążkami, w rękach niosąc cynie,
Pod ogrodu drzewami stajecie, Erynie!
To mojego dzieciństwa jarzębiny krwiste
I te już nie noszone szale powłóczyste,
I owo romantyczne głowy pochylenie,
O którym nie ma mowy już nawet na scenie;
Z klonów liście się sypią, a wy w moją stronę
Idziecie, o Erynie, wołając: "Stracone!"
Stracone, choćby jeszcze dni przyszły łaskawsze,
Pogrzebane, stracone, stracone na zawsze.
Coraz bardziej zamglone, z coraz większej dali,
Wiem z korali jarzębin, z powłóczystych szali,
Z granej w dali gdzieś starej francuskiej muzyki,
Z gęsi lotu, co teraz podniosły krzyk dziki,
I (skąd one się wzięły?) z żurawi, co sznurem
Płyną teraz nad wami, gdy wołacie chórem:
"Stracone, więc nadzieję porzuć bezrozumną!"
I ruszacie powoli jak za moją trumną.
O! dobrze, żeście w kwiatach, żeście się przybrały,
Bo przecież tak niedawno, przykuty do skały,
O dwa palce od serca czułem sępa szpony!
Jeszcze widzę tę chwilę, gdy padłem zemdlony
Pod głazem, którym darmo wtoczyć chciał pod górę.
To przecież ledwo wczoraj na całą naturę
Padła groza mnie strasznej przypisanej zbrodni

Erynyes

Old Furies, I knew you would come some day,
But I expected witches from the play
Macbeth, with wild, howling gales and thunder,
Instead, from a forgotten letter, under
Some garden trees you appear suddenly,
With ribboned hats and zinnia bouquets,
Those are the blood-red rowans of my youth,
With trailing scarves that no one wears, in truth.
And that head slant from the Romantic Age,
That is a bit much even on the stage.
The leaves are falling from the maple trees,
While you are walking toward me, Old Furies,
Calling "All is lost!" Lost, but better days
Are coming. Buried, lost, lost for always.
Ever more distant, ever more misty,
The berries and the trailing scarves convince me,
French music playing somewhere in the distance,
Wild geese are flying, honking with insistence,
Cranes (where'd they get them?) flying above us
In formation now call out in chorus:
"Abandon foolish hope, for all is lost!"
As if behind my coffin, you slowly plod.
I'm glad that you brought flowers and are so
Beribboned, for I was chained not long ago
To a rock and felt vulture's talons not
Two inches from my heart. I've not forgotten
How I fell in a faint under the boulder
Which I tried in vain to push with my shoulder
Up the mountain. And then there was the time
I was punished for that most forbidden crime,
And I walked in darkness with empty eyes,

I idąc wpośród blasku płonących pochodni,
Przez puste oczodoły widziałem noc ciemną,
I tylko Antygona jedna była ze mną.
I wszystko to, pomyślcie, w pysznych kolumn cieniu,
Wszystko na oczach ludzi, lecz wszystko w milczeniu.
Choć wszystkie razem brzękły gitary Grenady,
Ja jeden w czarnym płaszczu przechodziłem blady
I wśród masek tańczących szedłem w gaj oliwny,
Słysząc tylko za sobą: „Co za człowiek dziwny!"
Patrząc w lustro na twarz swą, zrytą wieczną troską,
Ten człowiek mówił sobie: „Milcz, na miłość boską,
Dociskaj tej przyłbicy, którąś wdział dla świata
I trzymaj mocno konia, o Gattamelata,
A tylko czasem nocą, gdy wszystko śpi wokół,
Mów o sobie tym wichrom, co biją w twój cokół!"
Piasek skrzypi i grabarz idzie między pinie,
Ale kto tyle milczał, co ja, o Erynie,
Tego żadne milczenie więcej już nie straszy,
A zresztą widzę z szalów, nawet z twarzy waszej,
Z uśmiechu, z ukwieconych waszych kapeluszy,
Że jeśli teraz pochód z mego domu ruszy
I złoży pod cyprysem ciężką czarną skrzynię,
Będzie ona tam leżeć przez dwa dni jedynie.

Under their torches, Antigone my guide.
In the shade of fine columns, all this violence,
Witnessed by men, but witnessed in silence.
If all the guitars in Grenada were strummed
At once, I alone dressed in black would come
To the olive grove through the dancing masques.
"Who is that strange man?" they'd ask as I passed.
Seeing in the mirror my care-furrowed brow,
My reflection tells me, "Be quiet now,
For the love of God! Lower that visor
That shields you from the world. Hold on tighter,
Oh Gattamelata, to your horse, keep
Silent till everyone is sound asleep,
Only then can you sometimes talk of yourself,
To the winds that batter your pedestal."
The gravedigger approaches through the pines,
But he whose silence has lasted long as mine
No longer fears any further silences,
And in your faces, despite your frenzies,
I spy a smile under your flowered chapeaux,
And if you process from my house and repose
The heavy black box under cypress trees,
It will remain there for two days only.

— Gerry Kapolka

Do Madonny nowojorskiej

Madonno nowojorska, mniej znana od innych,
Bo nie masz swych posągów i swoich ołtarzy,
Przed którą nie brzmią chóry sopranów niewinnych
I oliwne, mistyczne światło się nie żarzy.

Do której polnych kwiatów dobra woń nie płynie,
Przed którą prosty człowiek nie upada czołem,
Nie znana kalendarzom - też masz swą świątynię:
Stu wież podniebnych miasto jest Twoim kościołem!

Jak na szczytach gotyckich starej Europy,
Głoszących Twoją chwałę spiżowymi dzwony,
Na domach stupiętrowych opierasz swe stopy
I kominów fabrycznych słuchasz antyfony!

Z dna potwornych kanionów huczy Ci ulica,
Której głos ginie w górze jak dalekie gęśle,
A nocą Twoja szata poprzez sierp księżyca
Na mostów fantastycznych lekko spływa prześle.

Nie każdy Cię zobaczy, bo Cię kryje nocą
Jako dymy kadzideł czerwonych łun szaniec,
Lecz ja widzę po gwiazdach, kiedy się trzepocą,
Że to Ty Twój wieczorny przebierasz różaniec.

I zanim dzień zamglony noc czarną zwycięża
I księżyc blednie z wolna za fabrycznym dymem,
Widzę stopę Twą małą, która ściera węża,
Dłoń świętą, co krzyż czyni nad miastem-olbrzymem.

To Our Lady of New York

Our Lady of New York — Thou art little known.
No guiltless choirs cherubic chant Thy name;
Others have statues, altars of their own —
Before Thee glow no mystic lamps aflame.

No child's hand offers Thee the fresh-cut spray;
No simple soul falls down before Thee prone,
Yet fane Thou hast, if yet no holy day:
One hundred sky-hung steeples mark Thy throne!

As on old Europe's soaring Gothic heights
Whence praise of Thee from countless belltowers peals,
On soaring skyscrapers Thy foot alights
Amid factory-whistle antiphonies!

To Thee from concrete canyons the streets boom,
A faint rebeck that fading climbs aloft.
At night, along the sickle of the moon
And bridges' spans Thy mantle settles soft.

Not everyone can see Thee, for the night
Thee with its dusky-red incense conceals;
And yet I see, by the stars' flickering light
Thee telling of an evening Thy beads.

Before the misty dawn black night o'ertake
And the moon pale in factory smoke, I see
Thy little foot crush the head of the snake,
Thy sacred hand bless the giant city.

I w ciszy, kiedy tylko spóźnionych przechodni
Krok pośpieszny jak dzwonek na alarm kołata,
Wśród przepychu i nędzy, miłości i zbrodni,
Ja modlę się o cudy dla siebie i świata.

And in the quiet, when the hurried, late
Steps of the rushed ring like an alarm bell,
'Midst pomp and misery, love and crime, I pray
For miracles: for the world, and for myself.

— C.S. Kraszewski

Biografia

Z mych marzeń nie spełnionych, z mej dumy dziecięcej,
Z łez wylanych ukradkiem, o których nikt nie wie,
Ze wszystkiego, com kochał — zostanie nie więcej
Niż imię, scyzorykiem wyryte na drzewie.
Więc czegom nie powiedział — niech będzie ukryte,
Mych listów i pamiątek niech płonie stos cały!
I tylko jeszcze wytnę me serce przebite
I przy moim imieniu — twoje inicjały.

Biography

Of the unfulfilled dreams of my childish brain,
Of the tears no one knew of, wept secretly,
Of all that I have loved, nothing remains,
But a name carved with a penknife on a tree.
Let all I have not told remain in the dark,
Set all my mementoes and letters aflame!
But still I will carve, in my wounded heart,
Your initials, next to my name.

— Gerry Kapolka

Poeta niemodny

Mówią mi: „Nic nie wskrzesi czasu, co przeżyty,
Wkrótce o nim i pamięć wśród młodych się zatrze.
Zabieraj sobie swoje stare rekwizyty,
Bo nową będą grali sztukę na teatrze."

Cóż robić? Trzeba upić ambrozji się flachą,
Co jeszcze mi została z młodzieńczych bankietów.
Wychodzę z różą w ręku, z księżycem pod pachą,
A resztę pozostawiam dla nowych poetów.

The Unfashionable Poet

They say: "Nothing can bring back the time that has gone,
Soon even its memory in young minds fades with age,
Take away those old tricks you have used and have done —
By and by there will be a new play on the stage."

What can I do? Get drunk with the ambrosia flask,
Left over from the roaring banquets of my youth.
Exit: with rose in hand and the moon in my cask —
The rest I leave to young poets: let them do it.

— Agnieszka Maria Gernand

Wiersz do Williama Faulknera
spotkanego w Hotelu Waldorf-Astoria

Panowie jak zwycięzcy wchodzą do hotelu,
Służba szepce codzienne grzeczności pacierze,
Łukiem brwi strzela piękność do nowego celu.
I Pan tu między nimi? Skąd Pan tu się bierze?
Nie dlatego, byś miał być włożyć frak niezdolny,
Lecz przecież nie masz czasu. Ani chwili wolnej
Od słuchania umarłych, ani wolnej głowy
Od jęków, co Cię doszły z pól Bitwy Domowej.
Innym wiąz albo lipa, szumiące od dziecka,
Tobie — dom wspierająca ta kolumna grecka,
O który tak jak Edyp oparli się ślepi,
I liść zeschły buczyny, co się omknie, czepi
I w dusznym róż zapachu, co z ogrodu płynie,
Wolno sunie Jokasta w czarnej krynolinie.

To William Faulkner,
Met by Chance in the Waldorf-Astoria

As to a triumph, into the hotel
Stride the grandees. The help smile, cringe and bow;
Beauty lets fly a bolt from an arched brow,
And in their midst, do I see You as well?
It's not that you can't get yourself decked out,
But You don't have the time. Their idle chatter
Is drowned out by the moans, and martial clatter
That reaches you even here, from the war-scarred South.
Lindens or elms sing through the memories
Of some; for You, it is the Greek column
Of a brick portico, against which, the blind,
Like Oedipus, would lean, and dry beech leaves,
The humid musk of roses on the wind,
Jocaste in black crinoline, pacing, solemn.

— C.S. Kraszewski

***

Weroniko, nie myj plamy
Z twojej krwawej chusty.
Po niej tylko Go poznamy,
Gdy grób będzie pusty.

***

Veronica, wash not the stains
From out thy veil with Love engored;
By it, we'll recognise the Lord
When nothing in the Tomb remains.

— C.S. Kraszewski

II. *From Lechoń's Journal*

1949

6 September

[...] Returned to New York from Hunter by car. After a few miles the road wound through wooded mountains — still green. If it weren't for the steely and misty light — this might be anywhere in the mountains in Europe. Alongside the road, again and again, little stalls with peaches, apples, cider, honey, and signs along the road "Honey," "Peaches," "Cherries," "Italian-American Food," "Chinese-American Food." And of course hitchhikers thumbing a ride. "Tourist Cabins," "Bear Mountains," — lakes. Near West Point a huge panorama of forested hills — everything in a steely mist. A sense of great expanses, riches, and at the same time, the feeling that nothing here is unique, everything is some sort of reminiscence (I've got to control this feeling). Washington Bridge — our age's Gothic. A great aria might be written about this architecture. I wonder how one might build up a description of this trip from these notes.

13 September

[...] Central Park and Columbus Avenue in the evening, in a gloomy light and misty rain. Fog like a spider web, through which one can see the exceptionally lively contours of the buildings and trees, lights in the windows with their nimbus spilling about them like the moon in a fox-furred cap. Melancholy, so rare in this city, a London feeling, a very human feeling, creative somehow, a sadness full of compassion.

17 September

[...] There's a certain point on Park Avenue, where when I stand there gazing uptown I see only the sky, with no perspective. It gives one the feeling of a road to nowhere, something similar to the Place Van Dyck in Bruges. Only there — the sense of death refers to the past, while here — you feel it like a premonition, like a glimpse of future annihilation or nothingness.

18 September

[...] Rockefeller Center just before dusk. Steelyviolet buildings. Despite the lack of perspective — this place is the miracle of New York and the wonder of our times. Osbert Sitwell,[1] the *fine fleur* of English taste, wrote something not long ago to the effect that New York is the only place on earth that recalls the ancient imperial capitals. Despite a million "buts" that is really true. However many times I find myself on Wall Street, I always think of Florence, of the Pittis and Strozzis.[2] That's what Italy must have been like when it was the country of great bankers. It's not about architecture at all, but about the atmosphere, the poetry, you might almost say, of the quarter.

22 September

[...] The French idea, that without lifting another finger they are to be the avant-garde of literature forever and ever until the end of the world is just as infuriating and vulgarly provincial — as the conviction of some Lana Turner or other girlie from Hollywood that she is the summit of distinction and that the swaggering Queen of England is less a lady than she.

This Cocteau,[3] whose face-making, which lacks the charms of youth, can entertain no one except *précieuses* and pederasts past their prime, retirees from Les Ballets Russes,[4] is convinced that every blob that drops out of his already shaky pen — has a universal significance, and that if New York isn't crazy about it — well, that's just because at bottom it's just a capital of cowboys and gangsters.

---

[1] Osbert Sitwell (1892-1969). English poet and prosaist.

[2] Pitti and Strozzi — Italian banker families connected with Florence.

[3] Jean Cocteau (1889-1963). French poet, dramatist, painter, composer and filmmaker.

[4] Les Ballets Russes. An international ballet troupe creative between the years 1909-1929. It was founded and directed by Sergei Diagilev.

[...] I'm certain that it never occurs to Cocteau that there exist young writers and young people in the world, who are neither familiar with his works nor even dream of getting to know them. But why speak about Cocteau. When someone once related to Valéry,[5] who was a great poet and a charming gentleman, some compliments about myself, he asked me to my face if he had had a great influence on my writing. In an analogical situation, Mistinguett'[6] would probably act the same.

Why am I writing this and why am I getting so angry, more angry than ever since I began writing this journal? Because one would like to believe that after Sartre and all his humbug something really healthy in a literary sense would come out of France, something like Balzac and the brilliant degenerate Proust. But there's ever less hope for that. Hemingway is better than Jules Romains, Tennessee Williams than Achard,[7] and Truman Capote is younger and therefore more interesting than Cocteau.

24 September

[...] A lot is being said and written here about Arthur Miller's play, *The Death of a Salesman*, being a masterpiece. After all, our own countryman, the very intelligent and malicious Solski,[8] calls Miller a great writer in *Wiadomości*,[9] and compares the play itself to the best works of Gorki. At this moment, Miller

---

[5] Paul Valéry (1871-1945). French poet (first associated with the Symbolist movement), essayist and critic, friend of Stéphane Mallarmé and André Gide.

[6] Mistinguett' (Jeanne Bourgeois, 1875-1956). "Queen of the Paris Music Halls," French singer and entertainer.

[7] Marcel Achard (1899-1974). French dramatist.

[8] Not the actor, but the prose writer and essayist Wacław Solski (Wacław Jan Pański, 1897-1990). He spent the war years in London, and lived in New York from 1945 on.

[9] *The News*, an important émigré weekly published in 1946-1970 under the editorship of Mieczysław Grydzewski and then in 1970-1981 edited by Michał Chmielowiec and Stefania Kossowska.

is the Żeromski[10] of America and, just as that writer did for the Poles, so does Miller discover to the eyes of Americans their chief problem. Every day during that play, almost every man present in the theatre breaks down and cries. Everybody here is either a salesman himself, or the son of a salesman, and if he does something else for a living — like the salesman in the play he still dreams about a better life, which he will never achieve, having wasted his life in the very pursuit of the same.

There are a few scenes in Miller's play, especially the wife's monologue (delivered wonderfully by the actress) so full of human compassion, that the comparison with Żeromski and his role in Polish life presents itself automatically.

I don't know if Miller so wished it — the play is the tragedy of the grey man — I don't know whether that salesman might not have been able to change his fate, had he not given himself over to the idolatry of success, which is not fatalism at all, but the freely-willed insanity of America. But if Miller isn't necessarily, fully convincing, he certainly does move one to the depths. That confirmed Communist is so human that I wonder how long he'd be allowed to write in the USSR and if he'd be able to endure life there. As far as the eternal, artistic, literary merits of the play are concerned, its success, its importance for today's audience here and now mean nothing. But who knows if it is not to mark a great date in American life, the beginning of new desires and new thinking. In order for that to happen, it needn't be a masterpiece. *Uncle Tom's Cabin* wasn't, yet it had a greater significance for life here than did Emerson or Whitman.

25 September
[...] Today the air is as transparent as it is in Europe — and all of New York takes on a sort of poetry, as one can see all of its contours and colors. Maybe it's the humid mist here that blurs everything and makes Americans so completely colorblind. For this reason American painters (those whose paintings I've

---

[10] Stefan Żeromski (1864-1925). Polish novelist and playwright of an engaged social bent.

seen myself) are no more worthwhile than the fashionable tailors in these parts, and their clients, in love with such greens and reds that, as he saying goes, make the teeth hurt. Mary Cassatt always seemed to me to be the one important American painter from the perspective of color — and she's an exception. After all, she's French as far as art is concerned, just like our Gierymski and the Kapiści[11] were French. The landscapes in the background of Jacek Malczewski's[12] paintings had a wonderful color, not copied from the French so that one would like to call it Polish. I don't know if Pankiewicz[13] wrote something to that effect or said it publicly, but I remember that he held Jacek's landscapes in high regard.

28 September

[...] This morning, Riverside on the Hudson, my daily bus ride to midtown. Rusty red trees, ashen grey here and there, with no shine of light — a perfect painting by a bad American painter. But the Hudson itself, beneath that parapet of rusty green — is far from banal somehow, with that steely warship that just sailed up. Evening on Park Avenue. Such a crowd of automobiles that the whole street seemed to be some sort of fantastic parade with torches, flowing down the upper parts of the avenue toward the gate at Grand Central. In the darkness, the skyscrapers on Fifth Avenue, where in various offices single windows were still lit up, some white, some blue, looked like jewelry hung up against the sky. A uniform grey-red dusk past Rockefeller Center. This entire, gigantic adventure has

---

[11] Aleksander Gierymski (1850-1901). Polish painter associated with realism, impressionism and symbolism. The Kapiści were a group of young Polish artists in Kraków. They called themselves the Komitet Paryski (Paris Committee, hence the name), and remained together for study after traveling to Paris in 1925.

[12] Jacek Malczewski (1854-1929). Polish symbolist painter, fond of mixing naturalism with fantasy.

[13] Józef Pankiewicz (1866-1940). Polish painter and graphic artist, associated with the Kapiści.

something of its own mysticism. Just that there's nothing Gothic about it, not even the devil, no deities at all, whether evil or good. It is the mysticism of nihilism.

4 October

[...] Yesterday the playoffs in both major leagues ended, and now the victorious Yankees and Dodgers will play each other for a few days for the championship of America. For this reason the clinical frenzy of America regarding this game and its aces, who are lauded here more than the great military victors, is reaching its culminating point. Eisenhower never received even a portion of the welcome that, a few days ago, was enjoyed by Joe DiMaggio. Today, a full million of this crazy nation greeted the Dodgers with an inhuman baying. Thousands camp out near the stadiums, and even the *New York Times* prints baseball news before stories about China and the atomic bomb. The players' wives, generally of the same class as Warsaw kitchen help, are photographed as if they were Hollywood stars. This insanity — is truly proof that an entire nation can go mad.

9 October

[...] There are dramas around me, concerning Poles in emigration, which could enter into the annals of the martyrology of my nation. The shrivelling in misery and longing, and finally the death of the best is becoming the usual run of Polish life in banishment. This misfortune is just a drop in the ocean of New York, so much so that it goes unnoticed, the roar of this ocean drowns out our tears and cries for help. One says "It's all the same where you lie after death." And yet having been at so many funerals here my heart has been rent not only with sorrow for those who have passed on, but also by the view of that foreign grave.

[...] A little red leaf hanging from an invisible spider web, as if hovering in the air. The smell of the earth, but not so deep as in Poland.

*Tomorrow I've got to leave. I won't be returning home, because New York and my apartment here are not my home. Is it my fault, that I have no one who might belong to me and to whom I might belong? I think that in these last years I've done everything in my power to make that happen — but there are no such bonds with housing matters, kitchen, money, which could bind me really. And it's these that make what we call a home.

21 October

[...] Those who so easily sputter at America for her supposed lack of culture and *parvenu* nature ought to see this exposition,[14] not just its volume, its unheard-of organization, but also its openness — with both old ladies from Park Avenue and youngsters from Washington Square in attendance. This is just one of many, but so eloquent, proofs that America — if it isn't the center of artistic creation — is a young and enthusiastic student of painting. Her lack of tradition — so irritating at times — sees to it that new works are accepted here easier than even in Europe. Sometimes because of snobbism, but certainly not always.

26 October

[...] Those picky people who find fault with American barbarism too easily forget that — among the chosen few essential creators of the new feeling in literature, there can be found two Americans: Poe and Whitman.

7 November

[...] The floral shops of New York. What riches, what sumptuousness of beauty! Today for the first time I saw some

---

[14] Paintings by Vincent van Gogh.

sort of chrysanthemums with thin petals, light yellow and rose, with a hint of coral. And others of deep burgundy, and fantastic bouquets of orchids of all shapes and colors, coffeebrown as if moulded from wax, transparent, filigreed white-azure and those most familiar lilac and white-lilac, which against the backdrop of these others finally acquire the entire splendor of their color and shape, as if a surrealist had designed them.

Pansies, large and small, lose nothing in comparison. And the roses are really like the verses of Mickiewicz.[15] Who could ever get bored with their shape and color?

10 November

[...] Indian Summer. I can't bear the weather. There is something unnatural about it all: Winter was almost here, a serene Polish autumn, and suddenly this queasy warmth that makes one slack and lazy. This is one of those American specialties, which won't allow me to concentrate on any single mood and certainly, as many learned Americanists state in all seriousness, lead to the nervous instability of Americans.

19 November

[...] *The Battleground,*[16] the new war film which is the greatest "hit" of the season, disappointed me somehow, perhaps because so much is being said about it. From the times of Sherrif's *The Journey's End,*[17] it has become a cliché to present war as a combination of heroism and the mundane, both of which are narrated in the same tone. In *Battleground* this already seems fabricated, already cold-cut, and unfortunately (after all) as an artistic effect it has already seen its best days. Some great writer must come along who will find something in himself to freshen this template and make it again into a work of art.

---

[15] Adam Mickiewicz (1798-1855). Polish Romantic poet, generally considered the representative poet of his nation.

[16] Directed by Jim Layton.

[17] By British author Robert Cedric Sherriff (1896-1975).

It's another matter altogether that the American, or rather Anglo-Saxon, discretion in the face of death and great events, and perhaps in the expression of emotions in general — especially for a Pole who is used to a complete unfastening in such matters — is something very beautiful and moving. And beyond that Americans have some sort of exceptional finesse in male emotions. The scene where Johnson watches his young friend (Marshall Thompson)[18] closely, to see whether this babe, straight from his mother's care, is not too terrified by battle, is a revelation of this world of feeling.

21 November

[...] The Episcopalian cathedral on Amsterdam Avenue is just a few short steps away. The interior is similar to Chartres or Reims, only completely different. My Catholicism is now quite epidermic. It seems to me that only *our* cathedrals are real cathedrals.

22 November

[...] Ambassador Bliss-Lane[19] spoke today about Teheran and Yalta with a beautiful courage and an outrage that he controlled only with difficulty. His was the first voice I've heard in years, and from his milieu, in which one hears not only political common sense but also a real conscience. Nothing but simple truths, such as one hears so rarely. And among them, the most courageous: that if not for Churchill and Roosevelt, Stalin would never have been able to allow himself the yoking of eastern and central Europe, and that America will obtain a right to the leadership of democracy only when she denounces Yalta. [...] His speech gave me a sense of moral catharsis. And certainly — like everything else which is disinterested — some

---

[18] Marshall Thompson (1925-1992). Actor, director, producer of films.

[19] Arthur Lane Bliss (1894-1956) was American Ambassador to the Communist-led Provisional Government of National Unity in Poland from July, 1945. Between the years 1948-1951 he led the committee investigating the Katyń massacre.

sort of fruit will come of it. Mr. Poole, who was quite abashed by this real attack of Lane's on the US government in the context of readings, which, at any rate, were organized by that government, found a splendid exit from his difficult position, saying, "Ambassador Lane's speech this evening is an object lesson in democracy." And of course a lesson it is, and a beautiful one at that.

*My landladies, from whom I rent my dark room, are elderly unmarried teachers. They are Americans born and bred, but had been married to Germans and spent a considerable portion of their life in Europe. Among all of my very vexing problems, it was indeed luck that led me to them. They are the complete opposite of American, or rather Hollywood, indiscretion; they practice an old-fashioned cult of music, and they possess an old, quite amusing dachshund bitch. They are happy if I ask for a cup of tea, to which I am not necessarily entitled. With them I feel as if I were living in a salon from the very best prewar days. These ladies are named Mrs. Cora Lehman and Mrs. Estella Marburg. If ever I am deemed worthy of a broad biography, I here beg its author not to forget these ladies.

27 November

[...] Besterman[20] feels that Western Europe as a whole seethes with hate for America. In this great question may also be found that which abounds in common interpersonal relationships: the hatred of clients for their benefactors.

5 December

[...] In New York, in America, the Holidays have already begun, because everybody's buying presents, shipping gifts and mailing greetings. The stores are setting up splendid displays,

---

[20] Władysław Besterman (1903-1974). Polish diplomat assigned to Washington during the Second World War. After the war he remained in exile in America and worked for the House of Representatives' Committee on Immigration and Naturalization.

some of which are even brilliantly beautiful, huge green wreaths on the buildings, a gigantic, grey tree at Rockefeller Center with hundreds of colored ornaments, fellows dressed up like Santa Claus and stationed at the big stores — all of this has something fantastic about it, as well as the pomp and dashing breadth of America. Only, there's nothing of our holiday mood, which was religious and familial. "Christmas" here — is a wonderful rout, like the carnival in Rio.

8 December

[...] I've been used to the difference of America, its dissimilarity from Europe, for quite some time now. In some ways, the difference is greater than that which exists between us and China. I am really full of admiration for real democracy, for the vitality of this country and even from time to time I sense the difficult poetry of New York. The only thing that hurls me into a frenzy — is the indiscretion, the measureless boorishness in personal matters. Yesterday I saw an interview with Margaret Truman on the film news. Some hags were actually interrogating her in this manner: "Margaret! Is it true that you are interested in this and that fellow?" And the daughter of the President actually answered their questions, quite pleasantly, because otherwise the press would have made her life impossible. In our European conception, one of the attributes of happiness in love is its intimacy. Who knows how many madnesses in this country spring from the complete warping of this feeling.

9 December

[...] An exhibition of Walter Stuempfig's work, who is considered here to be the greatest American "Romantic" painter (these days, everything has to have its own label). All the influences one could imagine: Courbet, Vermeer and Thomas Eakins. Influences, that's stated blandly. The romantic effect is intended from the start and achieved by means which are rather un-painterly. There is no unplumbed mystery here as in the

75

work of Vermeer, who seemed to photograph nature, and yet despite that achieved so high a degree of poetry. Poetry in each art springs from the use of means which are particular to that art alone. Here — it's not so much poetry as literature. And all those naked boys again. Certainly America (and is it only America?) is going through a homosexual stage.

11 December

[...] Some Frenchman in *Le Figaro*, overeager in his synthetic zeal, attacked America for having no ideals. To which old Claudel,[21] a believer like Kasprowicz[22] and just as wide awake as Kasprowicz, replied more or less as follows: "France had her mission once. Russia believes that she has hers now, just as Hitler believed that he had his. But naturally — the role of the state is to guarantee its citizens the maximum of the good life and freedom. This role America fulfills like no other nation in the world." Claudel, who was an ambassador, and a perfect one, in Washington, has replaced with this one phrase all the non-existent American propaganda in the world. What a wise old duffer.

16 December

[...] I think that the famed American manner of childrearing, which is based on treating children as adults and on the so-called respect for their individuality, is a mistake from beginning to end; what's more, from it arise the basic errors of American life and thought. The difficulties of childhood — contrary to the viewpoint, upon which this childrearing is based — are not a cause for sadness at all, but rather the enriching and romanticism of youth. Take them away in love or work or any other life experience and nothing remains but emptiness, boredom, and quite simply weakness.

---

[21] Paul Claudel (1868-1955). French Catholic poet and diplomat.
[22] Jan Kasprowicz (1860-1926). Polish poet, one of the chief representatives of the Młoda Polska (Young Poland) period during the first few decades of the twentieth century.

The need for authority is a natural instinct, and the American school, in destroying authority, is not only not making children happy, not tempering them, but indeed stealing from them an essential charm of youth — not to mention the fact that it's derailing them.

I remember how Jacek Stryjeński[23] had a wonderful time at my place in Paris and was exemplary, when he accepted my authority without argument. All of this was destroyed in a single moment, when Wierzyński[24] lit upon the quite demagogic and unpedagogical idea of drinking *Bruderschaft* with the fifteen-year-old boy. On the next day, Jacek felt that he had all the pleasantness of life already behind him, began to look at me critically, and became so unbearable that I was happy when he finally left.

John Dewey, the great philosopher and educator, who feels that a philosophy must be judged according to its practical results, is a symbol of the unphilosophical nature of America, which has fatal consequences for real life.

The white man was formed in Greece, and enlightened by Christianity. These two teachings completely suffice for him to be really human. American education, wishing to elicit something else from him besides this, warps instead this one true virtue of the white race, which only needs to be carried out well in practice. Education ought to teach this very practice.

---

[23] Jacek Stryjeński (1922-1961). Painter, architect, scenographer, chiefly in France and Switzerland. Son of painter Zofia Stryjeńska (1891-1976) and godson of Lechoń and Maria Pawlikowska-Jasnorzewska (1891-1945), daughter of the painter Wojciech Kossak, a poet associated with the Skamandrites.
[24] Kazimierz Wierzyński (Wirstlein, 1894-1969). Polish poet, along with Lechoń one of the chief representatives of the Skamander group. After the war he lived long in emigration, mainly in Sag Harbor on Long Island. Like Lechoń, a member of the Polish Institute of Arts and Sciences of America.

Every year the store displays in New York get better and better — certainly influenced by artists from Europe. The most beautiful one that I've seen is in *baccarat* — nothing but glass, a silver Christmas tree and one splotch of color, two bottles of the golden perfume Chanel. Paris is full of such subtleties as this, but in New York it really strikes one.

1950

13 January
[...] I have got into the shameful habit of flipping through film magazines, which are a monument of the highest, specifically American, idiocy. I'm ashamed to pick them up, but on the other hand, one can learn from them what several tens of millions of people in this country are thinking about; people for whom film fills the role of the church in the life of a village woman in Poland. If divorce is not to become the chief plague of this entire country, if art and common sense are not to perish (to say nothing of decency and decorum) Hollywood should be burnt to the ground. These whores and gigolos[25] actually think that they are artists, and that the eyes of the entire world are upon them.

2 February
[...] It's hard for us Catholics to believe, but many American Protestants really wonder whether "Catholic totalism" — their term — might not be just as dangerous as Bolshevism. The fact that despite such moods Myron Taylor[26] officiated for so many years at the Vatican is both proof of the Church's power and of the wonderful diplomatic sensitivity of the Pope.[27] His recall shows that a great anti-Catholic wave is in the offing, which — though few suspect it — is always anti-Polish as well. Yesterday, at some meeting where the relationship of religion to sexual matters was being discussed, and at which the Catholic Church came in for a whipping from those assembled, the only defender of Catholicism was a rabbi. But that's quite natural. The Jews are closer to Catholicism than Protestants are — we

---

[25] *Pindy i gigolaki.*
[26] Myron Taylor (1874-1959). Lawyer, industrialist and businessman; from 1939-1950 US envoy to the Vatican.
[27] Pius XII (Eugenio Pacelli, 1876-1958). Elected to See of Peter in 1939.

are linked by mysticism. In the same way, because of their old traditions, the Chinese are closer to Europe than the Americans.

5 February

[...] These dues in American churches are a horrible thing. I understand perfectly that so it must be, but so it should not be, because the upshot of it is that he who has no money can't approach the Lord God. Priests in America have to recruit their parishioners, because they make their living from them. I wonder if something of these conflicts doesn't seep into the confessional.

9 February

[...] Naturally, no question about it, American literature is in fine flower. Artistically, it's today's avant-garde. Every week there appears some new, good book by a young writer, and every day, perhaps, a few helpful, wise books that open eyes toward Europe, explain the contemporary world. In politics, as in the social life of this country — there are no teachers. All this effort of observation and the art of the pen is carried out without compass and without any creative conviction. But it would be strange if no such a one appeared on this already very fertile ground.

11 February

[...] The obligatory American smile, the assurance that everything is "fine," the adoration of success, the panicked fear of failure, eternally spreading from advertisements and the photographs of the teeth of political leaders — what a cretinish, filmic conception of happiness! And how far from the real thing — toward which these smiling neuropaths and psychopaths can't even inch forward through all the drunkenness, automobiles and divorces.

[...] Lots of reviews of Hersey's[28] new book, *The Wall*, an epic of the Warsaw ghetto. Have to read it as soon as possible. One thing is sure. American writers ever more feel their significance, know that they are read everywhere; little is lacking for them to finally realize that, given this state of things, they also have obligations, that they've got to be conscientious towards literature, if not towards the world. Hersey already fulfilled this role in writing about Hiroshima. Now he took a trip to Poland, collected materials and documents — I can't imagine that anyone, in the most heroic years of French literature, would ever have set a foot outside of France for similar reasons. Naturally, the thought occurs to me: why does no one write about the Warsaw Uprising, as Hersey writes about the ghetto?

6 March
[...] Wacław Lednicki[29] writes to me: "One dies either for ideals or bread. For a comfortable toilet, no one will die." But America isn't a comfortable toilet. Her life — it is the nearly achieved ideal of democracy and the good life, equality, universal access to culture. What she's lacking is that about which democracies are silent, or about which they speak with hypocritical cant. True Christianity, a moral order based on something more elevated than social utility.

15 March
I saw an animated film yesterday, the story of a bird that cuts through all hard materials with its beak. I adore all cartoons, but this one was even funnier than others and at the

---

[28] John Hersey (1914-1993). World War II correspondent. Another of his famous titles is *Hiroshima*.

[29] Wacław Lednicki (1874-1967). Polish historian of Slavic Literatures. Since 1940 in exile in the US, where he taught at Harvard and Berkeley. Member of the Polish Institute of Arts and Sciences of America.

same time full of a discreet tenderness. When one sums up what America has given the world, one cannot overlook Disney. Not as an artist, because certainly many can draw one hundred times better than him, to say nothing of color and painterly invention. But Disney has given expression to certain forms of humor and American honesty, which have enriched the entire world and have become a source of deep joy for millions. Somewhere, there ought to be a place for this among poetry, the plastic arts, film and the world of "the friends of mankind."

17 March

[...] Today all the city is wrapped in a disgusting bright green color because of the St. Patrick's Day parade. What an ugly nation, these Irish: something like the worst of the Polish bourgeoisie, those encountered on afternoon walks along the Aleje [in Warsaw] or in Boy's[30] *Sunday*. But at the same time, what racial power, what strong bonds to that far-off, ugly, boring, agelessly unfortunate and — to many of them unknown — Ireland. These immigrants are a power in America. They've made their way to the highest offices, hold the Catholic Church here in their hands — oppressing by the way poor Polonia. And despite it all they've remained themselves, something detached in this new world and the green color of Ireland is something more for them than the red and white is for the constantly downtrodden Polonia. A parade like today's is a great lesson about what America is, how it unexpectedly finds a way out of the problems that have been making Europe tear her hair out of her head for ages. Because here one can be both an American and an Irishman at one and the same time, and equally good as either.

29 March

[...] A well-known, but not completely understood characteristic of American culture. That which was: past wars,

---

[30] Tadeusz Boy-Żeleński (1874-1941). Polish writer, satirist and translator of French literature.

ancient greatness, is for them unimportant. Important is only what *is* — today's happenings and the living. Now, this has changed a bit, it seems — this can best be seen in drawings — at least the expensively produced illustrations for articles in *Life* about western culture. But at the bottom of it all, the life of Napoléon seems to the average person here something *passé*, while he knows everything there is to know about Acheson and Artur Rodziński.[31] And he knows more about Nela Rubinstein[32] than about Josephine.

3 April
[...] *The Member of the Wedding*[33] — a very weak play. Truly boring dialogue and flaws in the setting of the main character. For two acts it seems as if the girl is a victim of her own family, perhaps American society as a whole, yet later this gets turned right around — she herself is a natural, wise, cruel egoist. And this is supposed to be the best play of the season. But set it alongside Tennessee Williams or Miller? Yet despite all this it's a fascinating show. The Negro girl, the hysterical girl and the seven year old boy are played in such a way that the whole uninteresting matter becomes moving poetry. There's a particular form of American acting, developed from nervousness, repression, and the cruelty of this life which yields theatrical effects nearly unknown in Europe. This is why it doesn't surprise me at all that Vivien Leigh or Arletty[34] can't cut it in American plays.

---

[31] Artur Rodziński (1892-1959). Polish orchestral conductor who won fame in Los Angeles, Cleveland, New York and Chicago.
[32] Aniela (Nela) Rubinstein (1908-2002). wife of world famed pianist Artur Rubinstein (1887-1982).
[33] Based on the novel of the same name by Carson McCullers (1917-1967).
[34] Arlet-Léonie Bathiat (1898-1992). French actress of stage and film.

[...] The theme, or rather problem, of *The Member of the Wedding* are the shallows of the lost souls in this country; those who neither belong to it nor anyone else, yet still thirst for participation in something and in some family, some society. Here, the family ends when the children aren't quite grown up yet. The social bonds have nothing in common with the feeling that gave birth to patriotism in Europe. Today I received an Easter card, which is like the cry of just such a very valuable yet abandoned soul for a group at least, if not a society, to which it might belong. The feeling that one means something to such a person — is an obligation, which one cannot simply shrug off, and which it would be a crime not to assume.

20 April

[...] A chat with Beckman Cothrel[35] about the American family, the madness of success, the loneliness of the individual, the mania of "personality". Despite the fact that he had spent several years in Paris, Beckman is an American not only by deep tradition, but also by a very primitive attachment to this country, which is almost a patriotism. That's why I'm very impressed with the fact that he agreed with almost everything I said on these topics. There is nothing stupider than a false generalization.

23 April

[...] The first greens. Seemingly the same colors as everywhere, and yet there's nothing of that freshness, health, or joy of a Polish spring in it. I recall how Sienkiewicz[36] discreetly bemoans in *Quo vadis* the laziness of the Italian spring, contrasting it to the Hellenic spring, thinking most likely of our own.

---

[35] One of Lechoń's acquaintances.
[36] Henryk Sienkiewicz (1846-1916). Polish novelist. He was awarded the Nobel Prize for Literature in 1905.

30 April

[...] Priests whose hands are greased with a few bucks to propagate films to their parishioners.[37] This is still nothing in comparison to the other strange things that go on, everywhere, in that circle. It surprises no one in America. The Church here is a private institution which has to look to its own survival. But according to European — and as we think — truly Catholic perspectives, this is scandalous and a horrible example. In Europe, alcoholism or immorality among priests — are transgressions — here, they're almost rules of thumb. The priest is a bureaucrat. No surprise, then, that the church becomes just another office.

3 May

[...] In the survey taken by *Wiadomości*,[38] which is above all an exhibition of graphomaniacs, the majority respond with: "My other fatherland is France." If I had to respond to this not very wise question, I would say, "France is the second fatherland of every European and when I came to know her, I came to understand how many of my thoughts, reactions and tendencies were awakened in me and made conscious to me in France. But in the last few of my Paris years I felt this ever more weakly, because France had ceased nourishing me, and became for me a museum and temple of souvenirs. I think that every free person who feels a bond with the world, belongs in the end to every

---

[37] In 1949, Lechoń served as a lector at showings of the silent film *Poland Now*, which took place in different venues along the east coast where large groupings of Polonia gathered. Portions of the monies gathered for the film *Blind Children* supported the activities of the *Komitet na Rzecz Niewidomych w Polsce* [Committee for the Blind in Poland], which aided the *Towarzystwo Opieki nad Niewidomymi* [Association for the Care of the Blind] in Laski near Warsaw.

[38] The survey was entitled "Profile intelektualne pisarzy polskich" [Intellectual Profiles of Polish Writers]. It was published in the March 1950 (13/208) issue of *Wiadomości*.

country in which he lives; if he is able to really love his country, he'll find something to love in others. My third fatherland, for which I long greatly — was Brazil, and America, despite everything, is ever more becoming a fourth. All of this is said with the *caveat* that we all have but one fatherland."

11 May
[...] France's war with Coca-Cola seems victorious. A few months ago, *France-Amerique* published a very insightful article which explained that Coca-Cola's invasion of France is an attack upon wine as a custom, a war declared against French taste. It seems that the victory in this war is (the more important than one thinks) manifestation of the Americanization of the world. To say that there is something Balzacian about this is an understatement. It's almost Shakespeare.

14 May
[...] The different types of Negro skin-color yield quite unusual combinations with other colors, and have too little, so far, inspired painters and decorators. Today in the subway I was once again struck with the subtlety of these shades as I looked at a chocolate-colored Negro woman dressed in a black suit, beneath which she was wearing a soft rose-colored blouse. She had a dark straw-colored hat on, garnished in flowers that ran the gamut of pastel shades, such as zinnias, and tied about with a light rose veil of gauze. She was a masterpiece of colorism.

19 May
[...] A few days ago, on a stroll with Zosia Kochańska,[39] we came across a Ukrainian, a worker, who, hearing that we were speaking Polish, attached himself to our conversation. When I asked him how long he had been in America, he said, "Thirty years. And I'd like to kiss the ground I walk on that I find myself in such a wonderful country." This is a wonderful

---

[39] Zofia Kochańska (née Kon, died 1960). Polish intellectual, expert in art, wife of violin virtuoso Paweł Kochański (1887-1934).

country for laborers, and for artists (who after all are an infinitesimally small minority) the country of freedom. Is it therefore not the best of all the not-best worlds?[40]

21 May

After her return from two years in France, where she had it quite good, Fela Kranc[41] said, "And yet to return to New York is to return home." I feel the same when returning here. I've now squatted out a place which is for me bearable. To so say "I love New York" — why, to whom could it ever occur to say such a thing? But I do have a certain comfort of being used to the freedom of this city, a feeling that one is at home, that one has the same rights as others here, something which I don't quite know how to put into words.

6 June

[...] Polish nuns in America, descendants of that same Polonia, whose "trademark" is an aversion to culture and a thick American skin, all have the same almost beautiful, worldly and otherworldly smile and cult of poetry and ideal Polishness. Almost all of them speak Polish with a refined purity and grace. The reading that I had a few years ago for the homeless in Reading, Pennsylvania, and the evening I spent with them there, remains one of my fondest and unique memories of this country.

16 June

[...] A poem in praise of New York is going through my head. About how it's impossible not to love a city, in which one's lived for ten years, in which one's gone through so many things, to speak banally, suffering and loving. But New York is after all an infamous vampire, a Babylon, a demon. Today, walking through the streets, sitting in the park, I felt the almost Parisian poetry of this capital of the world. Naturally, such a

---

[40] *Czyż nie jest to więc najlepszy z tych nie najlepszych światów?*
[41] Felicja Kranc (Krance, née Lilpop, 1908-1993). Personal friend of Lechoń; painter, wife of pianist Kazimierz Kranc (1911-1973).

87

poem would be difficult to write, because New York seems at least Rimbaudian to everybody. But maybe it will develop in some sensical form.

27 June

In the cinema today a very interesting review of the last half century, which without any propaganda shows the decisive role in world matters that has been thrust on America by history. And the necessity of the breakup of Russia by the States — this is as if the natural, cinematic sense resulting from the review. I thought to myself that America has realized the ideal of democracy in both social and personal life, in creating at the same time a presidential government independent of Congress. If the president were given a term of seven years without the possibility of reelection, he might do some wise things, simply because he would have no other pleasure.

28 June

[...] An exhibition of twentieth-century American painting. Eakins — is something like our Gierymski; Mary Cassatt — like something from Podkowiński[42] or Pankiewicz; after which it becomes hard to tell these painters apart from each other — that is, at least according to what was shown of their works at the Metropolitan. Americanness can be found in some themes and in the general colorblindness. A very pretty, graceful and poetic Chelishchev.

6 July

[...] It seems that the South Koreans are surrendering *en masse*. Yesterday, Eisenhower and Marshall alarmed public opinion by stating that Bolshevik propaganda is making giant advances in Europe and that no American counter-propaganda is felt. We believe — because how could one live, otherwise? — that America will win out in the end. But after what catastrophes

---

[42] Władysław Podkowiński (1866-1895). Polish impressionist.

still to come, and at what price? And will she still be truly able to enunciate the new, strong, salvific word of the white race — without which there will be no victory, only the conquering of the world by the yellows?

[...] Chaplin's *City Lights* — certainly a masterpiece which will outlast time. At times it seemed to me almost desperate, and therefore almost unable to provide a catharsis — but I left the cinema actually uplifted in spirit just like after a contact with a work of art. To achieve a feeling of depth, a penetration of life and its tragedy, through the aid of countless circus clowneries, that is a *Meisterstück*, perhaps even genius. I was afraid of being disappointed, of the quaintness of a silent film, the clumsiness of the costumes from that period of time. But I saw nothing of the sort, so transfixed, moved, and full of wonder was I. A marvelous evening.

8 July

[...] Frigidaire — for the average European, a symbol of American life, a symbol of the idolatry of the machine. But after all this same Frigidaire signifies hours of freedom for the housewife, economy of her effort and time. If an American woman wishes to read, attend concerts, have a human life, well she can do so thanks to Frigidaires and dishwashers and washing machines. The jealous French just don't want to understand that. They simply can't forgive Americans the fact that they are themselves living thanks to American dollars.

18 July

[...] Where is the army in Europe? There are only Moscow, its satellites, Tito and Franco. In other words, if the Russkis[43] wished to, they might in the space of a few days march to the Pyrenees, take Paris, and imprison the Pope. And all

---

[43] Lechoń uses here the pejorative Polish term popular during the Partition period, *Moskale*.

because Roosevelt thought Stalin a fine man and perhaps even a better democrat than Churchill, and also because American politicians kiss up to the electorate. The summit of the insanity which rules the world is the fact that America — despite even this — is saving the world and perhaps may even succeed at this in the end.

19 July

[...] Truman's speech, which is actually a declaration of war, an appeal for sacrifice, calling for soldiers — has something splendid in its naturalness, in that Truman speaks in the same tone about the security of America as he might of the purchase of some sugar. That familiarity and avoidance of pathos is one of the phenomena of American politics, which Europeans have to learn before they judge this "barbarian" country and make their forecasts about its politics.

28 July

[...] A discussion with Irena Wiley[44] about changing citizenship. Don't I think in terms of "our Truman," "our America"? Naturally I do — and I confess that, after twenty years of uninterrupted life in foreign parts one has become used to these other countries. But to toss fidelity aside, well, the sense of the importance of the oath, the shame of denying Poland in the present moment — it makes a breach in what we're fighting for, what we're defending. When I will have to — I will take that paper in hand, but only with the heaviest heart, with the sense of committing a disgusting lie.

---

[44] Irena Wiley (née Baruch, c. 1900-1972). Polish sculptor, married to American diplomat John Cooper Wiley (1893-1967), who was assigned to the American embassy in Warsaw in the 1930s. The Wileys were instrumental in arranging an American visa for Lechoń and his move from Brazil to New York.

[...] I return to New York almost in despair. Because this is not my home. Yet my honest old landladies did everything to make it seem as if I were returning home.

2 August

[...] The film *Men*[45] — is one of those artistic happenings which contradict the conception of America as one great Hollywood. One can't say that this is a great work, but it is an unusual work, shatteringly human and at the same time an expression full of artistic tact and simplicity. Marlon Brando — if he doesn't fall into mannerisms — might well be one of the greatest actors. He possesses a great romanticism, without which one can't do anything great in drama, fascinating looks, and moments that approach inspiration. After all, the whole cast possesses the splendid restraint and single tone, not to be counterfeited, of a very moving drama, covered over with brutal laughter.

4 August

[...] "The pursuit of happiness" — a very beautiful phrase, but I think that both it, and the veneration in which Americans hold it — are root causes of the misfortunes that this country has already experienced, and those which might yet visit it. Happiness cannot be an aim, since true happiness, such as reciprocity in love, the constant presence of those we love, and even health — are things that are independent of our will and constantly under threat. To build a philosophy of life on the thought that such a life can be achieved by struggle is egoistical nonsense. Now, what we might indeed acquire — material independence, a nice house and that proverbial refrigerator — is not, of course, happiness. To flee suffering, mourning, the sight of misfortune — thus the cruel American recipe for so-called happiness. And yet the entire theory of Sigmund Freud is based

---

[45] Directed by Fred Zinnemann (1907-1997). This was the first film in which Marlon Brando (1924-2004) appeared.

on the principle that we've got to suffer through everything consciously, because everything that we don't suffer through to the end will have its vengeance on us in the end and lead us to mental illness. America, being certainly a country of freedom, democracy, work and power, is also certainly a country of crazy people.

Life itself forced her to a change of philosophies, but for the time being only in practice — in the horrid practice of the war just under way. The American boys dying in Korea are not seeking their own happiness in that country, but are fighting for higher goals, of which they know nothing, and which have arisen because of the power of their country. These boys are dying heroes' deaths, without pathos. America owes them a revision of her philosophy, which led both to demobilization and the Korean tragedy. She owes them new slogans, which will not only strengthen her as a nation, but also cure the country's neurosis. Christ promised not happiness, only salvation. One can't be a real Christian and believe in happiness.

9 August

[...] American capitalism has something of the English aristocracy about it, as it is a fairy story for simple people about treasures open to everyone. Each Englishman carries a coronet in his briefcase — theoretically, of course — and in the same way every American imagines that he might become a millionaire. The history of millionaires is just as irreplaceable a part of the life of the average American as the history of the royal family is part of the life of the poorest Englishman. Since the time of the "New Deal," American millionaires have been above all figures in fairy tales for full-grown American children.

15 August

[...] In my imagination the Metropolitan Opera House and Carnegie Hall, same as La Scala, after all — were palaces of art, the very first external sight of which would be imposing. How miserable they are in comparison with even our late

92

lamented Teatr Wielki, the most beautiful theatre house I know outside of the Opera in Paris. Of course, the tradition of these places is their charm, their soul. But today I had some business at the Met and I thought, "What a shame that one can't simply come here to daydream, to hear with the 'ears of the soul' Caruso or Reszke.[46] I can hear nothing except the chaos of Broadway, I can see nothing except buildings, larger, yet equally disgusting as the worst stretches of Marszałkowska."[47]

20 August

[...] Must read Faulkner. And must read ever more "in American."

26 August

[...] Over my 114th St., a high moon, just like once in Warsaw on Boduena.

The City and the Pillar by the very young Gore Vidal was a very highly praised and often discussed novel two years ago. I read it yesterday with a horrible sadness, such as is never aroused by a real work of art. What is more, it's not literature, yet; only — a "long short story," valuable as a document, well composed, but pedestrian and shallow in the development of characters, and stylistically, I think, without any glow or inventiveness. The conversations, typically American, full of a "lot of fun" and "OK!" — are monstrously depressing like Sunday afternoons on the Aleje Ujazdowskie.[48] The hero — if one might so call him — comes to a tragic end, as he is a homosexual. I understand that not everybody in such straits can be a Michelangelo, but one can always find something valuable and enduring in life so as to lessen that particular drama. That Jim of Gore Vidal has nothing beyond his muscles and tennis with which he could both speak to himself, and battle out some

---

[46] Edward Reszke (1853-1917). Polish bass. Between 1891-1902 he starred at the Metropolitan Opera in New York.

[47] One of the main thoroughfares in Warsaw.

[48] A toney boulevard in Warsaw near the Łazienki Park.

sort of enduring love. The whole thing isn't the drama of a homosexual at all, but just one more "American tragedy."

1 September

[...] The dullwittedness of Americans is at times frightening. Just now they're going mad at every appeal for a "preventative war." What a stupid phrase. After all, Russia has already swallowed up half of Europe and almost all of Asia without firing a single shot, and now is waging an open war, if indeed through the hands of its slaves. So what sort of "prevention" are they talking about? Really, all of this reminds me, tragically, of that famous Jewish joke: "He punched me once in the kisser, and I'm waiting for him to start something. He punched me in the kisser again, and I'm just waiting for him to start something."

5 September

[...] A beautiful morning in the garden at Locust Valley.[49] Autumn flowers, dew, apple-tree lined walks. One could almost forget where one was.

10 September

[...] The vice of Americans, which renders them laughable in Europe, and even arouses hatred towards them, is their desire (arising from an inferiority complex) to show that they respect no European tradition, custom or protocol; that anywhere they may find themselves they feel at home and can behave like Americans. From this perspective, nothing has changed since the times of Ann Gould, the wife of Boni de Castellane.[50] The rich hags from the Middle West hold it as a

---

[49] On Long Island, the estate of Cecylia Burr (née Wasiłowska), widow of American millionaire George Howard Burr, Lechoń's *maecenas*. She patronized many Polish artists and Polish émigré politicians.
[50] Boniface Castellane (1867-1932). French politician, writer, and *bon vivant.*

point of honor to dismiss the great families of Europe; they speak to "royalty" in the most familiar terms, and shriek out "Hello" through the most splendid salons of Rome and Paris. The deep hatred of America, fostered by the Bolsheviks, the fables of the boorishness of the entirety of this splendid nation — take wonderful root in the soil of irritation and disgust aroused by this pathological, micromaniacal arrogance. Somebody ought to write this down in clear letters. A league of some sorts against this slovenliness, which of course is nothing but snobbery "à rebours," ought to be formed.

*Today in the *New York Times Book Review*, John O'Hara writes about a new book[51] of Hemingway's: "The most important author living today, the most outstanding author since the death of Shakespeare, has brought out a new novel." Accordingly, I'll have to read this new novel, which has been (delicately) run down by almost all the critics as a poorer effort from Hemingway's pen than usual. One simply has to see this phenomenon with one's own eyes, as it arouses so diametrically opposed opinions.

11 September

[...] City Hall like a toy among the skyscrapers, a wonderful little poem of Europe and of the old America, which was once similar to Europe.

26 September

[...] Broadway, between 70th and 90th is inhabited chiefly by Jews from Poland. Now and again one can find typically Warsaw names like Rapaport and Szapiro emblazoned on the signs. Along that very wide street the houses are chiefly of several storeys, and thus they remind one of Europe, like a suburb of Berlin or Łódź, or the old tsarist cities. In the grey, humid mist of this afternoon the huckstery, the loud cheapness of this quarter was redolent with the sort of dull sadness one finds

---

[51] *Across the River and into the Trees.*

in the poems of Tuwim.[52] Only in the evening, when the lamps are lit, can one bear this ugliness, weaving oneself fables on this completely un-fantastic theme.

29 September
    [...] Against a perfect theatrical backdrop, MacArthur handed Seoul back to President Syngman Rhee.[53] We have become so clownish and boorish that we don't feel the beauty of this scene, we don't think that, after all, everything hasn't been lost, since the utopian army of many nations, long the laughingstock of the so-called realists, came into being by itself, as an answer to the exigencies of the present moment, and achieved victory. The politics of the West are still mired in old mistakes, and go on committing new ones. But one would have to be blind not to see other signs as well: the splendid *sang-froid* of the Americans, the ease with which they put themselves in harm's way and sacrifice their lives, the fantastic swiftness with which they move from catastrophe to victory. Oh, give this nation a few first-class people, and they'll show the world that the entire splendid, wise and human future stands open before them.

1 October
    [...] The Pulaski Parade. Depending on one's point of view, it is either a moving and splendid thing, or something laughable and horrid. Laughable are the music-hall orchestras and the girls with their uncovered calves and cabaret contortions, the borrowed, poorly-fitting formal wear of the honorable gentlemen, the so-called marshals in their comically gigantic ribbons, the busty matrons and the provincial beauties tricked out as queens. If, on the other hand, one thinks that these gentlemen

---

[52] Julian Tuwim (1894-1953). Polish poet affiliated with the Skamander group. After spending the war years in exile, he returned to Poland in 1946. He and Lechoń quarreled over their respective political views.
[53] Sygman Rhee (Li Sygman, 1875-1965). Korean politician. Elected president of South Korea in 1946.

96

in tuxes, these girls and kids, are refugees from Polish misery, from one-room unfloored hovels where they, or their parents, would bed down with their pigs — and when one considers that they have made a life here worth the envy of more than one member of the prewar intellectual élite in Poland, and that despite it all they love their distant mother, who was never able to be even a stepmother to them, and yet for whom they are crying for justice to be done her, they send money to ease her misery. . . If one thinks of all that, there's simply no way not to be moved by so great and imposing a thing done in such bad taste, which speaks wonders of Polish biology and of America herself.

2 October

[...] The little square before the Plaza Hotel possesses something of the Comédie Française. I looked down 5th Avenue today, from Zolotnicky's store (on the corner of 60th), gazing with an immeasurable delight at the play of lights: silver, red, azure, all of them as if strung up in today's clear autumn air, without any mist. Completely different, but equally, if not more, beautiful than in Paris.

26 October

[...] The film about Grandma Moses — narrated by MacLeish — is one of the most moving things that I have recently experienced. I didn't expect from MacLeish such simple and deep formulaic statements such as that the painting of Grandma Moses, its poetry, arose from her life. The whole charm, the whole honesty, unknown to the world, the solidness of America is in this film, contained in the moving symbol of the unceasing, pious work of the old woman. Her paintings — and this is striking — profit from the cinematic repetition of their fragments. Through her very naiveté, Grandma Moses has boldly attacked one of the most difficult of all tasks — figures in motion. And these figures move with a wonderful stylization.

97

The colors too are very fresh and pure in a way that is not "American."

[...] In the morning, the view east from the Plaza — is a wonder incomparable to anything. In perspective — the skyscrapers sunk in a pearlish-auquamarine mist, the trees before Central Park yellowed to a color almost light green, and around the statue of Sherman (a very beautiful yellowish bronze) flowerbeds pied in the palette of Renoir, or rather Vuillard.[54] Around 90th a view towards a flight of stairs and bowers amidst all the finesses of yellows and greens, and in the evening, a view from Cecylia's windows in the Astoria of the most staggering féeries of our times — the lights of New York. This is neither Versailles, nor Rome, nor Nuremberg, nor Venice, but at the same time it is a pageantry of beauty, different and thrilling, and one doesn't know what to do with it or what it means.

11 November
[...] Faulkner was awarded the Nobel Prize, and I haven't yet read him. I confess that I don't have a great hunger at the moment for incest and murder. More to my taste would be a fable that would insult me with the suggestion that life is in our hands, that the just and suffering will have their reward here in this life.

18 November
[...] I have begun to read *L'Invaincu*,[55] a French translation of Faulkner, because it seems that I wouldn't be able to cope with the English original. Already I find vast perspectives and real poetry in what I've read so far. But naturally, we'll wait and see what happens next.

---

[54] Edouard Vuillard (1868-1940). French symbolist painter.
[55] *The Unvanquished* (1938).

[...] I finished Faulkner's *L'Invaincu*. It is certainly an exception in his work, deplored as immoral, because great, tragic morality is the very atmosphere of this strange and beautiful book. Even in translation there remains a powerful suggestion of this very individual, fascinating style and the aroma which infuses both its spiritual and physical air.[56] Naturally, one would have to know Faulkner better, this country, that South which is the fatherland of nearly all its distinct literature, in order to say anything meaningful about this book. At times it seems that it possesses the joviality of Huck Finn, while other pages are impregnated with something Hamsunish,[57] while the end of the story reminds one of the most splendid Villiers de l'Isle-Adam[58] and almost Norwid.[59] At any rate, this is a noble book, full of tragic feeing; the book of a conscious, original master artist. I've got to read more of this author.

*One of the most Faulknerish phrases: "The expression, which I have seen in the eyes of those who have already killed too many, who have killed so many, that they will never be alone again to the end of their lives."

21 November

[...] I am constantly under the impression of Faulkner's charm. I had expected everything from this American writer, except that intensity, and at the same time subtlety, of

---

[56] *Zapach duszący zarazem duchowego i fizycznego jej powietrza.*

[57] Knut Hamsun (Knud Pedersen, 1859-1952). Norwegian writer. Awarded the Nobel in 1920.

[58] Auguste de Villiers de l'Isle Adam (1838-1889). French writer of the Gothic-Romantic type, influenced by Poe.

[59] Cyprian Kamil Norwid (1821-1883). Polish Romantic poet mostly neglected during his lifetime; from the early twentieth century on considered an equal of the three great Romantic bards Mickiewicz, Krasiński and Słowacki. He spent some time in New York City before returning to Paris.

atmosphere, with which the last few pages are permeated. One could say that this is the very summit of Żeromski, only, unfortunately for us, it is more concrete, palpable, because it affords that uncommon sensation in translation which, as is well known, Żeromski loses, as everything in his writing is style, music. But there is something in the characters of this novel that recalls Żeromski's people, up to the glamour that murder has for Faulkner, just as it has for Żeromski. I already know that I am going to live with this novel for a while, with its charm and the problems that it sets before us.

23 November

[...] I think that, in the face of the inevitable Americanization of Europe (that is, as the best result of the fracas awaiting us) — Thanksgiving Day will be one of the things that will be adopted in the old world. It's a very beautiful holiday and, although like all holidays it is based chiefly upon eating (the meager turkey of this country), like all ceremonies, it gives occasion to concentrate on a thought often forgotten in daily life: that one has to thank, that there is something to give thanks for, that we are to such and such a degree happier than many others.

26 November

[...] The immeasurable provinciality of Washington. One waits around here for afternoon tea or the papers just like in the provinces back in Poland, just like in some manor house, a long way from the train station. He who doesn't belong to the few thousand truly important people in this city lives the deaf, dull life of the provinces. In Geneva at least there were the Alps.

27 November

[...] In Protestantism, and thus in Americanism, there does not exist "who" but only "what." And after all, every act is different in relation to who committed it. This very basic trait of the American psyche is not at first evident. But when one finally understands it, one understands better why it is so easy for us to exist here, and so difficult to really live.

28 November

[...] Morning in the Library of Congress. I met someone at the Declaration of Independence, which is something like the main altar of America's chapel, in the hall of the Library. Poles had other national relics, more theatrical: crowns, sarcophagi, coats of arms. In the American veneration for texts and standards there is something quite discreet, profound and eloquent at one and the same time. Their devotion to the Lincoln's Gettysburg Address has always moved me deeply.

8 December

[...] Malraux said of Faulkner exactly what I was thinking after finishing *L'Invaincu* that is, that he has introduced Greek tragedy to the police story. A trifle? No one could say that even about Dostoevsky.[60]

12 December

[...] Terrible things in the Polish translation of *The Cocktail Party* in *Wiadomości Polskie*. Terrible things not of the translation, but of Eliot himself. He is a thinking man, but completely lacking in talent. He's something like the emperor in Andersen's fable, but with the trappings of contemporary art. No one understands him, so everyone is afraid to say that the emperor has no clothes, that this Eliot spouts familiar truths, old morals, and that he is nothing but a complicated and empty old bore.

17 December

[...] In the literary addition to *The New York Times*, Marcel Aymé[61] explains the fame of Faulkner in France (greater,

---

[60] *Nawet o Dostojewskim tego nie można było powiedzieć.* The idea seems to be that, in Lechoń's opinion, Faulkner exceeds even Russian novelist Fyodor Dostoevsky (1821-1881) in this aspect of the art.
[61] Marcel Aymé (1902-1967). French comic writer.

by God, than in America). With joy, and with almost a sadistic delight I read in this article a comparison of Mauriac's[62] heroes, in whom, as Aymé puts it, there is completely no God, to the world of Faulkner, where one feels His presence at each moment.

18 December
[...] Visiting one of the galleries where sculptures are shown, Zosia Kochańska tried to persuade the owner to exhibit Zamoyski.[63] At which this fellow smiled indulgently and said that he's not interested in "that line," which means that Zamoyski is not "new art" and most likely this idiot thinks him "academic." Here is one of the most flagrant signs of the lack of true artistic culture in America (not the lack of an interest in art), this idolatry of "modernism" and the conviction that he who is not a Modernist must of necessity be a conservative. Zamoyski is just as much a Deformist as Maillol,[64] but for him to be understood in America, one would need to have that little — those few centuries of plastic culture — that lawn-mowing, everyday for a few hundred years, as in Versailles.

21 December
[...] The grand illusion of American indiscretion. This is only one of the forms of their straightforward speech, that might be laid at the feet of their lack of imagination. From my own experience I know that Americans do not have the spontaneous tendency to lie which is the province of so many Europeans, and the truth is always the first thing to spring to their lips. This real virtue becomes, after all, a vice, and sometimes even a crime, when for example we're dealing with such secrets that the European instinctually respects, while the people here discover them to others simply from that primitive impulse to speak the truth. This is even true of military secrets,

---

[62] François Mauriac (1885-1970). French Catholic writer.
[63] August Zamoyski (1893-1970). Polish sculptor.
[64] Aristide Maillol (1861-1944). French sculptor and graphic artist.

which find their way into the press and the Congressional Record simply because the American has nothing to hide. The matter of sexual hypocrisy is something altogether different, although even here the craze of divorce is in large measure the result of the uncovering and legalizing of that, which here is given the disgusting name "sex."

24 December

[...] A few days ago I was at an exposition of contemporary American art at the Metropolitan. A few hundred canvases, a few hundred names. Not even one painting that I'd like to have for my own. A few rooms cluttered with abstractions, for the valuation of which I lack the proper criteria, but which I consider boring aberrations. A lack of color in almost all of them. I was really well disposed to seek out something that would enrapture me. And nothing. One thing is certain: Americans really · desire an American tradition of painting. It reminds me of Huberman's[65] reply when some quartetists from Warsaw asked him what he thought of their play. "Well, sirs! You certainly play enthusiastically."

---

[65] Bronisław Huberman (1882-1947). Polish virtuoso violinist. Professor of music in Vienna, he also organized symphonies in Israel and the United States.

1951

[...] Once again on the very top of the lists of America's greatest athletes are to be found: the baseball players Jim Konstanty from Philadelphia and Vic Janowicz from Ohio. Stan Musial is a constant legend. It's incomprehensible that Poles in this sports-mad country have never been able to make capital out of this, have never used these boys in their cause, are constantly an ethnic minority that no one takes into account.

21 January

[...] A horrid wind from the Hudson this evening, quite enough to kill those with heart ailments like poor old Neumann.[66] At the turning between 110th St. and 5th Avenue, wondrous things against the aquamarine heavens. Grand ribbons of greyish violet and red, flamy mists. Beneath this the silver water, surrounded by a black colonnade of trees, and in the background that divine Gothic — the skyscrapers of new York; cathedrals — without God and not for God.

4 February

[...] MacArthur possesses the theatricality and pathos of the great men of Europe. There is something of Lyautey[67] in him. Americans hate this style. They can't bear people they can't slap on the shoulder. But this is a new American destiny, this European heritage of her tragical conflicts, which cannot be brought to a resolution by bankers and salesmen alone. And this

---

[66] Władysław Neuman (1893-1945). Polish diplomat. He held the position of Press and Propaganda Officer at the embassy in Paris in the 1920s before Lechoń. During the first three years of World War II he was made minister plenipotential to the Norwegian government in exile in London. From 1942 until his death he headed up the Polish mission in Mexico.

[67] Louis Hubert Lyautey (1854-1934). French marshal and one of the chief movers of France's colonial politics.

is why MacArthur's hour has tolled, the time rolled around for his pathetic gestures and incalculable inspirations. In Gunther's[68] book we constantly sense a fear of his intuition, a disbelief in his intuition. America must learn that irrationalities, even various imponderabilia, are the only wisdom with which man can face the mystery of destiny. Bismarck said that political reason is the talent for seeing when the Lord God is passing by, so as to latch on to the hem of his coat. MacArthur possesses this talent, which can fail one, but without which one cannot be a great leader or a man of history.

15 February

[...] The stalls and steps of the subway on 3rd Avenue are the remnants of the old, non-standardized New York. They are romantic fragments, which arouse one's fantasy. Yesterday, walking along 59th and looking at those stalls, I recalled the Rialto.

19 February

[...] Three-minute speeches by Cardinal Spellman in the cinema, during which he exhorts the audience to offer some money for the benefit of poor children all over the world. During these three minutes the *Leitmotiv* of "Only we can support them. What will happen to them if America won't help them?" returned again and again. And an old woman with a child's eyes and a childish voice rested her hand on a loaf of bread, our daily bread, of which so many people are deprived. Americans certainly constitute a chosen people now. And they are ever more aware of this fact.

26 February

[...] A Pole, even though he find himself in a country where no one has ever heard Polish spoken, where the sky, the

---

[68] John Gunther (1901-1970). American journalist and author of, among others, the book *Inside FDR* (1950), about which Lechoń is speaking here.

105

earth, the flowers are completely different from what they are in Poland — is always able to hear the voice of his Fatherland and feel its unrepeatable proud beauty. This miracle, which brings Poland close to the most distant and lonely exiles, is the music of Chopin. There is today no corner of the earth where it does not resound, where it is not borne by the mysterious machinery of radio. This afternoon, at war with my own self, lonely as I've never been before, being distant even from myself — I suddenly heard an étude of Chopin playing in one of the flats in this oh so unpoetic apartment house. And I shivered, as if I had been awakened from a bad dream by the voice of a close friend, the closest.

2 March

[...] The posthumous life of great people is almost always the evolutionary history of the societies which gave birth to them. Kościuszko was the idol of Poles during the period of their captivity, during the era of the myth of Racławice, when the intelligentsia, weakened and having become unused to uprisings, became inebriated by faith in the people, by the hope that the peasants, in some none too precise fashion would "work out" the independence of the nation.

Later on, when the state was reborn and the problems of a strong government and parliamentary control returned — Batory[69] became fashionable again, Batory seen somewhat through the prism of the Piłsudczyks, but rather spontaneous all the same. In America, Washington is now what Kościuszko was for us before the war — nothing but a portrait, an image to be celebrated, whereas Lincoln has grown into a symbol of America, in the life of which the necessity of grand politics are being melded with a grand ideological League, democracy and the idea of the state. Just as during the American Civil War — elevated idealism cannot be separated from tragic cruelty.

---

[69] Stefan Batory (1533-1586). Transylvanian prince who became King of Poland in 1576. He warred successfully with Russia over the Courland.

Lincoln, upon whose face all of these contradictions are etched, is the light which shines on and illuminates them.

9 March

[...] There is a very helpful synopsis of *South Pacific*, the legendary Broadway success, illustrated by Czermański,[70] in the *Coronet*. Helpful — because it speaks of what would never have occurred to a single European mind: that the uniqueness, the so to speak depth, of this operetta lies in its relation to love. In it we find startling comparisons *à la* Shakespeare, Racine, Goethe. These few sentences uncover to our eyes just how far that love, which transforms people by molding their souls — is a rarity in America, where one universally takes love as "a pastime."[71] In short, how different we are from Americans in this, which would seem to be so generally human a characteristic.

14 March

[...] Yesterday I was at a „dress-rehearsal"[72] of *The Green Pastures* by Marc Connelly,[73] a play which twenty some years ago was a big sensation and one of the biggest successes on Broadway. It is the Old Testament, as simple Negroes understand it, played by Negroes. This was at one time a real invention and a sensational idea. Today, when the audience knows what it's in for from the very start — the fable must be held together by something stronger — by real poetry. It is an Old Testament of completely watered down peripatetics. Its poetry seems to me quite narrow. It's lucky that the charmingly naive or subtly comical Negroes do what they can to make of it a

---

[70] Zdzisław Czermański (1890-1970). Polish graphic artist and caricaturist. In emigration from 1941. In this country, his drawings appeared in *Fortune, Look,* and *Life*.
[71] Lechoń gives this word in English.
[72] Given in English in the original.
[73] Marc Connelly (Marcus Cook Connelly, 1890-1981). American dramatist. This play won him the Pulitzer Prize in 1930.

real spectacle. As a result — it is folk art, plain and simple. In America, folklore is the Negro.

15 March

[...] Today at Litka Chandlers'[74] I met one of the editors of *The New American Mercury*, a 28-year-old boy spouting various ideal slogans, and *au fond* just a heap of complexes and bottomless neurasthenia. The strongest of the complexes was his American pride and antipathy to Europe, where he's never set foot. If I knew English better, I'd have started an intellectual brawl, because I'm convinced that I know one hundred times more about America than he knows about Europe. But maybe from such complexes results the subconscious determination of this country — to take responsibility for the world and knock out the Bolsheviks. Beyond this, the boy talks in pure scholarspeak,[75] nothing but syntheses, which after a certain time gives one the impression of insanity. But I think that he's a peaceful nut, of whom there are many in this country though people don't notice them — until they kill themselves or someone else.

16 March

[...] I took Whitman in hand. Incomprehensible, how little one speaks of him these days in the marketing of America. And after all — all of her greatness — is contained in his tirades, in his almost-prophecies.

18 March

[...] When thirty-odd years ago I first heard the name Whitman from the lips of Tuwim, he seemed to me to be the most exotic writer in the world. When four years ago, on my way to the Seghers'[76] in Huntington I suddenly saw his family home, it seemed to be the sudden incarnation of a fairy tale. My

---

[74] Personal friend of Lechoń.

[75] *Mówi samymi terminami naukowymi.*

[76] Lechoń's personal friends.

familiarity with English is so imperfect that I understand of this Whitman only what he's talking about — his ideas and nothing more — while the sense of his poetry, his art, escapes me. After all, there's a lot of cheap fanfaronniness and cosmic cabotineity in him, and now and again one is wont to be surprised by some unclarities in his biography. But one can also sublimate him, accept for truth the legend created about him by his adorers and somehow write it anew. In that case — he will be truly great, new, farsighted and prophetic. After all, in all contemporary art, there is something of a whiff of this legend, which discovered the poetry of things until then contemned by poetry.

28 March

/. . . / What idiocy this dependence of MacArthur on the United Nations, on all the great and petty idiots of all the nations in the pay of fantastic sums and able only to hinder something good, hesitate before something just. It is stupid and immoral to subject a man with such a sense of responsibility, a leader with — so rare today and indispensable — a vision, to irresponsible officials who see no farther than the tip of their own noses. In this war, in which there is no tragedy on the part of the West, no Shakespearean tone, MacArthur is by his own will and the will of destiny a tragic figure: Shakespearean.

10 May

[...] On the road to Sag Harbor various wonders of springtime color. Suddenly, the perspective of a green, far away, so bright and fresh and distinct — as if it were right in front of me — which stood out from dark greens and dark, greyish greens. Now and again apple trees in blossom, lily-colored lilacs looking as if they were freshly painted, rhododendron bushes. At the Wierzyńskis wisterias near the porch, still pale, still almost colorless. All of this seems unreal, like the memory of things seen long ago and no longer belonging to my life.

11 May

[...] On the train, a conversation with a young typesetter from Brooklyn. He told me of a trip he'd taken by car with his friends to New England, where they went to bars, swam, fished, played cards. His eyes were full of emotion at the very memory of these moments. Later, he opened up to me about all the doubts he has in life: about marriage, work, love, sports. He spoke about politics and not at all stupidly. We talked for the whole two hours. This is just one of millions of young people in America, who want something better and aren't going to get it, being unable to climb out of the anthill.

13 May

[...] On a newly mown little square in Central Park birch trees grow, rustling their leaves. That white bark, that rustle — is almost a voice from Poland; the air today was also so pure, as if I were standing right beneath heaven. I gazed into that transparent azure, listened to the rustle and felt such a peace, as if I'd already returned home.

14 May

[...] I sometimes think that the stars of New York and my own are crossed, that all of my battles, all of my struggles are written in those stars; that it would only cost me a trip to Mexico to leave all of my ills behind me.

2 June

[...] Wittlin[77] says that he can't write about Americans because he can't feel them as he felt and continues to feel for

---

[77] Józef Wittlin (1896-1976). Polish author and translator associated with the Skamander group. In exile from 1939 on (in the U.S. from 1941, where he worked for Radio Free Europe). Member of the Polish Institute of Arts and Sciences of America. His wife Halina (1900-

example all types of Poles, so that he's able to read their political affinities from the tone of their voice or the vocabulary they use. He's right from the Proustian perspective of great literature, and I share his scruples. But on the other hand the people in Balzac are certainly not differentiated; there is in them none of that Proustian finesse. One might even say that they have nothing French in them, nothing that would make them understandable to foreigners. One can, then, write without a knowledge of the finesse of a given milieu, as long as one has a vision of man. Given, of course, that one is Balzac.

17 June

[...] On the road to Sea Cliff, delicious hedges of purplish, climbing roses. And time and again a solitary hawthorn, of light or dark pink, reminding me of Poland like a thorn against my heart. I understand why the mighty Kasper[78] drew forth one of the most beautiful of his melodies from the heartrending poetry of this bush.

19 June

[...] American internationalists are most often communizing snobs or people without any instinct whatever, who discuss everything and believe in nothing. True Americans, solid, honest, with principles — if one scratches through to their essence — appear to be nationalists with inferiority complexes, constantly irritated by Europe. Whoever can't see this will not understand the foreign policies of this nation.

27 June

[...] I saw the play *Stalag 17,* one of the authors of which is Edmund Trzciński, a Polish-American, attached, as one can see, to his very uncomfortable last name. One of the play's

---

1994) was a Polish literary scholar, and his daughter Elżbieta (Lipton, b. 1932) a scenographer and interior architect.

[78] i.e. Jan Kasprowicz and his volume of poetry inspired by the beauty of the Tatra moutains *Krzak dzikiej róży* [The Wild Rose Bush] 1898.

111

heroes, "Staś" Urbaniak, an incessant clown and yet a courageous killer, is a rare example of a sympathetic Pole so infrequently found in the American theatre. The Łukaszek family, transformed later into the Negro American family of Anna Lucasta, and the wild stag Stanley Kowalski in *A Streetcar Named Desire*, were glaring examples of the bad press we have here, which identifies Polishness with misery, both material and moral. The play itself is a perceptive "slice of life," but this is better rendered in its moments of soldierly clowning than dramatic tension. Interesting that such war-plays, which imitate a soldier's life, are almost entirely "collective monodramas."[79] The whole cast was great — as if everyone was playing himself from those war years.

*Among the actors playing in *Stalag 17* there appeared, at a certain moment, a young man with a large nose and a not-too-intelligent receding double chin, who seemed to be a double for Gay Davis, that "first citizen of the world" who contemned American citizenship and for a certain time was loud in Paris. I looked at the poster and what did I see: that actor, that extra (because later on he had practically nothing to say), was none other than Gay Davis. It turns out that at day's end the citizens of the world feel most at home in New York, even in the role of a theatrical extra.

28 June

[...] In Cartier's[80] article on Franco-American relations, wonderful as always, I find a revelation of some weight: Roosevelt so hated de Gaulle that, during his visit in Casablanca, armed soldiers were hidden about, ready, in the event that de Gaulle should attack the President. This revelation clears up many riddles and displays the chasm of that ignorance of Europe

---

[79] Lechoń coins the phrase *samograje*.
[80] Raymond Cartier (1904-1975). French journalist. Lechoń considered him "the most intelligent great reporter alive today" (*Journal*, 19 November 1952).

found even among such European, Machiavellian Americans like Roosevelt. To imagine something of that order, does that not mean to understand nothing, either of people or of human matters? In the light of this discovery one better understands Yalta, as well as how Roosevelt might trust Stalin, believing that he'll "turn out all right."[81]

20 July
[...] Yesterday, a picnic on the Potomac with a very honest pair of elderly patriots from Maryland. When in Rome. . . What *Wianki* or jumping through the fire are for us,[82] thus for people here is holding a hot dog pierced by stick over a fire. I remember twenty some years ago the visit of Edgar Mowrer[83] and his wife at the Jackowskis[84] in Wronczyn. The first thing they did was to go to the lake, build a fire, and roast some hot dogs over it.

24 July
Today, saying hello again to New York, I was surprised to be feeling better than yesterday after arrival. But the blessed feeling left me before evening. I'm already both bored and exhausted, convinced that there is no escape in New York from New York.

---

[81] In the original: *poprawi się.*
[82] A reference to Polish folk traditions associated with the shortest night of the year, 24 June.
[83] Edgar Ansel Mowrer (1892-1977). American journalist and publicist. Lechoń was personally acquainted with him from this visit.
[84] Anna Jackowska (Izydora Wiesława née Schiller de Schildenfeld, primo voto Leszczyńska, 1884-1974). Polish actress using the pseudonym Anna Belina. Tadeusz Jackowski (1889-1972). Polish diplomat, her husband. The Polish intellectual élite, including Lechoń, were frequent guests in Wronczyn in the 1920s.

6 August

At eight o'clock the trip to New York — a fantastic road, divine air — everything like youth, only with the bitter taste of youth's loss. Later I wandered around New York, from which I will never extract myself as I once did from Paris. I'm already soaked through with this city and yet nothing of it is capable of penetrating me really.

12 August

[...] The priest in the little chapel in Margaretville celebrates Mass with precision and solemnity such as I have perhaps never seen since I have been in America. This is no petty matter, how one celebrates a liturgy, be it ecclesial, civil or military. The symbols they contain speak to us solely by virtue of their ideal celebration.

*I've always adored chipmunks, light brown creatures with black stripes, neither mice nor squirrels, agile, funny, greedy and very ready to be friendly with people. But ever since Disney introduced them to his films, where they exhibit wonders of industry and wit, making do in all difficulties and getting the better of all the larger animals, every time I see a chipmunk I have to laugh, as if it were true what Disney dreamed up.

14 August

[...] A stream like the Prądnik[85] or some other Zakopanian watercourse, those same boulders washed by the water, and above, Tatra-like slopes, with the same trees. It seemed to me that I'm gazing at it from afar, as if in a dream, from the great beyond, not as a reality, but as a vision of the past, full of sadness.

21 August

[...] For several days now, for a few minutes every day, I have been consumed by the sense that the world in which I live,

---

[85] As a child, Lechoń spent many summers near this river in southern Poland.

114

this New York and these hills, are a part of the same world as Warsaw, Pławowice or Wronczyn. This is effected by the similarity of this landscape to that of Poland, but that doesn't explain everything. Simply put, shyly for the nonce, as if aimlessly, there falls upon me the blessed, inebriating sense of being in contact with the entire world, a Christian sense of a sort of certainty that both there and here, God is above us.

27 August

[...] New York on a transparent autumn night, from the far side of Lincoln Tunnel. One sees every building individually and every single one of the millions of varicolored lights. It looks like some sort of conjured-up Chinese city, like an eastern fairy tale, like an America from a magic and positive fairy tale.

4 September

[...] The pale, thin sickle of the new moon against the autumn sky, over the wonderfully light colossus of the George Washington Bridge. I have known the pink and violet sunsets over Paris; I remember the purple sunset, brilliant past the dome of St. Peter's, as well as the shoals of diamonds which is night in Rio de Janeiro. But this New York sunset is also a wonder, one of the wonders of the world.

15 September

[...] The very middling, but solid landscape-artist Henryk Weyssenhoff,[86] cousin of Józef, once painted a picture displayed in the annual Zachęta salon in Warsaw and entitled, it seems, *Zacisze litewskie* [Lithuanian Retreats]. This painting represented a Lithuanian manor with a porch shaded by trees turning red in autumn, or perhaps woodbine, and beneath the porch two little bears tumbling about. It was a type of painting

---

[86] Henryk Weyssenhoff (1859-1922). Polish artist of the realist stamp; his brother Józef (1860-1932) was a novelist, who often employed themes from the eastern Kresy region of the old Polish Republic.

115

beneath the slovenly open,[87] but how pure-bred, plastic landscapes of Fałat or Wyczółkowski, not in the same league as Chełmoński.[88] But it possessed a mood, a scenography so moving to our countrified sentiment, that — despite all the mediocrity of this canvas — there was no way to forget it, to not recall it, to not love it. Gazing today on the autumn trees on Long Island I suddenly recalled that painting which so moved me in my childhood, and I began longing all the more strongly and painfully.

20 September
[...] In Faulkner's new novel *Requiem for a Nun*, one of the protagonists slyly turns to the dying heroine and asks, "Is there a heaven, Nancy?" She replies, "I don't know. I believe." Faulkner is a person possessed of a deeply religious psyche and each new reading of his works only deepens that conviction in me. Besides this I know of no other writer in our horrid times who should have such a European, I would say, feeling of honor, tradition, everything that the American understanding calls "imponderables." His cycle of novels set in the Civil War is a better work of art, unfortunately, a much better work of art, than Żeromski. I wonder what he thinks of Conrad.

4 October
[...] Over the past week, the baseball playoffs have been incessantly the most important matter in America. The most important among all the ministers and generals and peasants and schoolgirls. The victorious Giants are the greatest heroes of this country — no sporting frenzy in Europe can compare to what's been going on here over the past week, how President Truman and General Vandenberg were on the edge of their seats awaiting the results of the last few games. All measure of value becomes blurred on such days. One writes about a "homer" belted by a

---

[87] *Rozchełstane.*
[88] Julian Fałat (1853-1929), Leon Wyczółkowski (1852-1936), Józef Chełmoński (1849-1914), Polish painters.

player on the victorious team just as one would write about a victory in war or the discovery of radium.

15 October

[...] There is no joy or happiness, in exile. I am moving into a better flat, for me, a much better one. How I would enjoy this room, if I could only lean out the window and see — some familiar sight, hear truly Polish, Varsavian speech wafting up from the street below. Ten years in New York and still my greatest delight is the illusion that my street possesses something of Żoliborz,[89] which I certainly do not consider an urban wonder.

22 October

[...] Just as Park Avenue near 68th reminds me of the region around Parc Monceau and the Bld de Courcelles, 86th near East End has something of the Łazienki region of Warsaw. I don't know if it's the trees, or the view of some house across the river, similar to the Courdegard or barracks from the period of the "November night." Łazienki, thanks to Wyspiański's[90] *Night*, has always been closest to my heart, with the most moving atmosphere for me. — That is why, when I came to realize this association — I felt myself right at home in this neighborhood, in which I am to live, which save this is dirty and full of melancholy houses.

---

[89] A residential area in northwest Warsaw, developed during the twenties and popular amongst the intelligentsia and military officers.

[90] Stanisław Wyspiański (1869-1907). Polish dramatist, painter and theatrical director, perhaps the greatest light of the Młoda Polska period. Lechoń speaks of his *Noc listopadowa* [November Night], a drama dealing with the 1830 November Uprising, set in the Łazienki park and Belweder Palace.

2 November

[...] A letter from Stanisław Mackiewicz:[91] "It so
happens, unfortunately, that I've only just now read Your book
about Polish literature. What a wonderful style, what a charming
pathos, what a most beautiful — I can find no other words than
most beautiful — patriotism. How hard it must be for You in
barbarian America."[92]

I'd like to reply to him that God, in His
incomprehensible wisdom, had to know what He was doing in
creating America, and must have had something in mind when
He tossed me here. He alone knows how hard it is for me here,
but He alone knows, and knows best, how I would feel among
the ruins of culture in Europe.

10 November

[...] Not only in Warsaw, but in Paris too, I understood
everything and was myself comprehensible to everyone, even
though unknown to many. Here, I feel ever more that everything
I say, everything I do, can be understood diametrically opposite
to what I mean, not only by strangers, but also by my friends.
To the majority of Americans, we are what the Chinese are to us.

---

[91] Stanisław "Cat" Mackiewicz (1896-1966). Polish politician, publicist
and writer. In exile in Britain from 1939 until 1956, when he returned
to Poland. He served in the Polish government in exile in London, and
was Prime Minister of that government in 1954-55. The book he is
referring to in his letter is Lechoń's *O literaturze polskiej* [On Polish
Literature], published in London in 1942 and made up of lectures
delivered by the poet in the Polish Library in Paris.

[92] *Tak się nieszczęśliwie złożyło, że książkę Pana o literaturze polskiej
przeczytałem dziś dopiero. Cóż za cudowny język, cóż za czarowny
patos, cóż za prześliczny, nie znajduję innego wyrazu jak
„prześliczny", patriotyzm. Jakże Panu musi być ciężko w
barbarzyńskiej Ameryce.*

[...] I leafed through a book on Józef Konstanty from Philadelphia, last year's baseball revelation. Again, a Pole like Musiał, Borowy, Janowicz, Łuczak. And despite the fact that they are thus among the stars of baseball — which is the summit of the American hierarchy — Poles still remain a symbol of the ghetto and misery. It's already boring to say what the Czechs or Jews would do, if they had such a position.

28 December

[...] A conversation with an architect from Warsaw, who lived for five years in Paris. Everything he said about New York agreed with what I thought after a few months, and even after a few years, of being here. But that's only one side of the medal, and the other, more difficult to discover, is that despite it all the culture of this nation, standardized, cut to form, uncritical, though so in need of explanation — why, wherefore, whence — despite it being a vulgarization for the masses of our European culture, is that culture's preservation, and perhaps even continuation. Unfortunately! Like everything about America, this is not to be easily felt; it has to be learned.

1952

[...] In the monotony of New York, every now and then one finds flashes of poetry and a mood. 86th Street past Lexington is just such a slice of another world. It's a German district, but it looks more like a corner of Italy or Brazil. Full of lights, neon signs, but completely unlike the style along Broadway, rather like something from a theatrical decoration. And buildings as if from a fairy tale, like gingerbread houses, maybe some German elves are hiding in them from the days before Hitler began to exterminate them.

12 February

[...] England has preserved until today something Catholic, which despite all the Puritan hypocrisies renders them close, familiar to us. The mystique and splendor of the Roman Church was transformed into the mythical cult of the Crown, ceremonially speaking, in a fairy-talish naive faith in the monarchy. There is no mysticism in America, no ceremonial, and this is one of the certain and *à la longue* most essential reasons why the atmosphere of this country is so foreign to us.

21 February

[...] I could go on and on about this, what separates me from people like Gafencu, Ripka[93] and the dethroned East European grandees. But however often I find myself among them, I feel a solidarity with them; it's hard to say in what, exactly, but something that is simply a better, worse, perhaps completely outdated. . . Europe, but Europe all the same. Today,

---

[93] Grigore Gafencu (1892-1957). Romanian diplomat and politician, at one time ambassador to the USSR (1940), in exile since 1941. Hubert Ripka (1895-1958). Czech journalist and politician. In emigration since 1940; later he became Minister of Foreign Affairs and a member of the Czech parliament from 1945-1948. The Communist seizure of power in 1948 sent him into exile once more.

Gafencu spoke of the federalist[94] conference in London, and everything he said was full of things not expressed to the full, allusions, symbolical winks and such, which no American might understand, but which all of us caught on the fly — because we're Europeans.

[...] The sheepish parade towards Eisenhower is certainly a protest against corruption and petty politicians, and a longing for something better, more honest. The only problem is, they've chosen the most banal figure, with a smile for everyone and everything, as the fulfillment of these longings. Constantly smiling, even though — in contrast to horse-healthy Truman — he suffers from chronic ulcers. MacArthur wouldn't be elected, nor would Baruch, or any other truly great person. Democracies choose only between common villainy and common honesty. Which doesn't mean that with Eisenhower at the helm, the sharpies won't be able to make off with their loot.

6 April

[...] Wart sense is there to speak of man's free will, his control over his fate? I was such a confirmed Varsavian that my "office hours" in the cafés of Warsaw were almost proverbial, part of the city's landscape. And lo, a trip to Paris for a few months turned into ten years, and I became one of the most Parisian of Poles.[95] Not only living in America, but even a stay here was never in my plans. And now I've been living in New York for eleven years. In Warsaw, I was the incarnation of

---

[94] The Federalists of whom Lechoń is speaking envisioned a federation of East and Central European nations strong enough to withstand pressure from both Germany and the USSR. Lechoń himself was a founding member of the *Związek Polskich Federalistów* [Polish Federalist Association] founded in New York City in 1950.

[95] Lechoń lived in Paris from April 1930 until June 1940, just before the city was overrun by the Nazis. After a brief stay in Brazil, he came to New York City in 1941.

distraction, a Bohemian never to be reconciled to desk and office. And yet I sat behind a desk for ten years — without creating the slightest scandal, as even my enemies would be forced to admit. And I would say that it was not without advantage to the *sacrée* of propaganda. Somebody might say, you're just like a leaf, floating where the wind blows you. I've got a few more examples of that. Later.

7 April

[...] The critic in *The Illustrated London News* writing about *A Streetcar Named Desire* says that there is no food for thought in this play, which differentiates it from Ibsen and Strindberg. Of course, it has nothing in common with them, and that is it's very Americanness, for good or ill. This is an American invention, how they dangle before our nose a slice of living meat, as if they gave no thought at all to that life. Only, of course, it is a more complicated matter than that, and one needn't fling at them Strindberg or Ibsen right from the start.

15 May

[...] Oh, how I would *not* want to live in Montréal or any similar place. I've known for some time just what a blessing it is, the size and universality of New York, but today, after two days in this vacuum, of which it's impossible to say how to approach it — as there's nothing at all to say — I found myself longing for my room as if it were my very homestead.

18 May

[...] Ottawa is truly a phenomenon among capitals.[96] This is no garden-city like Washington, so strangely calm and

---

[96] Lechoń was in Canada from 13-20 May, 1952. Hosted by various Polonian groups, he delivered a speech entitled "O wielkich Polakach, których znałem" [On Great Poles Whom I Have Known] at Holy Trinity Church in Montréal, and subsequently at the University of Ottawa (on the anniversary of Monte Cassino).

provincial in comparison to the giant that is New York. It is simply a parliament and a few ministries set in a little city or a big town. Warm today, green, so that one might imagine that there's nothing more pleasant than to live in this Ottawa. And the Poles here are full of smiles, peaceful — they certainly must have better nerves than we do, the scurrying insects of New York.

24 May

[...] I suddenly recalled the morning I left Ottawa. It was warm, but shady, an atmosphere not of this hemisphere — I don't know if a different wind was blowing, or if the sky was clearer. Maybe so, coupled with the wonderful solution of life in such a village, which is at the same time the capital of a great nation. It possesses so much that it would fill volumes. And so close to New York, if indeed one would suddenly long for the frenzies which it's probably high time to bid farewell to.

2 June

[...] John Dewey has died, the man who more than anyone else left his mark on American anti-intellectualism, on the monstrous utilitarianism of this country's educational system, the horrendous heresies of the so-called philosophy it runs by. All of these things were put forward, of course, with the best intentions, but I don't know if there's anyone in contemporary thought who — like this worthy anti-humanist — might be equally responsible for such horrid and weighty errors.[97]

7 June

[...] Afternoon on the lawn at the Nagórskis in Tuckahoe.[98] The smell of freshly-cut hay, perhaps for the first time since I've been in America. Something of Europe in this

---

[97] *Potworne byki i tak brzemienne w skutki.*
[98] Zygmunt Nagórski (b. 1912). Polish lawyer, journalist and publicist attached during the war to the Polish Army in the West. He lived in exile in the USA with his wife Maria beginning in 1948.

landscape; to be more precise, something from the regions around Berlin — Dallen for example. How much I prefer this to Long Island, which is one disgusting, steamy laundry.

17 June
[...] MacArthur is an American patriot, that which in liberal slang is called a nationalist. But this only seemingly distances him from Europe, for at bottom his way of thinking, his one might say mystical sense, is European, i.e. it has been formed by the, if you will, European heritage of the West. The majority of Americans wish Europe well — only, they simply can't understand it at all. We might have differences of opinion with MacArthur, but we will always find a common language with him, that language which Lyautey and Piłsudski[99] spoke.

26 June
[...] My riverside neighborhood is made up of the most elegant new-fashioned buildings and, as one says in New York, only the best addresses. Not far away, on the other hand, are poor, peeling and smelly buildings, full of the poverty of (mostly) Central and Eastern Europe: Hungarians, Czechs and Germans. In the evening, when one can't see the puddling runoff and garbage, it has something of the atmosphere of Naples. People leaning out of windows converse with their neighbors, lovers or at least sympathetic pairs flirt in the courtyards. This is one of the tens of different New Yorks, closer than many others to Europe. Naples — or Chłodna.[100]

*Sometimes, when I think of the contempt in which elegant Frenchmen hold Americans, which is based on their pride in the famous French taste — I'd like to say aloud somewhere that it's not the Americans but the French, those subtle, overwise ironists, who seem barbarians to me. Their indifference to Misery, their amorality, their cult *de la haute*

---

[99] Józef Piłsudski (1867-1935). Polish patriot, military leader, and *de facto* head of state from 1918-1922, 1926-1935.
[100] A street in what was before the war a fairly poor region of Warsaw.

couture, is nothing but decadence, which neighbors upon barbarity, like Rome under Nero.

9 July

[...] Yesterday in Central Park a little, maybe thirteen year old shoeshine boy approached all of the men, one by one, vainly proposing his services to them. When he got to me, he asked "Were the Spanish kids here? They had to be, because everybody's shoes are already clean." I immediately understood the weight of the matter, and even though I had had my shoes polished just lately, I asked him for a shine. The boy, taking to his brushes and towels with vigor, began to sing under his breath something in a different language. It turned out to be a Yugoslavian song. Becoming garrulous, he told me that he's a Dalmatian, that his name is Ivo, that he came to America two years ago, and a whole lot of other things about himself, his family, his school. I handed him 50 cents after he finished, and he accepted them with a stunned joy and said "You are a millionaire." After which he told me that he once got 25 cents, once even 35, but never "half a dollar." "Half a dollar," he repeated, and moving off, said to himself, "Surely a millionaire."

10 July

[...] I listened on the radio to the Republican convention in Chicago. Songs, bellowing, shrieking, some comic voices raised over the crowd — all of this unthinkable in Europe, because you can't tell where politics ends, the will of the people, and where the shrieking mob begins. But does this mean that these elections are worse than those in Europe, that the average European voter understands better why it should be "this way," and not "that?" Of course not.

27 July

[...] After all the scandals, all the intrigues and behind the curtain deals and public clownery, both conventions picked the best of the possible candidates from each party. I don't think that Eisenhower was a star, but they made him into one, and more than that, his is a name that is famous not only in America, and one hundred classes better than the petty politickers. Stevenson is perhaps even an intellectual of the first class. These circus-like conventions and their perfect results are a classic example of the American paradox. Europe still doesn't understand anything, blithering on about comic strips, gangsters and Hollywood.

28 July

[...] On my way to Hunter, the scenery seemed to me exactly as in Europe, near Zakopane, Kraków, Burgundy, and yet everything completely different at the same time. We plucked thyme, so rare in these parts. The scent was exactly the same as in Poland — yet it grew differently. And I never saw any Alpine sedum or mullein.

5 August

[...] Right next to New York City, some Negro houses on the forested hillsides, almost as exotic as those in Rio. And all along the road, Negroes, almost naked, of different hues of black, in trucks and buses. For the very first time I had, here, in this heat, so near to Manhattan, a feeling of that folklore almost Southern in nature.

*For the first time since I arrived here I feel exhausted, not only by the heat, but by New York itself and America as well. To take a rest from it all, in some unknown country, among foreign, indifferent people; to feel as if one were not in the very center of the globe, but for all that, in every moment, to be with oneself, alone!

8 August

[...] Yesterday I listened to Stevenson's acceptance speech in the radio, which so lifted me in spirit when I read it. It was delivered excellently, too — but applauded at the most banal moments. What was most important in it — that phrase so

126

sensational in America, about materialism at home and the cruel tyrannical enemy without, was greeted with a deafening silence.

16 August

[...] People speaking about other peoples' business in a foreign language — that's what recalls us most strongly to our banishment. With what joy I gazed yesterday at a woodpecker, who drilled away at the tree and moved upwards as if it were on a spring — same as ours, at home. Thus, this country is just like ours, the whole world is our fatherland, ah! what I would give if I could not only say this, but believe in its comfort as well. I'm not comforted at all by Nikita Karamazov's words, *viedie yest' liudi.*[101]

29 August

[...] Very, very beautiful novel by Hemingway, *The Old Man and the Sea* — worthy its title. Everything in it is at the same time completely real and strikingly symbolic, as in poetry. That Sartre with his Genet[102] were nightmares worse than the plague — and now that great sea came to me like a salvation, like sailing out of the darkness into the sun.

8 September

[...] Cartier's article in *Paris Match* about the catastrophic effects of the American policy of liberation in the East, their blindness in the face of their agrarian ideas, their conviction that they can make American farmers of Arabs and Persians. Cartier rages with a barely controlled fury and even speaks of France's withdrawal from the UN, if she was to lose her case there concerning Tunis. I took part in that fury too — for nothing so sets me beside myself as that American overconfidence in progress, the conviction that they hold in their minds and hands the philosopher's stone for all that ails both

---

[101] Russian: "People are [the same] everywhere." Karamazov is a character in Dostoevsky's novel *The Brothers Karamazov* (1879-1880).
[102] Jean Genet (1910-1986). French writer and absurdist playwright.

Asia and Europe — while they will never change either Asia or Europe — because it's not just about standards of living, but also, and even above all, about imponderabilia completely incomprehensible to Americans. Despite the entire villainy of Yalta, there was present there too that overconfident stupidity, the faith that Stalin can't remain blind to such a beneficent light as the wisdom of American professors and research workers. One could write about this for hours, yearning for a Bernard Shaw and an Aristophanes. One might, but it's not necessary. So I end now too, shaking all the while with fury.

10 September

[...] Miss Rachel Giese,[103] an American girl who has been studying Polish literature for several months, said the most embarrassing things about me on the radio today: that I descend in a direct line from Spenser and Milton, that one can meet with my virtues only among the great masters, that "to read Jan Lechoń is to become certain of the vitality of European culture." Does she really think so? I suppose she does, because Americans generally don't spout such foolishness, which doesn't just occur to them. But at the same token is she really any sort of authentic, competent judge?

11 September

[...] One can adore Mark Twain even in Poland, but he will never be as well understood there as he is here. One must certainly *in Dichters Lande gehen.*[104] And one must be a Pole in order to judge not only Wyspiański, but even Prus.[105] And an

---

[103] Rachel Giese, author of *Erasmus' Greek Studies* (1934).

[104] Goethe: *Wer den Dichter will verstehen, muss in Dichters Lande gehen* [He who will the Poet understand, must take himself unto the Poet's Land.]

[105] Bolesław Prus (Aleksander Głowacki, 1847-1912). Polish novelist and short story writer of the Positivist period.

Italian — in order to feel the greatness of Manzoni[106] and d'Annunzio. Because every writer speaks to the entire world, but whispers and smiles only to his own.

3 October

[...] Santayana,[107] who died a few days ago, felt that America's leadership in the world is done a disservice by the fact that Americans wish to reform everything everywhere. This is true, of course. That mania is more of a threat, more hated than any tyranny that impresses with its strength, because that reforming zeal irritates in its naiveté.

10 October

[...] By now almost all new emigrants, who had the right to opt for American citizenship, have received it, so today they registered to vote and now struggle with the thought: Eisenhower or Stevenson? One can look at this from various perspectives, but it would be worst to look at it from the stage set. For after all, with the exception of a few cabotins pretending that their conscience requires them to forswear everything [from their past lives and identities], the rest of them couldn't help remaining Poles. And that is the phenomenon of America, that at the same time they can be both Poles and citizens — and very good ones at that — of America.

12 October

[...] Eisenhower spoke in Denver today, on the occasion of the Pułaski anniversary, and foretold the recall of Yalta, exhorting Poles in Poland to hope and endurance. His speech was seasoned with phrases to stroke both Polish pride and Polish vanity, such as those concerning "my friends Generals Anders

---

[106] Alessandro Manzoni (1785-1873). Italian Romantic poet and novelist.
[107] George Santayana (1863-1952). American philosopher and writer, an expatriate for most of his adult life.

and Maczek."[108] Supposedly, his text was prepared by Jan Karski[109] and Zaleski, Mikołajczyk's[110] secretary. It's also clear that if not for his need of Polish votes in Michigan and Illinois, Eisenhower wouldn't have expressed an iota of what he said. But for all these reasons, whoever would deny the importance of this speech and would not understand that it constitutes the resurrection of the Polish question, buried deep for seven years, would not be a clever realist at all, only the most naive of all political babies.

17 October
[...] Morning at the Library of Congress. Among the various colossus in America, there is this colossus too — a colossus of, well, say it — culture. A few thousand copies of books in all the languages of the world flows in here every day. Of course, one doesn't see this with the naked eye, just as one can't see the immensity of Rockefeller Center from up close. It is amazing that, in a giant such as this, finding a volume of the *Gazeta Polska*[111] from 1937 took all of twenty minutes.

---

[108] Władysław Anders (1892-1970). Polish general, leader of the Polish II Corps fighting alongside the British in the Western European Theatre during the Second World War. Stanisław Maczek (1892-1994). Polish general, creator of the Polish First Armored Division in Western Europe during World War Two.

[109] Jan Karski (Jan Kozielewski, 1914-2000). Polish courier and political emissary. He regularly smuggled important information from occupied Poland to the Polish government in exile in Paris and London. It was he who informed the West of the Nazi liquidation of the Jews. Beginning in 1952, he was a professor at Georgetown University in Washington.

[110] Paweł Zaleski served as secretary to the Polish politician Stanisław Mikołajczyk (1901-1966).

[111] In 1935-36 Lechoń published literary articles and correspondence from France in this half-official organ of the *Obóz Zjednoczenia Narodowego* [Camp of National Unity] — a Sanacja group.

[...] Today on the radio Edgar Mowrer said that neither France nor Germany will raise their own armies. I've known that about France for quite some time. The Americans ruined everything for themselves, tossing money about as if there were no tomorrow and for this reason they appear to be fools. Hoover and Taft were right. If one were to have been difficult to France — she would either have come to Washington on her knees, or it would be the same as it is today, but at a cheaper rate.

/ ... / A sudden strong gust of wind, cold, and half the trees stripped of leaves in the space of a few hours, as if snow were just about to fall. I sensed Warsaw, Łazienki and finally something in my heart, after so many dead and empty days.

[...] Of course, there have already been books like Hemingway's *Old Man and the Sea.* He has discovered no new truth or new form. But there simply *haven't* such books for some time now; rather, there were others that dissected a man into pieces, or rather into a pulp, most often a stinking pulp. Analysis, both Freudian and that which Sartre plays against it in his book about Genet, has achieved its zenith, beyond which one can't take another step. *The Old Man and the Sea* shows another path, one which reminds us of man's composition, of his synthesis, such as Balzac, Tolstoy and Conrad gave us. In this sense, this so unexperimental narrative is a sensational novelty.

[...] Day before yesterday I was at the Naturalization Office on Columbus Ave. Everybody in New York knows what that means. The main, highest boss, to whom I had a letter from Besterman, entrusted me to a naturalization specialist, an older, silent, dry gentleman whose gloomy expression boded no good. I was certain that, after a few minutes, he would prove to be the

131

sweetest fellow, to whom a person might entrust all his matters and concerns. I don't know where I've seen people like him before — perhaps in some film, or maybe I just felt it about him on account of that expression *Il est trop poli pour être honnête.*[112] That warning feeling has almost never failed me.

2 November

[...] Chaplin's new film[113] is a naive, sentimental history, and quite unbelievable. A scrounged-up cast, miserable music, uninventive camerawork, and a script overlong and repetitive. And for all that it's not only the most important film for some time, but one of the few which may well become immortal. Chaplin himself fills it up with such an engaging, daring comedy — so vital as in his greatest roles — and a sense of drama, almost a tragism, such as he has never before attained. This naive fable about an actor becomes, thanks to him, a truth about man, a great work of art, such as we have been unaccustomed to of late in the cinema. Chaplin has made better films, more inventive, better built, but he has never been better as an actor. One can't think of other films after this, and for a long time one won't be able to even look at other actors.

3 November

[...] A very pleasant, middle aged woman, leading a little girl by the hand, came up to me on the street and asked me about some voting formalities that she couldn't quite understand, because she's never before voted in New York, having lived in a little town. After this she said, as if she were looking for understanding and fellow-feeling, that she is very concerned about not wasting her vote, which she wishes to give to Eisenhower, and thinks that all American mothers have the same point of view. "My son is in Korea. He's still a child, really, a child. I believe that Eisenhower alone can help bring my little one home." Unfortunately! Eisenhower can do only one thing

---

[112] French: "He's too polite to be honest."
[113] *Limelight*, directed and starring Charlie Chaplin.

— bomb the Red bases. If he hasn't got that intention, he has taken upon himself a fearful responsibility in regards to the thousands of such honest, moving ladies like her, who confided in me day before yesterday.

4 November

[...] Both Eisenhower and Stevenson are without a doubt the most serious candidates that either party could have put forward. Despite the demagogy, and the moments of vulgarity in the campaigns, today one felt a certain Protestant-religious atmosphere. Seemingly everybody voted today out of a sense of obligation and, I'm convinced, the majority after consulting their consciences. Today is at the very least a good page in the history of America.

5 November

[...] It so happened that a few days ago someone asked me why I think that the Americans are a great nation. I replied that they are because they have a great destiny, and that evokes greatness from them. But as of yesterday I have another, less abstract argument as well. Those workers, who were able to withstand the political pressure exerted upon them by their unions, who do so many good things for them, are truly free people. The nation possessed of such workers, such a majority, is certainly a great nation.

9 November

[...] Whenever Americans, upon returning from Europe, complain about the enmity that they experienced there, I find myself feeling shame for European ingratitude and at the same time compassion for these — God knows — innocent tourists who are after all trying their best and paying taxes in Europe (unlike the majority of the French in their own country!) In my reaction there is both a sense of common guilt, and a kind of tenderness for Americans, as if they were weaker and more helpless in the face of those polished Frenchmen.

133

[...] Nothing can be covered up, no crime in the life of a people or in history. Not only did the corpses in Katyń become unearthed, but also all of the machinations of those who wish to blur the truth of this crime — they too have been exposed in their shameful crannies. One could really think that even in politics "there can't be too many injustices." Roosevelt winking at Stalin, smiling with compassion at his lack of "common sense" — what cynicism, what moral rot!

17 November

[...] Harvard, from breakfast to evening. A walk with Weintraub[114] in the library, full of the most original polonica: complete copies of the *Ateneum, Biblioteka Warszawska,*[115] Niesiecki, Stryjkowski, Estreicher, émigré titles, Długosz,[116] to say nothing of the newer white crows, then the poetry room, then the museum of art — just a little old college museum with Memling, Titian, Tintoretto, Poussin, El Greco, Delacroix, Botticelli. The reading room — no words can do it justice! On the street, every other face alive and thoughtful, and add to all this the ancient walls and the few yellow leaves still on the trees. I'd already forgotten that there can be such oases in America, oases of Europe, the mother of us all, Europe.

---

[114] Wiktor Weintraub (1908-1988). Historian of Polish Literature. A diplomat associated with the Polish government in exile during the Second World War. Professor of Slavic Languages (later, of Polish Literature) at Harvard from 1950. Longtime PIASA member.

[115] *Ateneum* was a bi-monthly cultural magazine published in Warsaw from 1938-39. *Biblioteka Warszawska* [The Warsaw Library] was a literary and scholarly monthly published from 1841-1914 in Warsaw.

[116] Kacper Niesiecki (1682-1744). Polish Jesuit, genealogist and writer. Maciej Stryjkowski ("Strycovius,"c. 1547-bef. 1593). Polish historian and poet. Karol Józef Estreicher (1827-1908). Cracovian librarian and literary historian, initiator of the monumental *Bibliografia polska* [Polish Bibliography]. Jan Długosz (1415-1480). Polish chronicler.

18 November

[...] New York at dawn. Probably the last time I saw it like this was when I lived in the Hotel Lafayette and went around with films at the most ungodly hours. Every city has some hidden mystery which becomes visible only then, when one sees neither people nor artificial lights. Odd, that even in New York that mystery should seem better than the content visible to us during the day.

*Ever since yesterday I've had Harvard constantly on my mind. How great it would be to settle there, the master of those wonderful Polish treasures in the library, teaching at least a few young people that Poland, at least in poetry, is a "great thing." I'm sure that I'd be a very good professor.[117] And even, which for such people as me is easier — a master, a mentor.

22 November

[...] The Polish ghetto in London and even here, where there are much fewer of us, is perhaps a sad reality, but now I know for sure that it is an inevitable one, the only reality. After thirty five years of emigration, the White Russians, on the whole more resourceful than us and better masters of their foreign environment, live really only amongst themselves with their Russian language, Russian superstition, Russian vodka and *kulebiak*[118] — in a word, in a Russian ghetto. Only geniuses and bastards might live otherwise — the ones creative for all, for the foreigners, and the others aping them. The quarrels of London Poles, those provincial Polish grandees, their *tam-ta-ram* ceremonies — this is actually the only true life, among which a Pole might forget about his chains, become anesthetized to the horror of Polish fate. That's why it's wrong to laugh at the Polish ghetto. One should rather poke fun at those who love

---

[117] In 1949, supported by M.K. Dziewanowski, Wacław Lednicki and Oskar Halecki, Jan Lechoń unsuccessfully sought an appointment to Harvard's Slavic Department.

[118] A Russian dish of pastry stuffed with cabbage.

nothing and thus squeeze themselves into a foreign skin, where they still don't understand anything and in which doors are slammed in their face at important moments.

26 November

[...] Someone told me that, catching sight of New York upon returning from Europe, he experienced a shock, although he had earlier lived here happily for ten years. He experienced, as he said, a feeling of terror, that he might live his entire life through in this city, in which one doesn't really "live." Come to think of it, New York is actually a city of death, if we're speaking of individual life, such as one lives in Europe. But if one begins to think of the hugeness and social sweep of America, of what is commonly held — and thus what is truly American — one can experience a different sort of shock — the shock of discovering a life splendid in its risings and fallings, virtues and mistakes — a life new and completely different from the life of Europe, but just such a rich, moving life.

6 December

[...] The thought of the great destiny awaiting America, which fills her as if with inspiration, an instinct which projects nothing but simply acts, let us say, in an historical trance — has been my *idée fixe* for some time now. Around this all my other thoughts concerning the future of the world group themselves in a logical system, in which everything is explained and finds its proper solution. And only through this thought do I perceive a light in the darkness and absurdity of our days. This doesn't mean that America is an ideal. But it is a creative force, an explosion of historical biology, an historical epic, full of both splendid and horrid things.

12 December

[...] It's Soviet Russia that has made of America a worldwide power, the arbiter of the world, and has given her a grand national, political idea; I'd even risk the statement that it is

Russia that has made of the American peoples a single nation. And in history, where ages are what years are in our individual lives, perhaps this will be acknowledged as the secret sense of that horrid experiment.

25 December

[...] The priest from Indonesia, whom I saw a few weeks ago celebrating Mass, had a sermon today. It was obvious that he was at a loss for words in English; I'm sure he's much better in French. Despite that, it was the best sermon I've heard for a long time. he spoke of the mystery of "birth" like a true mystic. For Americans, religion is morality beneath the whip of God.

27 December

[...] Little houses, old furniture in Georgetown,[119] past the window: trees without leaves and a wind like that on the Aleje Ujazdowskie. Acquiescence to everything, not joy, not happiness, but despite it all perhaps the only good of life itself.

---

[119] Lechoń spent his Christmas here at the home of Maria (née Rosen) and Jan Wszelaki (1894-1965). The latter was a diplomat assigned to Washington during the Second World War. Subsequently, he taught Political Science at both Georgetown and American University. Member of the Polish Institute of Arts and Sciences of America, of which he was Executive Director from 1962-1965.

1953

[...] The article in *Life* about France, which conjured up such a storm — almost an armed incursion of the borders — sets out in an oversimplified and scandalous way what I am trying to consider in my essay — from many perspectives, if not objectively. I've been behind the times more than once, and expressed things not expressed before — right when others had it on their lips as well. Despite this fact I will finish this article[120] and even this polemic will at least flush out what I've already said about the opposition of France and America.

3 February

[...] As I was entering the Waldorf, it so happened that Mrs. MacArthur was coming out. Among all the ladies of American politics, she is the most ladylike. Actually, she looks French — but that's how "Southern ladies" are supposed to look, I suppose. Such a beautiful and dainty wife of a great man, a splendid military leader, always seems to me the apotheosis of natural selection. These days, I think about America in Shakespearean categories, and today's coincidental meeting made me dream of a scene from a grand historical play.

21 February

[...] Eisenhower's appeal to Congress for a declaration that America did not wish the subjugation of the peoples behind the Iron Curtain, and that she does not recognize this situation, but refers it to the Atlantic Charter, is the summit of all that Poles could hope for themselves. There is no word concerning

---

[120] *Aut Caesar aut nihil*, which first appeared in *Wiadomości* (Nrs. 45-47, 1954), then in a pamphlet edition published by the London Oficyna Poetów i Malarzy (1955). The English translation, entitled *American Transformations* first appeared in *The Polish Review* (New York, 1958/3) and in pamphlet form by Voyages Press (1959). It is reproduced in this anthology.

borders in this speech, thus, the matter of the Oder and Neisse is open; there is no polemic with Roosevelt, who would reduce everything to an internal matter. It does not bind the English, nor create any immediate diplomatic complications.

2 March
[...] I saw Faulkner on the street today. He had the look of a Polish squire. They could be so small, thin, and noble. He was wearing a completely un-New Yorkish overcoat and a brown felt hat cocked at a rakish angle. It's my opinion that in Faulkner's work one can find atmospheres, figures, ideas not from Conrad, but Żeromski. He himself looks like somebody from *Wierna rzeka* [*The Faithful River*][121] — somebody closer to Traugutt[122] than New York.

6 March
[...] The form of Eisenhower's condolences on the occasion of Stalin's death,[123] the underscoring of the fact that this is an "official" act and thus has nothing to do with his real feelings, is perhaps the first example of such a thing from the very beginnings of diplomacy — perhaps the very negation of diplomacy. And thus it is a great political event.

13 March
[...] I wonder whether those Poles, who have already made a life for themselves in the States, and accepted (one sometimes wonders why) American citizenship, some even changing their names — are not a bit abashed at the fact that everything points to the possibility of an eventual return home. Because it's one thing to be an American when there is no Poland, and another — when Poland again comes to be. But I

---

[121] Novel by Żeromski, 1912. It deals with the January Uprising of 1863.
[122] Romuald Traugutt (1826-1864). Polish General, *de facto* dictator of Polish state during January Uprising.
[123] 5 March 1953.

think that the majority of them believe that it will be a sort of second-class state — and thus it'll always be better to be a Yankee.[124]

17 March

[...] Upon leaving Tatiana de Plessis', Pierre Frederix,[125] whom I hadn't seen for perhaps 15 years, was going in. After a few minutes of conversation (he hasn't changed a bit), he asked me how I'm feeling in New York, in the hopes that I'd say horrid, and how I'm pining for Paris. With what pleasure I told him that I love New York, and that I feel better here than in Europe!

18 March

[...] Three pages, a bit too journalistic, timely, but in sum more or less what I was looking for. I ought to go on about democracy, the actuality of Lincoln. At the very end the thought that in America there is no problem about the end of culture and that the social conscience is purer here than in Europe.

30 March

[...] Some naked thoughts.[126] Who would have supposed, fifteen years ago, that I'd be living in New York for more than ten years and that I'd even grow accustomed to this city. This wonder isn't all that stupid, as I was the very last Pole suited to life here, and never even planned to visit New York. God proposes, God disposes.

---

[124] Lechoń uses this very term.

[125] Tatiana de Plessis was a personal friend of Lechoń. Pierre Frédérix was a French journalist, writer, and literary scholar.

[126] *Myśli adamity.* The Adamites were a Christian sect of the second century AD, who taught the necessity of returning to the state of innocence enjoyed by our first parents. The sect re-emerged several times in the modern era, most notably in Bohemia during the fifteenth century, when the group's views were notoriously expressed by the public renunciation of clothing.

[...] *Kak sam syebya nye pokhvalish, kak oplevanny sidish.*

So I have to brag, that I am able to separate my personal matters from my judgments on more important issues. America is not the country for me, I'd never be able to make a so-called career here, and quite a few thorns have been thrown in my path here, probably unthinkable elsewhere. Despite it all I understand this country and value it better than all of the wise-guys I know, who made careers and fortunes here. The consciousness of this fact is a pleasure of a special kind, something like splendid dinners *a la cena delle beffe.*[127]

10 May

[...] Mother's Day. A beautiful thought, but like all such holidays in America, spoiled by the commercial madness, the bouquets of flowers pinned to all the mothers' coats, and even flowers in the boutonnières of their sons, such as clever salesmen have been able to force upon various bachelors thirsting for such medals. And besides this, the mothers here are no European saints, who didn't sleep throughout the entire childhoods of their sons and daughters, who thought it a shame to pass the lot over to the "baby-sitters;" no, these are the severe "bosses" of the home hearth, happiest when their youngsters leave home for their own *pieds-à-terre* and who, if they have tenderness for anyone, it's for their seventeen year old sons — Mommies-boys hysterically adored and thus entering life burdened with complexes. Love for one's mother, that is a feeling so discreet that, every time I read confessions on that theme, they always seem improper to me, not excluding the much-overrated letters of Słowacki.[128] For this reason these

---

[127] *Kak. . .* Russian: "He who doesn't praise himself, sits covered in spittle." *La cena delle beffe,* Italian: "dinner of mockers."

[128] Juliusz Słowacki (1809-1849). Polish Romantic poet, rival of Mickiewicz.

brooms of gardenias or orchids, gathered together with disgustingly shiny-bright ribbons and decorating the busts of New York mothers, seem to me an unnatural manifestation of true feeling, nothing but an indiscreet and vulgar form, without any content.

24 May

[...] A tropical sun in New York, which saddens the purest weather for me, as it has no European freshness to it. At bottom I like light frosts the most — cloudy days without too much humidity. Then I'm reminded of how it used to be at home.

19 June

[...] What Faulkner said at Wellesley about man saving the world and the quality of people "at home" seems no revelation to me — surely someone somewhere said this in another manner. But it's quite another affair that only a writer, who takes responsibility for the world, and not some scribbler like the majority of the thoughtless liberals who constantly spout empty phrases 200 years old, could say this — only a man who is in constant conversation with his own conscience. Add to this the fact that he is an American in the best sense of the word, which means a person truly believing in the future, whether or not he's Faulkner.

25 June

[...] Rising above all Polish provincialism, Sambor[129] in *Kultura*[130] advises Polish authors to take up foreign themes,

---

[129] Michał Sambor (Michał Chmielowiec, 1918-1974). Polish writer and journalist. He was affiliated with the Polish government in exile. and later worked for the Voice of America and Radio Free Europe, among others. Editor in chief of *Wiadomości* from 1966 on.

[130] Polish émigré monthly published in Paris (1949-2000) under the editorship of Jerzy Gedroyc; rival of *Wiadomości*. Lechoń was critically oriented to it.

because Hemingway after all, and Koestler[131] after all . . . Now Koestler is exactly that sort of bad literature, those fake people, who will reveal their falsity some day, at which time all thought of Koestler will evaporate. Hemingway, on the other hand, I'm sorry: he wrote not about any foreign matters, only about his own, about what he experienced himself — it's all one whether in America, Italy or in Spain. Same as Conrad. Well, but somehow I don't see any Conrads or Hemingways in London, peeping up behind the shoulder of Dakowski.

29 June

[...] A walk in the evening along a route with a view of the sea. A rose-lily light, the warm scent of caprifolium, one might say: just like in Poland. Only totally different.

3 July

[...] The humidity has suddenly vanished. A sky like in Athens, or at least like in Warsaw. The little square at Rockefeller Center looks just like a portion of the Piazza san Marco, the horrid Library on 42nd like the Acropolis, and the laughable giant blocks to the west of the park like a fairy tale about America. But what of it? *Que faire? Faire to que*,[132] as once poor departed Teffi[133] wrote somewhere.

22 July

[...] For quite some time I've felt that in my Hungarian-German neighborhood, above all in the poorer section where life is carried out on the street — I am seen as a figure from another

---

[131] Arthur Koestler (1905-1983). British novelist and essayist of Hungarian extraction. Like Hemingway, he wrote of his experiences during the Spanish Civil War.

[132] French, then sarcastically Polonized French: *What's to do? Do that what.*

[133] Nadyezhda A. Teffi (Buczyńska, 1872-1952). Russian humorist, sister of the poet Mirra Lokhvitskaya (Maria A. Zhyber, 1868-1905), whose verses Lechoń translated into Polish.

world and all the same I don't arouse any good will. But yesterday I became convinced that such a reputation, being equivocal, is not the worst one could have. Because as I was walking along my 82nd street, full at the time of amused youngsters, still wet behind the ears,[134] I heard a cry in my direction which was only half-contemptuous: "Einstein! Einstein!"

31 July

[...] Senator Taft, who died today, was an American political phenomenon. He wasn't interested in pleasing anyone, he spoke and acted against public opinion, with no regard to either America or foreign lands. This is a great lesson for the dishonest and those worse than they, the political sharpies, that by acting in this way he not only won popularity for himself, but also respect such as no other American politician, perhaps, might boast of. What is more, he always knew what Poland is, and defended her exactly because of that knowledge.

1 August

[...] The spontaneous and general apotheosis of Taft is proof of the fact that the American nation is different and better than banal opinion paints it to be. Not only the Democrats, but also the union bosses are honoring his memory, although his name was often a red flag for the demagogues. Such is the prestige of character and that most rare virtue on earth: disinterestedness. Today's papers uncover one more thing, which had escaped the notice of us, guests in America, yet, it seems, absorbed all Americans. After his unsuccessful campaign at the convention in Chicago, Taft stood next to Eisenhower and the ever more powerful medium of television showed this scene from Epinal to the entire nation. Thus writes the *New York Times* about him: "His good sportsmanship in rising above these disappointments was so admirable and relentlessly examined by

---

[134] *Rozmemlane.*

the television eye in his last defeat for the Presidential nomination in Chicago — so authentically genuine, that it was almost painful to watch."

I encourage those who constantly speak of American brutality, who do not understand the emotional discretion of these people, to consider well those words, which say more about American honesty and morality than long scholarly treatises.

16 August

[...] I did nothing today, because we were on the way back to New York. It was warm, but already autumnish. The roads were not yet crowded, which always makes one angry and doesn't permit one to enjoy the landscape. As it was, I enjoyed it more than I can remember ever having done. The scent of the meadows and woods, some sort of little romantic lakes, with tiny islands of lily-colored herbs, the Hudson silvery-green like the canvasses of Manet, the beauty of the George Washington Bridge — in the mist today like a cathedral of lace floating along above the earth.

19 August

[...] Again in the park today one could make out each individual branch, almost every single leaf. I thought of Corot and Ruisdael, and one could fall to dreaming as if on the Prater, the Bois de Boulone, the Villa Borghese. I almost wanted to say — and as if in the Łazienki Park.

21 August

[...] The so-called Kinsey[135] Report, and above all its reception by the American media, is a scandal so revolting that I have to restrain myself from drawing from it conclusions concerning American politics and cry "We're in bad shape!"

---

[135] The American sexologist Alfred Charles Kinsey (1894-1956) published his controversial *Sexual Behavior in the Human Male* and *Sexual Behavior in the Human Female* in 1948 and 1953, respectively.

Kinsey is a zoologist and treats people like mammals, pure and simple — which is proof of his stupidity — but I'm afraid that beyond this he's a sex maniac, or a sharpster, or both together. The confessions of 5,000 women, shameless women, who, unconstrained by any illness, uncover to strangers' eyes the things that even animals cover with their tails prove nothing more than the bestialization of these very women. The fact that the press greeted this load of manure as a scientific breakthrough, as a lamp of wisdom, that the *Herald Tribune* dedicated a few pages and a front page story to it, is a revelation of depthless naiveté or such hypocrisy, as from the time of the famous Martian invasion of America[136] has not made of this country such a clownish laughingstock in the eyes of the world.

19 September

[...] No literature is truly comprehensible if one cannot feel an entire nation, an entire culture behind it. Despite all their raving over Tolstoy and Dostoyevsky, the French actually know nothing about them, which can be deduced at the very least from their imitators. Slowly, very slowly, after learning something about America, I have begun to savor their writers — to understand their common relation to one another, and their relation to the history and life of their country. And because of this discovery, everything in their writings seems deeper to me, more interesting and beautiful.

28 September

[...] The view from the Falenckis'[137] window — the very center of Manhattan so composed that Cézanne himself couldn't do a better arrangement. And no Monet would be

---

[136] A reference to the (in)famous radio broadcast of H.G. Wells' *War of the Worlds* by Orson Welles' Mercury Theatre of the Air on October 30, 1938.

[137] Władysław Falencki (died 1991) was a Polish financier and philanthropist, He and his wife Karin Tiche-Falencka, a Warsaw actress and cabaret performer, knew Lechoń since before the war.

147

capable of thinking up such colors — that silvery-navy sea of electric lights, surrounded by the aureole of the red sunset. Venice, Paris and Rio are lovely in different ways, but not more beautiful.

1 October
[...] Again I began a new thought, which dissuades me from a conclusion. To end it — necessary. I think that America is "sentenced to greatness."

14 October
[...] I'm having a lot of trouble with the title for this sketch. It can't be a political title, and there's too little literature in it for a literary one. Today it somehow occurred to me to call it *Wieczór nad Hudsonem* [Evening on the Hudson], but it seems to me that this would be pretentious, and that one would after all have to add some sort of introduction, for which I no longer have the animus, dreaming as I am to finish it.

18 October
[...] Jamestown[138] is a fairy tale incarnate. Fenimore Cooper — on a little square the Confederate fort, the old tumbledown Methodist church, a 300-year old cemetery, the statue of some Smith or other and an Indian girl, the purl of waters and an old Negro right out of Uncle Tom's Cabin leading one around these relics. And amidst it all the legend of Polish pitch burners, who arrived here 300 years ago, proved to be wonderful craftsmen, and didn't allow anyone to pull them around by the nose, faithful to the arch-Polish motto *Ja mu pokażę* ["I'll show 'em"]. The ceremony per se itself could have been better, but this combination of Poland, the Indians, and the Civil War gave me lots to dream about. If I were younger, I'd write a book about it all for young readers.

---

[138] The Polish Club of Washington D.C. organized a celebration to commemorate the 345th anniversary of the arrival of the first Poles to America in this year.

20 November

[...] The George Innes[139] exhibition. Lots of literature, like our Ruszczyc,[140] but these canvasses are full of a true, plastic poetry, not expressed in literary-wise. And what is so rare among American painters — in several landscapes one finds such a light, not impressionistic — which always means French — but American, such as painters here just don't see. In this light, colors compose themselves in gamuts completely different from those in Europe; they play as they do on the best French canvasses.

28 November

[...] It's obvious that death has its own rounds to go, now visiting one sphere or profession, and at another time — another. Bernstein[141] was only a great master, O'Neill, on the other hand, a great tragic writer — but the theatre is in mourning for both. An entire epoch ends with the death of one, while the other — departs like the proper creator of the true theatre of his nation. O'Neill was, after all, the antonym of all rules, principles, mathematics, and dramatic writership — from which Bernstein grew and amassed a great fortune (though of course I don't believe in the sum of $8,000,000). Like almost all great American writers, he was a bit of everything, vain and lazy, a wandering bum, a reporter, and an actor before he began to write, and this is why his theatre is permeated with a strong breath of life, such as the French maestros know only from books and glances. His time will yet come, when soapy eyes grow clear again, and the public ceases to chase after what supposedly never was, and much smaller, after all, masters than Bernstein. And when one considers who from our era might remain for all time in the theatre, one begins ever more to doubt

---

[139] George Innes (1825-1894). American landscape painter.
[140] Ferdynand Ruszczyc (1870-1936). Polish landscape painter and scenographer.
[141] Henri Léon Gustave Bernstein (1876-1953). French dramatist.

in Bernard Shaw and think less of Pirandello, while there is no way not to think about O'Neill.

29 December

[...] Walking around Radio City I saw a queue two blocks long from Sixth to Fifth Ave. and back again along another block. Several thousand provincials have been stamping in place for two hours without a complaint, and even joyfully, only to see a very stupid film and a very effective, but cheap show, and especially to be able to brag back in Tennessee and Nebraska that one was present at wonders. And yet I'm not certain that this patience and this prestige of praised things does not contain something quite edifying.

1954

[...] I've made a determination to read the entire works of Saint-John Perse.[142] So far, various soundnesses,[143] suggestive images, even inventions. Yet right next door artificiality, unbearable quirks invented "by force," and, devil take it, why isn't this called prose? I'm going to read more tomorrow afternoon.

24 January

/. . . / It's banal to say, and yet it must be said, that Hemingway died[144] the way the author of his books should have, and certainly would have wanted to finish his life. The valleys in his writing were embarrassing, but whenever the simoom of his passion rushed through a novel of his, this broke through his simplemindedness and blew all sentimental-arrogant trash from its path. Uneven, it almost seemed *passé*, yet Hemingway was from time to time truly a great writer, and thus he was in fact a great writer. In prose, in the very art of narrative, he was a great inventor who blew a strong, fresh breath into the moldy, consumptive, heartburn-sterile analysis-novel[145] of our century. And for all this he was not a litteratus — horrible word — which means less, the more one becomes proud of it and uses it to elevate oneself above others, who are so much more unusual writers — for being more usual folk.

---

[142] Saint-John Perse (Alexis Saint-Léger Léger, 1887-1975). Innovative French poet and diplomat. He lived in the USA from 1940-1959, and received the Nobel Prize in 1960.

[143] *Trafności.*

[144] Hemingway and his fourth wife Mary actually survived two plane crashes on the 21st and 22nd of January. News out of Africa that they had been killed quickly spread, to be corrected shortly thereafter.

[145] *Zgagaciałej w bezpłodnej analizie.*

25 January

[...] Hemingway was saved by an improbable working of fate, like the most improbable event from his books. I wouldn't change my necrology a bit in a few years even if, of course, "the old man" leaves no true masterwork for his old age, which I wish him from the bottom of my heart. Amen.

13 March

[...] To speak the language of Sanacja, they're "driving McCarthy to death."[146] But in my opinion there never was any McCarthy, and perhaps — no McCarthyism either. The Bolsheviks furiously convinced both learned and unlearned idiots that he was a future Hitler. But how can that be, in an America victorious and full of well-fed workers? McCarthy existed as long as Eisenhower agreed to his existence. Rightly or wrongly, he is America's goad. "Eisenhowerism" — now that's something. That's a psychological state, a temperament, superstition — something like our Endecja.[147]

21 March

[...] *America* is finished — that means, I have rewritten and corrected the end, which was perhaps a bit too clear, and thus unnecessarily "prophetic." I gave it the title *Aut Caesar aut nihil*[148] but I'm sure to change it. *Byk i Europa* [The Bull and Europe] would be just what the doctor ordered, but maybe a bit too frivolous for this sharp-toothed serpent.[149]

---

[146] *Wykańczają.*
[147] The prewar National Democracy Party.
[148] *Either Caesar, or nothing*, subsequently entitled *American Transformations* in its English version, reproduced in this volume.
[149] *Kolubryna.*

[...] At the discussion-evening "Poland and America." Mierzwa[150] quite splendid. Of course he said Polunia and not Polonia, but that peasant boy, who as he confesses himself didn't know in his Limanowskie that such a thing as Poland even existed, speaks a pure Polish, simply put, pure, and at times attains a French finesse. At the start he said, "I have been living in this country for forty years now, so I can't speak objectively about America like some of those who got here two days ago." The subtlest Frenchman couldn't achieve a more elegant nastiness. And only a great speaker could risk the joke, "Professor Halecki,[151] who lives in Scarsdale, because he's afraid of atomic bombs," without worrying that he might insult Halecki, and moreover certain that he'd make him chuckle. Bravo, Mierzwa!

25 March

[...] I watched the Oscars ceremony, sitting in front of the television at the Falenckis'. Bronek Kaper[152] got the award for best musical illustration, and I admit that it wasn't with indifferent eyes that I watched him ascend the stage to receive the rather vulgar (in any case) statuette. I had the feeling that it wasn't only Warsaw, but the "Ziemiańska"[153] that was receiving that grand and world-

---

[150] Stefan Paweł Mierzwa (1892-1971). economist, professor at Drake University in Iowa, founder (1925) and president of the Kościuszko Foundation.

[151] Oskar Halecki (1891-1973). Polish historian, professor at the University of Warsaw, and, later, Fordham. From 1939 in emigration (in the USA from 1940). One of the founding members of the Polish Institute of Arts and Sciences of America, which he led as President until 1962.

[152] Bronisław Kaper (1902-1983). Polish composer and pianist. Settling in Los Angeles, he worked for Metro Goldwyn Mayer studios.

[153] A café on Mazowiecka St. in Warsaw, especially associated with the Skamander group.

renowned award. And in the spirit of the old Ziemiańska I sent Kaper the following telegram: *Unjust sentence...*[154]

13 April

[...] In the introduction to *Faulkner's Reader*, Faulkner writes that the most beautiful conception of a writer's role that he has come across, was that sentence of Sienkiewicz's concerning the invigorating of hearts,[155] which he read in his childhood, and which we have found so laughable. It's odd, perhaps, that gloomy Faulkner was so struck by this, but I have this little journal and my scribblings to testify to the fact that I have always considered him a Romantic, and in his Civil War cycle akin to Żeromski. And — as the prewar journalists of Warsaw would put it — What would Mr. Gombrowicz[156] say to that?

1 May

[...] Nothing which is American is completely the same as ours. Their most human reactions are, in a human sense, different than ours. If the content is the same, the style is different, just like our style — Poles and Frenchmen — is different. But here the differences are larger and it's more difficult to find a key to that style, without which it can't be understood. And the mistake will be larger than if we were prying into the souls of Chinamen. Because with them we know from the start that they're different.

1 June

[...] On Madison Avenue, first Greta Garbo — old and with mussed hair, but always Greta Garbo — with her usual

---

[154] *Wyrok niesprawiedliwy.*

[155] *Krzepienie serc.*

[156] Witold Gombrowicz (1904-1969). Polish novelist and essayist, in exile from 1939, chiefly in Argentina and France, where he died. Perhaps the most well known Polish literary figure beyond the borders of Poland.

entourage: an older, greyheaded gentleman (I knew who he is, but I've forgotten it, upon my word!) A few paces further Marlon Brando, without a jacket, in a very common blue shirt, unshaven and — in the American sense — with unkempt hair. Who knows if those two persons are not a symbol of the heights of the American theatre. And maybe it's no coincidence that both of them have broken with American elegance, the banal standard.

20 June

[...] In the Polish church in Glen Cove young gentlemen and misses, grandees and boys just the same as in our country and suburban churches. But everyone's so spruced up, coiffeured, fresh-bathed, with hats, dresses and suit-coats, that the spirit sings. Some of them, and certainly the majority of their parents, had put on shoes in Poland only to go to church. I love the stripes of Łowicz and the ribbons of Kraków, but when I think of those peasants a few miles distant from the city, where people lived right among the swine, I find beauty in these standardized dresses as well, which signify one's own little house, a car, and the refrigerator for everybody, which so many make fun of.

22 June

[...] Two walls of an aluminum skyscraper — set up in one day on the corner of 57th — that means, a skeleton to which aluminum plates have been fixed. This is of course no wonder of architecture, but it is certainly a wonder of efficiency, such as no ancient or medieval mind dreamt of, to say nothing of the Renaissance. As far as beauty itself goes — the figures on the Concorde are likewise not beautiful, and despite it all the whole square is one of the wonders of the world. And this skyscraper, illuminated, will also be part of the towering wonder of our times — New York.

11 July

[...] Just as there are figures particular to Rubens, Leonardo and El Greco, so are there trees instinctively Ruisdael, Poussin, Watteau, Corot and trees of Chełmoński, Wyczółkowski, Jacek.[157] Through the window I see Corot-trees, whispering above the mob of American bushes. And I think, and dream, of seeing once more Chełmoński's Mazovian pine or Wyczółkowski's Tatra fir.

20 July

[...] The gorgeous cemetery in New Haven, gorgeous because tree-filled like ours in Poland, in Europe. It's inconceivable, but only there did it occur to me that there are no trees whatsoever in American cemeteries. The bastards don't plant them, because that would mean so much less space for the dead.

30 July

[...] I've lived in New York for 13 years now and day before yesterday I was on the open sea for only the second or third time. It did me good. The sea, which tortured me in youth, is now my element. I thought of the beach in Połąga[158] 45 years ago, of the happiness of the Mediterranean Sea and of the pages

---

[157] Jacek Malczewski.
[158] Połąga (Palanga). Seaside resort on the Baltic in Lithuania. As a boy, Lechoń vacationed here once with his family.

of Przybyszewski[159] in Boy's anthology, as beautiful as *Anhelli.*[160]

[...] Among various "nevers" and "too lates," today I have discovered one more. I'll never learn English to the degree that I might truly delectate the genial laconicity of Shakespeare. I can feel it through Paszkowski,[161] and even Pajgert,[162] but that's not the same thing. Thank God that even in translation the world-vision remains the same, for the sake of which Middleton Murray[163] blasphemously compared Shakespeare to Christ. But beyond this, the greatness of Shakespeare — are words, words which like those of Racine and Mickiewicz are unique and impossible to translate.

21 August

[...] Margaretville again, and I am resigned to the boredom of a familiar landscape, to memories of two years ago, when I was tortured with various uneases. For now everything is different — no one and nothing irritates me, and some light began to shine in my head, like a thought of the future. But there can be no word of writing, and here I might repeat the famous

---

[159] Stanisław Przybyszewski (1868-1927). "Demonic" Polish writer, first associated with literary movements in Germany and Norway. Upon his return to Poland, he settled in Kraków and became one of the main movers behind Młoda Polska. The anthology referred to is Boy's *Młoda Polska. Wybór poezji* [Young Poland. A Selection of Poems], Lwów, 1939.

[160] By Juliusz Słowacki (1837), inspired by his religious experiences in the Holy Land.

[161] Józef Paszkowski (1817-1861). Polish translator and poet. Many of his translations of Shakespeare are considered classics.

[162] Adam Pajgert (1829-1872). Polish translator and poet, mostly from the English.

[163] John Middleton Murray (1889-1957). British literary critic, married to New Zealand author Katherine Mansfield until her death in 1923.

phrase from letters written home by cooks in Warsaw: "And now I report to You, my dear parents, that I have nothing to report."

22 August
  [...] I've done nothing, but I feel that such empty lazing is just what I need. I lost myself in New York, like so many people, like so many millions of people, and I want to find myself, as our honest Polish dreamers used to say, "on the bosom of nature."

1 September
  [...] Evening in a cloudless sky above the woods, rising from the autumnal exhalations, the sickle of the moon and next to it Venus so pure, cut from the heavens by such a wonderful silver-gold light, as if painted by Chełmoński. I stood with Józio Wittlin and we spoke of frighteningly banal things, and heartrendingly sad things, none destined for other peoples' ears, torn from the very depths of exiles' stomachs.

15 September
  [...] Styka's[164] funeral in St. Patrick's Cathedral. Ten years ago there was hardly a single great house in New York where you would not find a portrait by his hand hanging on the wall. Except for a few virtuosos, he alone among Poles made what one calls a career in this country. And yet there wasn't a single American at this beautiful ceremony. And if there was, he was engulfed in the mass of Poles, used to giving honor to the dead, and having been taught that an artist is an unusual person, and more interested in ecclesial pomp than kicking a ball around. For those who dream of American triumphs, who laugh at the Polish ghetto, this service was one great, gloomy lesson.

---

[164] Tadeusz (Tade) Styka (1889-1954). Polish painter active in Paris and New York, to which he emigrated in the late 1920s. His father Jan Styka (1858-1925), also a painter, is the creator of, among other things, the panorama *Racławice* (1899).

18 September

[...] On the way from Manhasset to Locust Valley, so many "schools" of trees, which in this country are called nurseries. So many glass houses with dahlias and chrysanthemums of American dimensions, which fit so well alongside those splendid, but somehow millionairishly magnificent flowers. Just beyond Cecilia's garden gate, on the other side of the road, one hears the gallop of horses and voices from a megaphone describing the progress of dressage. Here, as in England, autumn is the season of "society," the members of which have a grand old time whereas others don't even step off their treadmills after Labor Day. But God forbid one think of America as a "society" land. Just the opposite. America belongs to those others.

26 September

[...] At Washington Square in the afternoon with Solski. What a relief to gaze at people, almost every one of whom is different from the other — to see at last the oddies, *les folles, les folles de Washington Square*, Bleecker St., Charles St., all dressed up in moth-eaten pre-deluge stoles, in slapping slippers and torn stockings. Painters exhibiting their canvasses for sale on the walls of buildings and fences, old *cabotins-pompières*, not even *pompières* but the usual hacks and young Surrealists, Abstractionists, more often than not handsome boys with anxiety in their eyes, more often than not on sale themselves.

1 October

[...] The World Series, the final playoffs in baseball. Even though this time it is taking place in Cleveland, and not in New York as every year in the past, it's driving all of New York, indeed all of the country, to complete abstraction. Don't ask me to explain what a "homer" is, because I don't know myself — it's enough to say that there's some sort of quick race through

159

the field at record time, because of which the runner's team amasses a very great amount of points. Thus yesterday, the day before yesterday, and again today a fellow named Dusty Rhodes made such homers for the New York Giants. This immortal feat was recorded by the following headline: "Rhodes did it," illustrated with a photograph in which Rhodes kisses his bat. Why should we be surprised at the papers, after all, when the mayor of New York City himself, Wagner, greeting a few days ago these "Giants" at City Hall, stressed that the city greets them as it had other "great ones" such as Lindbergh and Eisenhower. And I'm not sure that even Eisenhower would think that an exaggeration.

19 October
[...] Yesterday I was at the Capitol in Senator Fergusson's office. I'm very fond of that entire quarter of white buildings, not necessarily wonderful architecture, but having something Roman in its mood. American congressmen and senators are no great patterns of virtue, and the majority of them are wild simpletons when compared to the culture of the French and English. But Congress as a whole, as an idea, is for the average citizen something more than the parliaments of Europe are for their peoples. And, walking among these piles, one feels that the great fathers of the Republic live on in them despite their unworthy and unwise grandchildren.

22 October
[...] Only one great nation has emerged during our times: the United States following the Civil War. And there was only one great founder during those times: Lincoln. What the poets, beginning with Whitman, have written about him is a fantasy of history. In their lines Lincoln is not a living man, he is a sort of Piast or Krak.[165] In these times of constant decline and demise, what an encouragement it is to see some sort of

---

[165] Piast and Krak are legendary figures associated with the myths of origin of Poland and Kraków.

beginning, and thus, what I constantly say about America, some sort of future.

28 October

[...] Hemingway received the Nobel. Before God and truth I don't know how anyone among the contemporary writers that I'm familiar with could have got it, if not him. In France one can speak seriously of Duhamel[166] (for his past), and Malraux, in England of Morgan[167] and Somerset Maugham (but is this really first class, or first among second?) It's enough to say that in Italy Moravia[168] is seen as a possible candidate. I am ever less surprised that every year in October Kuncewiczowa[169] has her sleep broken by moans, to say nothing of the fact that Melchior[170] can't even sleep during that month.

2 November

[...] Faulkner is really the contradiction of all that one thinks about America. And since he is from the South, a symbol of the South, one can say that the South is not America. First of all, money plays no role in his world, as if it didn't exist — at the very least it is not the demon it was for Balzac and is for many American writers. But now Hemingway occurs to me. He too has little to do with money, even though he's not a Southerner. So maybe after all we don't know America, and she doesn't even know herself. Maybe America isn't America.

---

[166] Georges Duhamel (1884-1966). French physician and writer.

[167] Charles Langbridge Morgan (1894-1958). British author and theatre critic for the *London Times*.

[168] Alberto Moravia (Pincherle, 1907-1990). Italian author, whose traditionally-styled works are suffused with eroticism.

[169] Maria Kuncewiczowa (née Szczepańska, 1895-1989). Polish author. Lived in exile in London (1940-1955) and the USA (1956-1968), where she taught at the University of Chicago before returning to Poland.

[170] Melchior Wańkowicz (1892-1974). Polish journalist and writer of travel reportages and war correspondence. In exile from 1939 on (in the USA from 1949-58 before returning to Poland).

[...]   The most improbable evening that I ever experienced in America: dinner and an evening of poetry at the Pen and Drust Club, where various old hags, some even quite rich, exhibit their paintings — some of them even abstracts, and where they recite their works.   Grace Humphrey dragged me there, an honest old dame, and professional friend of Poland, something like an American Różyczka,[171] enthusing over Zakopane and Zuzanna Rabska[172] with equal fervor, Cardinal Sapieha[173] and old Kraushar.[174]   At dinner I sat between two younger ladies, one of them a confirmed Polonophile and the other an asthmatic painter; in a word, a monstrous torture, and I cursed honest old Humphrey for jamming me into such a pre-deluge affair.   Later, a half hour straight out of *Babbitt* or the best scene of Ruth Draper.[175]   The old hags sitting in a row read their poems written under the direction of a professor and which — as the president of the club emphasized more than once, a huge, stout woman, and it seems the richest of them all — have already all been "sold" to various magazines.   I admit that after these emotions I was waiting to see how far the next number, our countrywoman madam Ogrodowska-Bristol, who wrote a novel in blank verse entitled *Let the Bird Sing* and for whom poor old Grace dragged me there, would outdistance these grannies in foolishness.   And here comes a poorly-coiffed lady, dressed in some old-fashioned evening gown full of cocards and lace.   She

---

[171] Rosa Bailly (1890-1976). French poet and Polonophile, propagator of Polish culture in France. Lechoń's friend since before the war.

[172] Zuzanna Rabska (1888-1960). Polish author.

[173] Adam Stefan Sapieha (1867-1951). Archbishop of Kraków, known for his heroic defense of the Church and Poland during the Nazi Occupation and the post-war Communist persecutions.

[174] Aleksander Kraushar (1842-1931). Polish historian, co-founder of the *Towarzystwo Naukowe Warszawskie* [Warsaw Academy of Arts and Sciences], 1907.

[175] Ruth Draper (1884-1956). actress specializing in monodramas.

begins to speak and after a few seconds I become aware of the fact that she was once beautiful — she reminded me somehow of Modrzejewska.[176] I fall under the charm of her voice, her real English, and am charmed by what she says. She speaks humbly, but certain in her opinions on poetry; cites, not to show off, but in order to back up her theses, real authorities, including some of the most recent ones, and time and again refers to her father, who "killed himself, in order to find himself," who, in a word, was a truer Pole than either Żeromski or Conrad. Everything that she later read from her book pleased me — not as art, because I can't judge it fairly due to my problems with English, but as a part of the author's personal saga, which I am piecing together like the revelation of a beautiful human being. I have rarely been so moved and comforted in these past times as I was by the words of this strangely charming woman, who bade farewell to me with the words "My father liked so very much your poems that appeared in that *Tygodnik*."[177]

8 December

[...] Irena Piotrowska,[178] congratulating me for my *America*, said that "I was born anew." That's a compliment, of course, but I understand what she meant and I dare to think that there is something true in this nice bit of praise. Writing these articles was like crushing stone for me, and yet I felt that I had to write them, and I finished them despite the fact that I was near despair as the different formulations weren't quite working, and I was bothered by so many contrarieties. But the best of

---

[176] Helena Modrzejewska (Jadwiga H. Misel, 1840-1909). One of the most talented and famous Polish actresses. She came to California in 1876 and became popular on the American stage as Helena Modjeska. American citizen since 1883.

[177] *Tygodnik polski* [The Polish Weekly], weekly journal published in New York from 1943-47 by the *Koło Pisarzy z Polski* [Circle of Polish Writers], edited by Lechoń.

[178] Irena Piotrowska, Lechoń's friend. She wrote on art for the *Tygodnik Polski*.

everything that I wrote was brought about with great birthing pains, and in the horrid self-doubt that is indivisible from real creation. In these few pages about America there is certainly something new, which hadn't yet been said; at least not like I said them. This something is me — not completely new, but I feel able to still experience something new and toss something off from me which is not dead or decomposed.

25 December
[...] Yesterday, when I went to Cecilia Burr's for Christmas Eve Supper, little old Faulkner, in some sort of cape, in a somewhat comic brown quasi-Tyrolean hat, looking like a kind of Polish country aristocrat who happened to wander into New York City, entered the Waldorf just ahead of me and, as I entered the elevator (constantly glancing over my shoulder), I heard him say to the porter "Mr. Stein, please." And a moment later, "I am Faulkner." Among the tuxedoed gentlemen and ladies in diamonds and furs, nobody recognized him; in that hall he looked like some sort of figure from Hoffmann: a spirit from another world. I felt a bit stupid for being dressed for the evening, although I'm a poor fellow while Faulkner is fame itself and a rich man. I thought about how much I have lost thanks to all those evenings throughout my life spent in tuxedos, and I wasn't far from tugging Faulkner by the sleeve to tell him this, like the Warsaw drunks in the Astoria or Adria,[179] bewailing their misery, drenching with tears the vests of various Polish greats.

---

[179] Warsaw restaurants, the first patronized by government officials and other élite types.

16 January

[...] To Atlantic City with Bejtman[180] by car, where I will suffer through a very difficult screenplay (not mine) for a whole week. For the nonce at least a novelty: the American Ostend is unfashionable already and at this time of the year completely empty, but I have so grown into New York that even such a change is entertaining. But this week of leaving poetry behind, leaving myself behind, frightens me, although this is an old obligation and there was no way of getting out of it. I've written nothing.

22 February

[...] I've written three pages on Mickiewicz[181] and one strophe of the "Madonna Nowojorska" ["Madonna of New York"] — two, three more and it will be finished. This is real Catholic and New York Baudelaire, but if I finish it as I have been writing it so far, it will be truly a Polish Baudelaire, who is understood and taught in New York, in the New York of his master Edgar Allan.

4 March

[...] This is neither a fad nor a mass hallucination, but Marlon Brando is actually an actor such as there are none here, such as existed during the great, legendary times of the theatre. One must compare his roles of Stanley Kowalski in Tennessee Williams' play, Marcus Antonius, and this last one, splashed about with all the advertising paint in the world, *On the*

---

[180] Wincenty Bejtman, film producer and distributor associated with PIC Films Inc,. Producers and Distributors of Motion Pictures, 117 W. 48th St. in New York. Lechoń cooperated with Bejtman in many projects, including the writing of screenplays for and commentaries on films produced by PIC.

[181] Written for the one hundredth anniversary of the poet's death in 1955, and first published in Paris under the aegis of the Polish Library.

Waterfront, in order to realize that he does not play conditionally at all, but always differently; that he can play both a wild animal, a grand tribune, and, beneath the mask of a rough from the docks, the most tender human person. Who cares that his Marcus Antonius wasn't in the Shakespearean style and had no patrician gestures, if he alone among all of those Masons and Gielguds[182] with their A plusses in Shakespearean recitation, was a real man and only through his not completely enunciated words one felt the grand breath of tragedy? In *Waterfront* he is completely different than he is in all of the roles he has played up until now — he has a simply surprising tenderness, so unexpected in this so-called "tough guy" specialist. The scene with the gangster's brother, who wants to kill him — a melodrama in the style of old theatrical bombs — is a great masterpiece of acting, full —- as Bataille wrote — not of fitting accents, but rare ones, the rarest.

5 March

[...] Already in the memoirs of old Prince Andrzej Poniatowski[183] I knew how great an influence Sienkiewicz, especially through *Ogniem i mieczem* [With Fire and Sword] had on Theodore Roosevelt, which means, on all the people whom he in his turn taught Skrzetuski's virtues and Kmicic's rowdiness. Today Gabriela told me that Archibald Roosevelt once told her that his father taught him and his brothers *With Fire and Sword*, and how he constantly had them return to that book. To this very day Archibald remembers all of the heroes, not only Zagłoba but also Skrzetuski, and Wołodyjowski, with whose names, of course, he had no little difficulty.

---

[182] James Mason (1909-1984). British actor of stage and screen. John Gielgud (Arthur Gielgud, 1904-2000). Great British actor and director. Of Polish descent, his family emigrated to England from Lithuania in the nineteenth century.

[183] Andrzej Poniatowski (1865-1954). Polish industrialist and financier.

[...] In the film *East of Eden,* [184] the one scene full of the greatest poetry is when the hero, a young, clumsy boy, stalks after his unknown mother, a professional lady, the owner of a public house, as it turns out. For the first time in color film I saw such discreet mistiness and half-tones. The content itself, taken from the novel by Steinbeck, is quite a unique matter, pathological and for this reason I cannot say that I was very moved by it. For all that Julie Harris is once more simple, moving, constantly the same, it seems, and yet one can listen to her and look at her endlessly. And James Dean as that young boy, unloved and longing for love, who still so desires to give of himself, is revelatory. Despite what so many critics of the film say, I don't think he resembles Marlon Brando at all. He has indeed that same passion, that same intensity in acting, but this should be after all A B C for every good actor. On the other hand, his movements, his smile, his way of speaking, all of this is his own, similar to no one, and very moving. All of his accents are *les accents rares*, upon which, as that wise master of theatre Bataille said, everything in the art of acting depends.

6 May

[...] I prepared myself to speak about Wolfe[185] and felt something like inspiration — as if my knowledge of American writers, of Mark Twain, Whitman and Melville, and contemporary readings, had already created in me an entire poetic world, where all these persons, the Mississippi of Huck Finn, Whitman's walks on Long Island, the Biedermeyer South and the fierce, cruel saga of New York, mixed into one, became my subconscious and were ready at any moment to explode — like Polish symbols did at one time. This might well turn out to be, of course, only one poem, but I think that this essence, this perfume, could suffice for a good one.

---

[184] Based on Steinbeck's novel, directed by Elia Kazan.
[185] For a radio audition on Radio Free Europe.

9 May

[...] Neither Wolfe, nor Faulkner, to say nothing of Dreiser, are pessimists. And this again not in the sense that they find delight in their art, but because — as Faulkner has said — they are of the opinion that the world is not yet ready to end. Thus the various horridnesses of America that I feel are akin not to the fall of Byzantium, but to the cruelty of the Renaissance.

20 May

[...] I have a feeling, so incomprehensible that I don't know if I might express it in words suggestive enough. Yesterday, climbing onto the bus on the corner of 79th, I glanced at the sign above a kiosk with newspapers, a sign in English above a kiosk which didn't resemble Varsavian or sub-Varsavian kiosks at all. Yet suddenly Pruszków[186] stood before my eyes, the whole time we lived there, the whole feel of those two years — so dramatic because of my emotions, rather than events. And myself from those days — as if I'd returned to those places, that time.

5 June

[...] Have I changed here in emigration? Not a bit — and yet completely. All of my instincts are the same as they were thirty years ago in Poland, but my opinions about the world are already taken from the entirety of my life — not only from Polish dreams and French culture, but from America as well. I am a true, confirmed democrat, because I know what haughty-lordliness[187] is from Poland, and this is why I live in America.

12 July

[...] I was sitting in the park under the trees, in front of a wooden house such as might have been a miserable little cottage somewhere in the eastern marches of Poland. Rustlings similar

---

[186] Pruszków, small town in which Lechoń lived with his family in 1911, before returning to Warsaw via Milanówka in 1912.
[187] *Wielkopaństwo.*

168

to those trees, and I felt as if I had already died, was in a Platonic world, where there is no suffering, but where everything is also as if wrapped in mist, a mist which separates us from all intense feelings, and thus from happiness too.

25 July

[...] Dr. Józio Gertner[188] gave me a shot today in his office, where he tends to Negro children. Such a pleasure to gaze at these wondrous beings, so much more amusing and vital than whites. One little infant of a *café-au-lait* skin carnation, tiny, maybe only a couple of days old, was sleeping completely naked in his mother's arms with an expression of adult suffering on his beautiful little face. He looked as if sculpted from some unknown, precious material by the hand of a most tender master-artist.

1 August

[...] I received my first copy of my thing on America, beautifully published by the Oficyna Poetów. Still and all, some sort of bad luck is plaguing this little book, because despite Grydz's[189] intervention, the publishers printed subtitles not of my own hand, which changes everything into a propaganda-rag. I looked at these comments once more and I'm happy that they won't be lost, even though I've been jumped on quite a bit on account of them. In formulating them, I put myself through quite a bit of difficult thought — and such, as one says, "doesn't walk about in exile on foot."

3 August

[...] I woke up around six and saw something I haven't seen for years: the strawberry-colored sunrise over Manhattan, shot through with light from within and broadening with

---

[188] Personal friend of Lechoń.

[189] Mieczysław Grydzewski (Grycendler, 1894-1970). Polish journalist and publisher. He was active in both Poland (the journal *Skamander*) and in postwar exile in Britain (*Wiadomości*, among others).

brilliance more and more with the passage of each second. I was alone in a narrow hotel room,[190] and for the first time since I can't remember how long I didn't feel alone. Aubrey,[191] who can't come to terms with any existing religion, says "Of course God exists, because the sun goes up and down."

4 August

[...] For the last three hot, humid, trouble-filled days following that horrid Sunday, I have fallen in love with New York. In that little hotel room I felt like I did in Paris, and walked about the streets without any boredom. Something has changed in me, and I hope it remains: as if death had stepped away from me and I felt that I still have something to do, something unexpected, true and necessary.

God help me!

28 August

[...] The boarding house[192] in which I spend the summer along with about fifty exiles of various types is an entire world, unreal, despite the fact that the majority of guests are well-off and already on their feet in America. But their enthusiasm for Polish specifics, their constant comparing of the landscape of the Catskills to our own, the constant reminiscing of Lwów, Kraków, Hawełka and Szkowron[193] bears witness to the fact that they aren't living a real life; that they have remained there, whence they shall never return, and perhaps don't wish to return. This helps me in my self-delusions as well. Once more I say, and believe: "Life is a dream."

---

[190] At times, Lechoń lent his little apartment on East 82nd St. to friends passing through New York. At such times, he rented a room for himself in a hotel.

[191] Aubrey Johnston, intimate friend of Lechoń since 1941.

[192] At the time, Lechoń spent his vacation in Highmount.

[193] (Antoni) Hawełka and Szkowron were famous restaurateurs, in Kraków and Lwów, respectively. Hawełka's restaurant, on the Rynek Główny in Kraków, still bears his name.

[...] I never watch television, but today I surrendered myself to watch the *Quiz Show*, which has sent all of America into hysteria and in which today, for the first time, 64,000 dollars constituted the stake. A young Marine lieutenant was answering questions about his hobby, cooking. If he gave the right answer, he would win 64,000, at the risk of losing the 32,000 dollars he had already amassed, if he were wrong. The question concerned five dishes and two wines served during the Auriol[194] party in Buckingham Palace. Assisted by his father, the lieutenant answered correctly, winning the pot and disproving the myth that Americans know nothing about fine food. This whole contest is a commercial advertisement for the Revlon cosmetics firm. It is a game, but one that has something fantastic about it, apart from the sums there to be won. A shoemaker who is an expert on Shakespeare, a baker whose specialty is opera, an old lady who can name the roster of a baseball team from thirty years ago — this too is America, that America which any given European idiot takes for a country of troglodytes.

29 September
[...] I like Truman a lot. Bullitt[195] once said, venomously, that "There ought to be at least one such Truman in each little town." I think that there is. And that's why one can have faith in America.

1 October
[...] Returning after midnight from Forest Hills, I saw Chevalier on Lexington. He was heavier, greying, but not at all so changed as one might think from looking at his photograph.

---

[194] Vincent Auriol (1884-1966). French politician, first president (1947-1954) of the IVth Republic.
[195] William Christian Bullitt (1891-1967). American diplomat, envoy to the Versailles Conference, first American ambassador (1933-36) to the USSR. Later, he served in the Middle East and France.

A few words spoken by him to the huge old hag accompanying him[196] and suddenly Lexington seemed Montmartre to me — the Boulevard Pigalle. For a moment, that Paris, dormant in me, awoke, and I had to give my head a good shake in order to shape myself up and return to New York.

15 October

[...] *The Philadelphia Story*,[197] a film held to be a classic masterpiece of American cinema, fantastically played by Katharine Hepburn and Jimmy Stewart, entertaining and not stupid, but for all that it's more difficult to understand the drunkenness of the female lead. Women who drink constitute an American specialty, which turns Europeans off to life here. I'm certain that a lot of Americans suffer on this account, not realizing why.

23 October

[...] I saw Faulkner on the street in a jacket with leather elbows, pants too short and looking as if he'd had a few glasses in him. Meeting him always moves me and makes me conscious of the fact that New York is not just the capital of exiles from the whole world, but also the greatest city of incomprehensible America, and that in this America there live not only Babe Ruth[198] and Buffalo Bill, but also Whitman, Melville, and Hawthorne, and that in these latter days there lives a great tragic writer — that little gent in the jacket with leather sleeves.

30 October

[...] McKinley Kantor's new book *Andersonville*, again about the Civil War. How can one be surprised at the Poles with their *Trilogy, Popioły* [*Ashes*], martial poetry and the fact that after five hundred years nothing's made such a shout in our literature as that, given the fact that this one war and its greats

---

[196] *Jakiegoś idącego z nim babska.*
[197] Directed by George Cukor.
[198] Most likely. Lechoń has "Bebe Rull."

will not let the historians and writers in America sleep at night. I understand that it was an ideological war, that it was the business of every American, just like the Dreyfus Affair concerned every Frenchman. Still and all, in the land of Rockefeller and Al Capone, more is written about Lincoln than about them. Food for thought for all those who bark at America from Europe.

23 November

[...] Against a backdrop of well-polished, well-pressed official guests at the Sunday ceremony (to which I was also invited), Auden[199] in a grey suit and yellow shoes. At one time I would have thought, doesn't he have a black sportscoat? Why doesn't he look like everybody else? But all those blacks, those creased formal pants, those standard phrases have already begun to bother me so, the desert of all formalities has already begun to so bore me, that I was simply overjoyed with the vision of that true poet who — alone on the whole stage — was from the world of poetry, the world of Mickiewicz. And he read his beautiful translation of "Romantyczność," [Romanticism], the translation of a real poet, and thus a Mickiewiczean translation.

5 December

[...] Thornton Wilder's *The Matchmaker* — a continual laugh and again and again "deeper meanings" and even poetry. I think that I will more than once reminisce about this wonderful farce and will see it several times more. It is the work not only of a great master, but a great artist, who made a gem out of the nonchalant ideas of Shaw, who gave an artistic answer to the craziness of life, which might be the "story of an idiot" as well as the poem of a delightfully crazy man. An excellent show.

---

[199] W.H. (Wystan Hugh) Auden (1907-1973). Important British poet, who lived for a time in the United States. One of the chief English language poets of the generation directly following that of Eliot. The invitation was to a celebration of the 100th anniversary of the birth of Adam Mickiewicz, held at Hunter College.

[...]   After a busy and exhausting day, a calm and pleasant Christmas Eve supper at Cecylia Burr's.   A conversation with Larry Parker, Cecylia's grandson, about painting, Poland, Melville, Hawthorne, such as only in America one might have with this sort of young person — that means, with a person unfamiliar with many matters with which every European has been familiar for so long, but who has a desire to learn such as so few of those Europeans feel any more.

1956

10 January

[...] A sudden desire, or rather a dream, to really come to know, feel, understand the literature of the American Transcendentalists just as I had understood the French. Thoreau, Hawthorne, to say nothing of Melville — whom I almost know now — how they looked, who they were, for after all I know for sure who Victor Hugo, Balzac and Baudelaire were.

21 January

[...] At McBurney's[200] today I looked at Auden, who's only 45 years old and isn't a young man any more, after all, but who has his disciples and his creativity past him, and I couldn't forget that I am older than him, that for his disciples I would seem nothing more than an old poet. And yet it constantly seems to me that I have something yet to write, which hasn't yet been written. I know how old I am, I think of death, but still I expect, still it seems, that I'm about to start life over again, a different, better, and — what I never even in my youth dreamt of — a happy life.

12 February

[...] Warm puffs of wind just like before Easter in Poland. I recalled the painting by the forgotten Wojciech Piechowski[201] entitled *Święcone* [Blessed], meadows, willows, crowfoot and the Resurrection Mass in the countryside. And all of this came to me in one breeze from the river, one springtime moment among the slush of winter.

---

[200] Clark McBurney (b. 1913). Translator of Polish poetry (using the pseudonym Clark Mills). Lechoń wrote the "critical appreciation" to his *Adam Mickiewicz: Selected Poems* published in 1956 by the Noonday Press. A planned edition of Lechoń's poetry in his translation was never realized.

[201] Wojciech Piechowski (1849-1911). Polish painter affiliated with the Viennese *Sezessionstil*.

[...] I caught myself at something unusual today. Since I have kept it hidden from my fellow Poles that I have had my naturalization hearing, I have kept it hidden from this journal as well. So I had the hearing and it came out horribly, so exhausted was I, and after all my knowledge of English doesn't include an understanding of quick speech. I couldn't understand even half of the questions and if I've "passed," as I hope I have, it's only thanks to the protection of people in high places. I had to do it, since all of London was breaking apart and laughing at me, but it was neither easy, nor a pleasant operation.

The gentleman in Immigration who interviewed me set off into such a conversation with me as women in buses who lay their souls bare to the drivers. He had been a war correspondent at the time of the surrender of the Japanese. He was a friend of Ernie Pyle's,[202] and, despite it all, called himself unintelligent; and told me that on the other hand his son, who is at West Point, is unusually bright and that I should really see him and have a talk with him, after which he wrote down his address for me. All the more did this make me feel bad for letting him down, that I didn't understand a few of his questions, that I didn't know where Lincoln was born.

8 March

[...] I saw Orson Welles' film *Citizen Kane* today for the first time. It was made fifteen years ago and — as is well known — is based on the life of old Hearst. I won't say that I was delighted with the camera work, the ideas and entirely cinematic tricks. None of the actors played exceptionally well. As far as cinema goes, it is a pretentious, average film. For all that, I was delighted with the script, the drama itself, and what one here

---

[202] Ernie Pyle (1901-1945). Reporter, managing editor of the *Washington Daily News*, popular war correspondent in practically every theatre of World War II, for which he received the Pulitzer Prize. He was killed in a Japanese *kamikaze* attack.

calls its "message." *Citizen Kane* is not in the least a satire on America, as they shout in Europe. It is a powerful, moving human drama in which that Kane or Hearst isn't a caricature at all, but rather a great person of splendid passions and a hero, if not a positive one. Everywhere outside of America one finds people similar to him, but only in America can one find them of his stature.

30 May

[...] One can always find in one's intelligence, will, heart, something that will help one in one's struggles with life, with other people. For the struggle with oneself — there is only prayer.[203]

— *Translated by C.S. Kraszewski*

---

[203] With this, Lechoń's *Journal* ends. He committed suicide eight days later.

III. *American Transformations*

Lechoń's American Transformations
A preface by Kazimierz Wierzyński

We were five poets who began our literary careers together
— four of us were twenty-four years of age — and there was young
Lechoń, a nineteen-year-old. We started a literary cafe in Warsaw
— At the Sign of the Picador — and every evening at eight o'clock
we recited poems before whatever public happened to have gathered
there. This was toward the end of the First World War; the Germans
were still in Warsaw, but the breath of freedom that was soon to
pervade the earth was already in the air. Lechoń amazed us by his
maturity and, even though such things were not usually discussed
among Bohemians, it often occurred to us that he was something of
a genius.

At about this time Lechoń published a collection of verses
entitled *Crimson Poem,*[1] which only confirmed our impression. The
little book contained seven poems, but it resounded throughout
Poland like a triumphant polonaise. It marked the end of the
Romantic period — the epoch of Polish martyrdom — and the
beginning of a new period that dawned in the glow of freedom,
recovered by Poland after 123 years of captivity. Lechoń came out
for the new life, and rejected the oppression of the past; he called
for the demolition of the palaces of the former Polish kings. He
wrote that he wanted "in Spring to see the Spring itself — not
Poland."

In spite of this, inwardly he represented a synthesis of these
two trends; he wrote poems spiritually akin to Romanticism, but in
the modern manner. He always preserved the classical stanza, did
not resort to assonance, and became a master of condensed
metaphorical expression.

His second volume of poems, *Silver and Black,*[2] contains
lyrics marked by a surprisingly balanced gravity and permanent
structural solidity which call to mind Michelangelo's sonnets. It is
as if the words that comprise them could not be shifted — they are
arranged once and for all in a rational order, monumental in their

---

[1] *Karmazynowy poemat* (1920).
[2] *Srebrne i czarne* (1924).

wisdom, although they seethe with passion, are torn with despair, and conceal a living and profoundly human sorrow.

After the publication of these two collections Lechoń ceased to write for ten years. It was only the Second World War, and the tragic fate of Poland, which having fought on the side of the victors found itself in the end among the conquered nations, that released a second creative phase in him. He wrote of Poland's heroism, of the wrong done her, and reached his peak in short three-stanza poems of astonishing eloquence and scope. They are like three-act dramas, each with a prologue, a culminating point, and a shattering finale.

I do not know whether these poems can be made accessible to the foreign reader — so inseparable are they from the Polish spirit and its history and symbolism; but they will retain their resonance forever in the literature of his country. His poetry lives a hermetic life of its own, and in this respect is reminiscent of that of Paul Valéry. Lechoń wrote little, as did Valéry; like the French poet, he tended to delicately chiseled effects, which resulted in work that possessed the unephemeral qualities of marble and bronze.

Lechoń's interests ranged beyond literature. He was a connoisseur of paintings, he had a well-developed understanding of music, he wrote critical and polemical essays, and took a passionate interest in politics. His mind was not only brilliant; he possessed a rare intuitive gift. Perhaps his intellectual endowment surpassed even his unusual poetic talent.

The essays presented here to the English speaking reader under the title *American Transformations* voice the thoughts of a European who saw in America a champion and the hope of civilization and the culture of free men. In a way, it is the testament of the immigrant of Western orientation who died recently in tragic circumstances. Perhaps it is more than that. Perhaps it is a warning that should be heeded.

American Transformations[3]

Today it is almost an accepted fact that every recent major international event reflects a change in America's attitude toward other continents and in their attitudes toward America. Sixteen years ago, when the mysterious and dynamic Wendell Willkie emerged as an apparent threat to President Roosevelt's re-election, Europe misread the contest as one between two fundamental world views and believed that American entry into the war hinged on its outcome. At that time idols in many countries were collapsing in unimaginable disaster. Blind reliance on such respected institutions as the French General Staff or British Secret Intelligence proved a dangerous delusion. England was no longer an unassailable island, nor France a grotto of last-minute miracles.

In the eyes of proud, unimaginative Europe, American help was then to consist only of material aid. Because of America's so-called inability to grasp the world situation, Europe was willing to accept nonchalantly American support of decisions reached without United States participation. Europe saw in America a kind of rich but naive Uncle Sam or, perhaps more an amiable, prosperous niece who in the end never refused to pay the price of incorrigible Aunt Europe's follies.

Even those who today rebel against the complete reversal of roles in the family relation between Europe and America well know that within a few crucial years the United States, once a remote and almost legendary economic power, has become one of the two decisive political forces in the world. Continual American interventions in the quarrels on every continent have shifted a balance of power that had seemed an absolute constant. But few are yet fully aware of the truth that, despite many traditions of varying age and force that still hinder its acceptance, this change is

---

[3] First published in Polish under the title *Aut Caesar aut nihil*, *Wiadomości* (Nrs. 45-47, 1954); subsequently in a pamphlet edition published by the London Oficyna Poetów i Malarzy (1955). The English translation, entitled *American Transformations*, first appeared in *The Polish Review* (New York, 1958/3), and subsequently in pamphlet form by Voyages Press (1959).

irreversible. Occasional hesitations of American policy or surface evidences of European weakness or strength cannot alter this fact. The change is an historical phenomenon that defies pedestrian political arithmetic and the horoscopes of shallow specialists in ideologies, and it moves as if governed by the objective law of a biological, almost geological process.

I shall not consider this phenomenon from the viewpoint of an academic historian or statistician. I shall not go backstage of the political arena, nor haunt the retreats of political writers with their ears out for rumor or glued to the headphones of secret intelligence listening posts. In its very nature it is more like the emergence of new stars, the eruption of volcanoes or the appearance of genius in art, than what journalists now view as politics — for instance, the continual unsettlement of the French government or the relative stability of the British regime. (The fact is that the latter are unimportant not only in world politics but in the real life of these nations themselves).

One cannot express in precise formulas or exact weights and measures the deepest reality of an organism as powerful as America. The tremendous vitality of this country, as well as the creative contrast of its basically contradictory origins, guarantee its continued vigor, capacity for growth, and inevitably extraordinary future. Analysis of such factors might lie even beyond the powers of a writer whose experience was not confined to the émigré margins of American life. In my attempt to unravel the fascinating riddles that confront us I cannot turn to exact scientific method. I can only place my hope in that intuitive grasp of reality which I believe is the means and purpose of genuine thought and real art.

I must state at once that I do not expect to eliminate from this discussion an impulse toward what the British describe as wishful thinking and what Poles disparage as pious hopes. I doubt in fact whether this would be desirable or wise in creative thought. One of the most eloquent proofs of America's importance in every walk of life is the fact that opinions about this country differ enormously. Whether held by a Frenchman, Englishman, Pole or Burmese, they are violent, subjective and invariably colored by such wishful thinking. To almost everyone, whether he plays a conscious role or merely acquiesces in the changes of our times, America and the American way of life symbolize in many ways the abandonment of old habits of action and thought, and embody a transformation not only of the political hierarchy of the world but of our very lives.

A not trivial, though in some ways comical example of this subjectivity is the recent Homeric battle waged over Coca-Cola in France. More was involved than the particular product: here was an attempt to resist an ever-growing power that threatened to move into areas abandoned by others and to drive out hesitant or weakening forces. The bottle of brown liquid, whose taste is still debated, seemed a kind of Sixth Column, and may indeed have been just that. For cultures express their force in terms of the unquestioned, conventional authority of the customs and forms of everyday life, based on legend and tradition, and they range from kitchen and cellar to the realm of moral principles.

The horror that met the invasion by Coca-Cola of areas under the ancient sway of Burgundy, Champagne and Perrier water — as well as the sharp sarcasm vented on real or imaginary shortcomings of the American cuisine, the worship of great baseball players in America (inconceivable to the European mind), the discomfort of drugstore breakfasts and the directness of American social protocol — were more than a defense of Perrier water, *paté de foie gras* or the aristocratic manners of the Faubourg St. Germain. In posters advertising American cookies and drugs on some highways in Europe, appalled European intellectuals and socialites saw the ruin of the only culture they regarded as genuine. Logical order could never enter into such a dispute, which has separated a Europe preoccupied with verbal formalities from an America not quite aware of its instincts nor able to decide whether the foundations or merely the superficial aspects of its culture were at stake.

The fact is that the invasion of Europe by American tourists, reinforcing their demands and whims with the beneficial and therefore hateful dollar, is reciprocated by the influence of Europe, of France above all, on the same tourists. Americans often remain in Paris until they have lost the shirts off their backs. They are often brutally insulted. Nevertheless, infected by the bacillus of Parisian charm, persuaded of their ignorance in matters of art, and with a truly American faith in the magic powers of study, they train their eyes and ears to respond to all the artistic and musical novelties of Europe. The miracles of the Parisian cuisine are to be found nowhere else, except in New York. Fifth Avenue shopwindows show gowns that in subtlety of hue and inventive refinement equal the most famous displays in the Faubourg St. Honoré. America, or New York at least, imports every masterpiece of the cuisine and of the art and theater of Europe, the plays of Giraudoux, Sartre, Anouilh, Roussin and Cocteau,[4] and exceptional films, as well as some sadly inadequate in their Parisian provincialism. Here one also finds stars and meteors from Montmartre and St. Germain-des-Prés, every outstanding composer and conductor, even the most freakish, unacademic elements in painting and sculpture. Clearly America is especially susceptible to novelty, but "novelty" here includes European biographies and critical studies that give new luster to past writers and artists.

The arrival of America in Europe and of American products in all the capitals and beaches of the Old World is thus accompanied by an ever more thorough penetration of Europe into American life. If Europeans bewail the Americanization of Rome and Paris, inveterate Yankees might equally lament the Europeanization of New York.

A Parisian or Roman provincial regards European influence on America as the light of Athens descending on Boetia. Justly proud of the giants of his native art, he usually knows as little of the tremendous sweep of American popular knowledge of painting, music and the theater, as of the number and splendor of American symphony orchestras, museums of classic and modern art, traveling exhibitions and theatrical groups. Still less does he know the great literature of America, which had influenced Europe long before its discovery by the Nobel Prize Institute. Melville and Thoreau, known to European intellectuals only by name, were not only masters of the literary craft but, like Tolstoy, Balzac, and Conrad, creators of their own worlds — worlds in no way more exotic for Western Europe than the Russian cosmos. Who but the moonstruck

---

[4] Jean Anouilh (1910-1987), modern French playwright. André Roussin (1911-1987), actor and theatrical director.

New York madman, Edgar Allan Poe, initiated the most refined disciplines of modern European prose? Who was the forerunner of a revolution still struggling for victory, and a patron of genuine poetic feeling and expression, if not the great Walt Whitman, spokesman for the social and political essence of Americanism? Henry James, a model for Conrad, who might also be called a precursor of Proust, became English by his own choice. But he was born and raised in an environment that became the field of his Proustian observation. We Poles, who find so many of our native elements in Conrad's view of the world, and who are so proud of the Polish exoticism of his style, should be well able to sense the depth of the problem of double nationality — not only in the great James but in T.S. Eliot,[5] a man ever moved by the noblest disciplines and motives.

No one with a critical sense will deny to modern American literature a powerful vision of reality and its own irresistibly suggestive conception of prose style. And while genuine writers everywhere have become aware of their calling and developed it in the light of such great beacons as Balzac, Tolstoy, Dostoyevsky, Stendhal, Flaubert and Proust, we must also admit that a young writer finds ever fewer such beacons on the road European literature is now traveling. He must now often search for them outside Europe.

The influence of Hemingway and Faulkner on European prose was the result not only of the revolt of young writers against Olympian deities too long enthroned and too sure of their rule: it also grew out of the need these writers felt for new elements to replace their hermetic literary cliques, the need for unity of feeling, thought and style — in short, for a new literary continent. Europe here began for the first time to identify this continent with the utterly novel political and geographic continent — America.

It would be too simple and too academic to find in the art of great American prose writers merely another powerful expression of the extreme pessimism that sums up the experiences of our era and bears witness to our cultural collapse in the face of increasingly

---

[5] Both Henry James (1843-1916), the novelist, and T.S. Eliot (1888-1965), the poet, were American expatriates who took up residence in Great Britain.

total mechanization. One might as unreasonably seek the source of Shakespeare's tragic sense in the brutalities of the Elizabethan age or trace the origin of Racine's masterpieces to the ills and abuses of French absolutism. The power of O'Neill, Faulkner, and other American playwrights and novelists less known in Europe resides in their instinct for tragedy which finds in the life of an American farmer, beachcomber or traveling salesman the same contrasts of nostalgia and destiny, love and death, will and fate. Earlier great writers discovered these on a different plane, in the history of royal successions. Others, like Balzac, found them in the brilliant careers and failures of the conquerors of social and bourgeois Paris. Among modern novelists, Faulkner is a tragic writer in the purest sense. Despite the remote world of his origins and the uniqueness of his literary craft, he is of all great prose writers Conrad's closest psychological counterpart. One might say after reading his Civil War series that he most nearly approximated Conrad's conception of creative pessimism.

As we approach American writing we must remember that the chances for an interpenetration of the European and American literatures are not equal. The style of life and thought in Europe, the manifold peculiarities and associations that form the climate of a play or novel written there, acquire in America a halo with which the equally attractive peculiarities of American literature cannot hope to be crowned abroad. Americans who seek to penetrate the strangeness of European art can, if they are determined, find innumerable clues and explanations. Unless he is carried away by the novelty and power of an American work, a European cannot and does not wish to ask himself whether he is prepared to comprehend it, whether his sensibility has not missed qualities, meanings and allusions that require a knowledge of America and of the style of feeling and life of this country. With no key to these mysteries, he loses interest in a work that appears utterly alien to him.

To take only one example, Europe regards Mark Twain as a mere humorist who managed to force on the French or Polish reader a new and, as some believe, not the highest form of a definitely American humor. The truth is — Americans generally know this — that he was not only a great humorist but simply a great writer. To recognize this, Poles and Italians would have to cross the barrier of the American atmosphere and way of life, both as closed to them as are to an American the mysteries concealed in the melodies and cadences of a Żeromski or a d'Annunzio.[6]

The essential error of Europeans who criticize the United States does not lie in their ignorance of American artistic achievement or in their reluctance to recognize it. Mistakenly, they identify an entire culture with only certain of its manifestations, which, even when they are of the highest order, cannot encompass its totality, just as the flower of a plant cannot live without the whole plant, stem, leaves and the roots. Western European culture, which many sophisticated provincials identify with refinements of literary style or collections of past curiosa, holds moral canons which bind equally devout Catholics and skeptical liberals — concepts produced by the dual heritage of Christian revelation and Roman law and embedded in a complex of Humanist ideals and the watchwords of the French Revolution. Never codified, the laws of this culture have lain somehow dormant in the instincts of every conscious European, and both the moral sense of great creative artists and the collective conscience have reacted infallibly to all deviations from them and to all offenses against their spirit.

With no attempt to define precisely all the elements of this culture, to which Jules Lagneau's[7] remark applies — that the meaning in the French watchwords is understood by the heart but remains an enigma to the mind — all will probably agree that one cannot detach from a concept of European culture the ideal of the equality of man.

This ideal, despite skeptical "capitalist" columnists and the alleged incompatibility of material prosperity with the eternal good, may not lead inevitably to utopian economic equality, but at least it maintains the principle of a minimum prosperity open to all. In contrast to the mystics, who are dedicated to ideals of renunciation and the privileges of the chosen few, the Catholic Church long ago launched a struggle for social progress, envisioning an earthly realization of the equality of man before God and regarding it not as

---

[6] Gabrielle d'Annunzio (1863-1938). *fin-de siècle* Italian writer.
[7] Jules Lagneau (1851-1894). French philosopher.

189

an obstacle to the Kingdom of God on earth, but as one of the very foundations of that Kingdom.

In the center of Western culture the whole array of its creative forces thus formed an alliance in order to achieve a purpose. On this alliance the authenticity and further development of our culture now depend. Christian Democrats, orthodox and Fabian Socialists, social sentimentalists and collectivist Utopians have vied with each other to spread prosperity and evolve a system able to withstand the onrush of destruction that, in the form of an illusory social paradise, now threatens the entire West.

Today there nevertheless remains a dangerous failure of real action, a crippling repression in the so-called universal social crusade of the West. The failure is portrayed clearly in the concluding line of *Waiting for Godot*:[8] The characters repeat for the last time, "Let's go," as the curtain falls and no one takes a single step. Social psychoanalysis could find here, as in every other inhibition, reluctance to face simple reality. For it is a delusion to assume that the inevitable social revolution in Europe can take place under the benevolent glances of philanthropists, in a gentle transition from one system to another, in the course of which "capitalists" will continue to enjoy all their wealth together with the comforts of a clear conscience — or, in other words to hope, as in the French saying, that things can both change and remain the same as before.

Europe, which cannot be called capitalist, since social phenomena are not that simple, is unable to submit to such a social psychoanalysis today; exposure of the roots of the disease would require remedies that it could not now accept. And in the present state of European morale it could not really be expected. Some Europeans, who cling with stubborn folly to their old prejudices and who still equate Soviet materialism with so-called American materialism, unconsciously blind themselves to the truth in order to avoid the trials of sacrifice and redemption.

Thus Europe cannot or does not wish to confront the dangers at hand. The cause of this lies primarily in the world of its

---

[8] Absurdist drama by the Irish-French playwright Samuel Beckett (1906-1989).

prejudices and habits: its way of life, modeled on the French bourgeois virtues, which had triumphed in the Revolution and later degenerated into class egoism, retarding all social progress in a country whose very motto vowed to defend and to spread that progress. Democracy, the child of the French Revolution, developed to maturity on the fringes of the Western world and became the way of life of monarchal Norway, Denmark and Sweden, while in its native Republic of Liberty, Equality and Fraternity it was despoiled of its name and relegated to the servant quarters by its illegitimate offspring, the very bourgeoisie born on July Fourteenth. The middle class identified itself with this cruelly betrayed democracy, and middle class egoism arrested its final growth. Thus was perpetrated one of the great historical follies, which eased the way for Communist propaganda outcries against the total subjugation of Western culture to capitalism and its debasement into an instrument of class oppression. Today France embodies and is the standard-bearer of the cultural entity of Europe; but France cannot survive the disasters of our time without recognizing that ours is a social period, just as the Middle Ages were mystical, the eighteenth century intellectual, and the nineteenth century, which lingered until World War I, an era of nationalism.

In a nation that so clearly typifies the bourgeois era, a socially decisive resolution of this supposed incongruity could resemble an ordeal by fire. When patchwork will no longer suffice, the social structure must be transformed. The egoism of the great French bourgeoisie must be overcome if there is to be a victory in Europe of genuine democracy based on the material well-being of the laboring masses.

The American social experiment, the economic emancipation of American workers, was effected in a different way in a society without feudal traditions, where democracy was becoming a tradition in itself.

The field of this experiment was a capitalist empire of breath-taking dynamism, indomitable in its youthful power. In bourgeois European terms this involved the ability to resist successfully not only scruples of conscience but especially the power of organized labor — and this without bringing on the distant threat of revolution. In this land of private wealth, filled even today

191

with magic possibilities for every bootblack and street vendor, where fortune may smile on the poor adventurer as on the most intrepid Argonaut in quest of millions, in the very world where capitalism might have acquired an almost romantic halo and thus been absolved of its crimes, there took place an abrupt change which reconciled the economic, didactic and myth-breeding values of capitalism with social development and justice. If this change did not establish a permanent balance between the empire of capitalism and the new empire of labor, it did persuade both to effect a compromise that made possible a realization of the most daring and instinctive potentialities of the American dynamic.

The New Dealers of Roosevelt claim the credit for this revolution. Basically, it was carried out independently of their doctrine or of Marx and the Fabians. Through a mighty expansion of the American economy and in an explosion of American vitality, it overcame all barriers in the path of its plans and destinies. The wrongs suffered by labor — latent with possibilities of widespread strikes and vengeance — hindered it no more than mechanical difficulties or problems in the supply of technical skill.

Americans are innocently unaware of the broad significance of this achievement. The inflamed labor issue has been quieted by a remedy of tremendous consequences not only for America but for the world. Americans see in the agreement negotiated by Secretary of Defense Wilson[9] with the workers at General Motors nothing more than a laudable professional action within the automobile industry. They do not suspect that this social peace, concluded between the doges of Detroit and the consuls of the republic of Labor, ensures that near-paradise with which the noblest Utopians and most erudite social reformers of the old continent try in vain to enter.

A paradise is not of this world; it is an ideal. Querulous or petty minded people can easily demonstrate that the American worker's prosperity does not bring him the well-being for which European theoreticians of happiness have spilled so much ink and even bourgeois and proletarian blood. If he knew his Aristotle, an

---

[9] Charles E. Wilson (1890-1961) was Secretary of Defense in the Eisenhower administration (1953-1957).

American worker could reply by quoting the aphorism about the theater — the play was marvelous even though it did not observe the three unities. Nothing expresses better this non-classical happiness than the spontaneous reply to this writer of a Ukrainian worker who, even when asked how long he had been in America, said: "Twenty years already . . . and every day I want to kiss the pavement for being able to walk on it."

The *litterati* of Paris, London, and pre-war Warsaw, who complain speciously of the artistic and intellectual "backwardness" of America, suffer here from a lack of atmosphere and find it impossible to draw creative inspiration from the soil of a country without ancient cathedrals, honest *vins de pays*, and tables at sidewalk cafés. These are the crusaders of Western culture who, unconsciously and also inhumanly, would restrict that culture to a few insignificant gourmets absorbed in intellectual Chinese puzzles, in little games that amuse the readers of scattered and rather old-fashioned literary monthlies. It has never occurred to them that this country, which their oversensitive nerves find so uncomfortable, and which in fact may not be comfortable for Europeans accustomed to an old-world scale of values, has bestowed a decent life on millions of people. In European capitals of culture and refinement these millions were thrust aside from any culture and condemned to an infamous struggle — for mere light, heat and crumbs of bread. A few steps away from the touchingly beautiful cathedrals and inspiring cafes, they lived the lives of outcasts and could look forward to nothing but the charity of their betters or a Bolshevik massacre.

A pamphlet on the noble French attempt at Boimandeau to build a utopian European community speaks of the humiliation and sense of inferiority from which French workers suffer. We read this in America and can scarcely picture it. We meet American workers every day. We know that they have their own homes, their cars, their Frigidaires, their television sets and their tuxedo. Here the idea of a worker looked down upon, defenseless against exploitation and deprived of comforts reserved for wealthier citizens, seems a specter from a far-off world, somehow compounded of *Uncle Tom's Cabin* and Zola's fiction.[10]

In the United States the acute problem of social distinctions has been blunted by taxation. In proportion to their fortunes, men of fabulous wealth have been taxed for the benefit of the state, which is to say, the mass of its individual citizens.

So heavily taxed, the rich man is no longer envied by the increasingly prosperous workers. If there were bitterness among the workers today such as existed before the era of Theodore Roosevelt and even up to that of Franklin Roosevelt, it would be a pathological excess in the mind of a basically well-off property-owner, whether he were a mechanic in Detroit or a steel worker in Pittsburgh. Naturally not all American laborers dwell in what a newcomer from the Renault or Citroen works in France would regard as an Arcadian idyll. Pennsylvania miners, like the Polish miners of Katowice and Dabrow,[11] still pass their days in darkness and coal dust. This problem has not been solved even by those who have brought down nobles, peasants, and burghers to the very depths of misery in order to open a "paradise" for the workers, and who now explain to them that this paradise requires overtime hours spent in the bowels of the earth to win the title of hero of labor, or, as Mickiewicz would say, hero of slavery.

Communism, which can often rely on the weakness, satiety or snobbishness of intellectuals and the rich, finds that American workers are the social class most decidedly opposed to the Soviet. Whereas they might be expected to accept readily the ultimate practical objectives of Soviet policy, the fact is that they respond instinctively to every offensive and initiative of American foreign policy vis-à-vis Russia.

When the somber, magnificently theatrical General MacArthur entered New York like a triumphant emperor, in European, almost Oriental pomp, he was welcomed by more than a politically unthinking mob, avid for the spectacular. He was welcomed by New Yorkers who recognized in the great tragic

---

[10] Émile Zola (1840-1902). French Naturalistic novelist, whose works often deal with brutally objective depictions of social misery.

[11] i.e. Dąbrowa Górnicza.

Commander petty envies and hatreds not unlike their own disgruntlement over government taxes, as well as by ordinary morally sound citizens, sensitive to the spell of greatness and ashamed of the wrong done to a famous American. In that crowd of millions he was also greeted by American workers who lined up on the dock in solid ranks. They shouted their welcome and paid their homage. In face of the dangers that threatened the United States they felt a strong sense of solidarity with the great Proconsul and shared with the whole nation the deep emotion evoked by that historic return.

Franklin Delano Roosevelt seemed as accessible and straightforward as a character in a morality play; he was in fact mysterious and complex. He was a patrician worshipped by the common people in a way that no other such leader of the American nation had been since Jackson. He was the undoubted though only partly knowing, creator of a new class of contented, politically independent citizens capable of defending their rights and property. To paraphrase a French saying, this class might be called the infantry of the great Republic. Here, as often happens, a large task undertaken for a definite purpose achieved more than that purpose and served ends never intended by its author.

If we can hope to see the fateful results of the monstrous Yalta agreements repaired in the future, if America abandons the illusions there consecrated and perseveres through winding paths toward the great highway of its policy, it will be because that policy is not opposed by hungry masses swayed by the Communist mirage and ready to resort to strikes and other forms of pressure on behalf of their self-styled Moscow ally. On the contrary: contented, prosperous workers will continue to urge the government to act to protect their gains against an emancipation laden with horror, a Pyrrhic victory of the proletariat.

Well acquainted with its friends and enemies in the United States, Moscow persistently attacks President Eisenhower, the late Robert Taft, Governor Dewey, Secretary of State Dulles, and a host of others. It is not difficult to persuade a French or Polish factory worker that these names are symbols of a plot hatched by Wall Street and the Pentagon to forestall the victory of the proletariat. But such names, so easily used for propaganda, are not the only ones on the Moscow blacklist. There are many others, mentioned reluctantly because they are those of the most determined opponents of Communism, of leaders who won their spurs in the struggle for the rights and prosperity of the workers.

William Green and Philip Murray, the two late leaders of the largest trade unions; John L. Lewis, the Napoléon of the miners and scourge of mine-owners; and young Walter Reuther,[12] who many believe is destined for greater future tasks and who is the one distinguished American singled out for a Bolshevik murder attempt — these four men were and are enemies of Communism, the more formidable because they command powerful and disciplined armies in a field that the Bolsheviks would like to regard as their own.

In the anti-Communist stand of the majority of American workers lies the fundamental difference between the American revolution and the experiment in Great Britain, where, in contrast to France, so much has been done for the well-being of the laboring masses. The difference lies in part, of course, in the differing geographical situation of England and America. American prosperity results also, however, from the loose-jointed unity of feeling, thought and action that might be described as Americanism, as well as from its natural wealth and dynamism. It is irrelevant that the English reforms were undertaken in the name of Fabian morality and summoned the propertied class to sacrifices considerably more painful than the burdens of taxation imposed on American millionaires. The vitality of the American experiment is conditioned and fully safeguarded by its organic structure and growth, by an intermingling of good and evil, by all sorts of contradictions and upsurgings that elude every theory, and by the irrational, which has always determined the power and novelty of epochs and empires.

This lack of order even in major industrial centers makes it difficult to predict the future course of efforts that have produced the prototype of the American worker, reconciled capital with labor,

---

[12] Walter Reuther (1907-1970), president of the UAW and CIO, knew the Soviet Union from the inside, having worked in a Soviet automobile plant for two years in the 1930s. He violently disliked the lack of freedom in Soviet society, and battled Communist elements in the UAW and CIO upon his return to the United States.

extended both prosperity and personal freedom, and given to trade unions power in matters affecting labor conditions without allowing them to exercise more than a trifling influence on the political views of the organized workers.

During the past fifty years these men and women left their homes three times, abandoned their riches gathered by hard work or ingenuity, and despite all official isolationism of the nation, shrugged onto their traditionally pacifist shoulders the military uniforms of an army that grew in the space of that half-century from volunteer ranks of armed cowboys into the greatest military power the world had ever seen — an army that today remains the sole guarantee of freedom where it still survives and the only hope of its revival where it now lies overwhelmed. Pershing's regiments that turned the uncertain scales of victory in favor of a liberal Europe, Eisenhower's armies that routed the Germans on all the battlefields of the West, or the divisions of MacArthur, Ridgway and Van Fleet, which, though entangled in most unfortunate political factors, yet shed their blood in distant Korea for the sake of that liberty which is indivisible for the entire world — all these veterans, celebrating their soldierly anniversaries in ribald songs and hard drinking, the dead and the invalid, who are never remembered in songs or poetry — have they not all accomplished great things in common? And can there be any doubt that their brothers and sons, without a trace of pathos or bravado, will accomplish great things in the future? And must we not acknowledge that they have already passed through the baptism that Renan[13] ascribes to societies that are determined to become nations?

At the root of almost all false and therefore dangerous judgments in our times lies the lack of imagination of those charlatans and soothsayers who are unable in the parallels they draw to reach beyond periods in history that are supposed to have shaped Europe's course, such as the Middle Ages or the French Revolution. They seem unaware that a generation is still living that came into this world while an empire, which once embraced one half of the world, was being finally destroyed in the Spanish-American War. That generation still remembers the time when the Princes of

---

[13] Ernest Renan (1823-1892). French philosopher and writer.

197

Bulgaria and Rumania were vassals of the Sultan. It remembers imperial Vienna competing with Paris in the charm of its attractions and in its pomp and carefree life, remembers the power of the Tsars, the dazzling wealth of St. Petersburg and the realm of the Hohenzollerns, so full of raw force and preparing for new conquests. Before the eyes of that generation the star of the Ottomans was extinguished and Turkey, once the terror of European capitals, declined to an Asiatic state with shrunken frontiers, without memories and without dreams. The few years that followed the collapse of the Hapsburgs sufficed to turn a leading center of attraction, a pre-eminent center of music, into a provincial city, scarcely able to hide its poverty from the eyes of a diminishing number of tourists.

The thesis advanced here in an attempt to define the phenomenon of Americanism rests on the notion of an instinct that reaches beyond theories and in fact usually precedes them. This is the collective, scarcely developed instinct of a people that numbers as many nationalities as the Soviet Union, an instinct of wealth, of fullness of life and love of innovation, which can find a social solution independently of European doctrines and thus enable the Genoa, Venice and Florence of the American continent to integrate into a modern equivalent of ancient Rome.

Pessimists who doubt the existence of this sound instinct will naturally oppose the hope of such a solution. They will cite instances of average Americans whom they find completely indifferent to public affairs, inherently isolationist, and unable even to adjust themselves to military service, that necessary shield of a foreign policy of wide range. The answer to all this lies in the last fifty decisive years, when the American people gave proof of an altogether contrary tendency and went to war twice, although American territory was not threatened. In World War I, as in the Korean War, American soldiers fought for aims that lay far beyond narrow national interests or that, at least, interpreted those interests very broadly. While it is true that America was attacked in World War II, the response to this attack was a battle on all fronts, the offer of material and military aid to every ally and the transformation of an initially defensive war into a great crusade that

198

vanquished the direct enemy and brought about the crushing defeat of the European oppressor of that time.

It would be absurd to assume that three wars in a half-century could have been imposed on the American nation by its leaders through an abuse of public quiescence and of their own high position. It would be as futile to pretend to measure the spirit with which American soldiers three times acquitted themselves of their duties. Optimists, along with pessimists, may choose to be scandalized by the clamor of American soldiers to be sent home after the Second World War — but they may also wonder why these soldiers, enjoying the comforts of prosperity and brought up on the Monroe Doctrine, were ready without fervor but also without protest to fight in theaters of war, more distant than was Pearl Harbor from Los Angeles or New York.

The seductive political genius of Franklin Delano Roosevelt prepared and sustained the great effort in World War II. His great personality, endowed with the ability to move the spirits of men, ceaselessly exerted a suggestive, almost magnetic influence. We find the condition altogether changed, however, when we reflect on the entry of the United States into the Korean War. In this case the decision was made by a man who had been judged in most contradictory ways — violently ridiculed by his opponents, and overwhelmed by the sympathies of the common people, for what were the undoubted qualities of his character; a man who could not exert moral leadership even within his own party. President Truman, who will present great difficulties to future historians seeking to correct wrong evaluations by some of his contemporaries, took the risk of a dictatorial if admittedly legal decision to meet Soviet aggression with active resistance. He was not guided by vision, but by the impulse of an average American to act not only in the immediate interests of the country, but also against more distant dangers and in terms of still undefined future tasks. President Truman, like Queen Victoria, thought exactly as did the majority of his fellow countrymen; his solid mediocrity had the gift of feeling the common pulse. He knew that a Texas farmer or a worker in Detroit would not rush into battle like a Polish lancer or a Warsaw newsvendor, yet would let his sons and brothers go off to the war, and would pay the taxes needed to sustain it, if in a challenge to the United States the Soviets were to cross the intangible line that cannot be infringed without stirring ordinary Americans to action.

"To be a nation," said Renan, "means to have done great things in common in the past, and to wish to do them in common in the future." Great things obviously include the achievements of industrial genius, great commercial undertakings, scientific expeditions, a system of schools, a profusion of museums and hospitals. Surely the multitudes of immigrants who were driven by poverty from their native lands and found in America prosperity and a sense of unlimited opportunities, have long ago been cemented into a great nation, proud of its gigantic cities, its riches as if in a *Thousand and One Nights*, and the astonishing dimensions of its productivity of goods and machines.

However lofty the dreams, however cherished the ideals of the American nation whose Constitution sanctified the pursuit of happiness as one of the foundations of the state, the unity suggested by Renan is never complete until it has been tested in hours of common struggle, victory, defeat and mourning: until — not to shrink from the terrible, hackneyed phrase — it has been cemented with blood shed in common. America, emerging as a philosophers' Republic and the heir of the Encyclopaedists (for America was that heir, not France of the great Revolution, born in the bloody confusions of Rousseau's follies), found no other path to freedom and the longed-for rule of reason than the blood-soaked roads of war that forever testify to the unreason of man.

Fought at a time when the population of the United States was ten times smaller than today, the fratricidal Civil War between the North and the South devoured half as many American lives as the hitherto inconceivable weapons of World War II. Margaret Mitchell, in her excellent *Gone With The Wind*, a novel neglected by European connoisseurs, has convincingly rendered the tragedy of that cleft, the scars of which have not yet healed today. This tragedy still moves the imagination of the greatest American writers, like Faulkner, and seems to open forever like an abyss between the vanquished aristocratic, poetical and impractical South, and the Yankee, that ruthless, self-made victor who is enemy to all tradition. This cleavage weighs even today on the internal politics of the

200

United States. Only the sentimental legend of Eisenhower could break the century-old traditions of Southern support for democratic party candidates, escaping the old stigma of Republican as plunderer. The Confederate flag, which Jefferson Davis unfurled, still appears from time to time at the rallies of belligerent and riotous "nationalists" from Atlanta or New Orleans.

Nevertheless, these and similar displays of the stifled superiority complex of the separatist South do not in the least mean that the unity of America, gained at the price of the tragedy of Civil War, is not the property of the whole American nation, or that descendants of Scarlett O'Hara, however debased the traditions of their former splendor, would ever voluntarily renounce the unity that was imposed on them by violence. They themselves regard it by now as a guarantee of their prosperity and as part of their own legitimate history. Lincoln's Gettysburg Address, a political and literary document unequaled in the history of any other nation, has shown with unique simplicity the depth of the tragic paradox that high aims cannot be achieved without the use of physical force, and has given new meaning to an old truth: the value of struggle and sacrifice. With the Declaration of Independence itself, Lincoln's address became for the American people the most important expression of their united aspirations. In speaking of a government "of the people, by the people, for the people," it gave the most perfect definition of political democracy, and made heartfelt the ideal embodied in constitutional forms — permanent, sensible and free from demagogy and extremism. That historic speech, equally great as an action and as a literary monument, laid bare the inevitable and tragic contradiction of tendencies in conflict: on the one hand, the dream of rule by the people as an embodiment of the "pursuit of happiness" inscribed in the Declaration of Independence; and on the other, the urge to struggle and sacrifice, which, if not denying personal happiness, removed it to a realm of almost mystical vision.

The Civil War was both a confirmation of the ideals of American democracy and tragic doubt of the possibility of an integral idealism. In this sense it cannot be said whether its lesson points to the lofty aims that inspired it or to the cost of a victory gained by means incompatible with the pursuit of personal happiness. The fact remains that the Civil War never became an embarrassing page of history, but is an event deeply fascinating to men of letters and students of history. It is not the magnificent, handsome, and conventionally moral Washington, the father of the American people, but the physically strange vessel of spiritual and perhaps other secrets, Lincoln, doomed to a life of ceaseless struggle and to death at the hand of a murderer, who embodies for the average American the secret of the greatness, contradictions and essence of the American people.

The number of works that appear year after year to swell the vast literature devoted to Lincoln and the Civil War should convince European skeptics that their deep-rooted idea of an American aversion to the past, or of the priority Americans give to what is and will be rather than to what once was, is somewhat over-simplified. Nevertheless it is certain that the American reader, even if he is not always aware of it, searches in the biographies of Lincoln and histories of the War of Secession for links with the present and for signposts of the future. Besides fortifying his faith in democracy, he could not help learning the difficult lesson that the road to great achievement is often drenched with blood and strewn with the bodies of the dead.

Americans, who are the descendants of Pilgrims and heirs of the first Mayflower passengers — farmers of Anglo-Saxon stock interbred with the Indian natives they all but exterminated; who include the children of unemployed landless exiles from Italy, Poland and Yugoslavia, and of German colonists and Jewish shopkeepers born in Czernovits, Kaluszyn[14] or Berlin (millionaires with fortunes that exceed the annual budgets of many a European state), the Irish, who have grown in America into a powerful, conservative clan still loyal to the hatreds and myths of their native land, and the Negroes who, despite the continued opposition of the South, in spite of all obstacles and restrictions, move onward along an ever less stony road, from Uncle Tom's Cabin to the offices of

---

[14] Czerniowce, a town in the eastern reaches of Poland, since the Second World War in the possession of the Ukraine. Kałuszyn, a small town in the Mazovian reagion. Before the war, its population was chiefly Jewish.

municipal administration and federal delegations — all these men and women of different races, nationalities, conditions, beliefs, superstitions and manners, carrying in their blood the heritage of European rivalries, hatreds and national and social animosities, have produced, if not an entirely new and solid nation, a great society bound together by common interests and opportunities, by the blessings of liberty cherished in common and by room for life open to all. To stress that these people want peace, and that they will do everything possible to keep it, is not merely to repeat a propaganda commonplace, but to state the simple truth — the deepest instinct of American democracy.

The malachite palaces of the Tsars, the spell of the St. Petersburg carnival amidst the sparkle of candelabras and champagne evoked in the verses of *Engene Onegin*,[15] the orgies, cruelties, crimes and attractions — even the very name of Peter's capital — became but a legend of a dim past, incomprehensible to younger generations. Berlin, which twice dispatched its armies to conquer the world and was twice on the threshold of victory, was reduced to a heap of rubble. Our time has seen the awakening of Asia brought about by the pressures of the Bolshevik imperialists and well-meant sermons on democracy from across the Pacific — an awakening of incalculable consequence, that cannot be repressed. Our times have seen the undermining of the remnants of European colonialism, which could exist only as long as its very principle had not been questioned.

All these revolutions have occurred within the memory of a single generation and, like the eruptions of scores of mighty, hitherto dormant volcanoes, have changed the shape of the world. We are the witnesses of a transformation that cannot be held within the narrow borders of European history. The European traditions, criteria and taboos, which had seemed to us the measure of the universe, have now been decisively bypassed by universal history; all the possibilities of the so-called European chessboard, which once decided the fate of all continents for centuries, have been

---

[15] Novel in verse (1823-31) by Aleksander S. Pushkin (1799-1837), generally seen as the masterpiece of Russian Romanticism. It was later made into an opera by Tschaikovsky.

exhausted. The cards with which the political game has been played have dropped from the hands of the former masters of that game, and the game itself is now taking place at a different table. To measure this transformation one would have to reach back far beyond that Revolution which once seemed great to us, even beyond the somnolent models of the Humanism of the Middle Ages, as far back as the migrations of nations and the growth of the empires of antiquity.

The Soviet conquest of eastern Europe, a center of powerful demographic forces that adheres naively and fanatically to principles we feel are a monopoly of the West, is one symptom of history that has upset the political, cultural and moral equilibrium of Europe. Liberation from this subjugation is the first condition of a moral renaissance in Europe and of the preservation of Western culture on the continent as a whole.

"Cultures die like human beings," said Paul Valéry, the most skeptical observer of our time, who yet remained most faithful to the heritage of our culture. Cultures die when they have said their last word, when they have given final and perfect expression to their content; like human beings, they die of the exhaustion of their biological potential, and like human beings, they find immortality in their works. Buried under the ruins of their monuments, under the tomb of their vanquished defenders, after centuries of oblivion, they can suddenly reappear from beneath the earth in the marble-hewn, torn limbs of their gods, demigods and saints, and their voice, stilled centuries ago, resounds again and forever, handing along the marching centuries names and works cleansed by death and winged by legend. The symptoms of this biological decay of culture are of course not as measurable by learned physicians as the exhaustion of the human heart. It would be easy to confront various prophecies of the end of European culture by facts that demonstrate the unceasing artistic creativity, the technical progress, the bliss of millions of human beings who swarm into the capitals, temples and beaches of that so-called dying world, and who draw from its "exhausted" springs a beverage of indefinable sweetness and unequalled flavor.

Optimists can draw comfort from the mistakes of others who have for so long predicted the end of Europe. They can point to the cloudy, learned discourses of Spengler[16] that come after the pedestrian Zola, who at the end of *Nana* symbolized the decay of our world in a prostitute dying of a monstrous disease while drunken crowds stagger through the streets of Paris greeting a war that will end in their destruction. Sober men who put no trust in prophecies will answer: And what then — ? The Paris of Zola's naiveté survived the disaster of German invasion, the shame of betrayal and the misfortune of annexation. Not only did the walls of its churches, museums and palaces defy these calamities of defeat, but at the turn of the century France itself rose from them stronger and happier to one of its most glorious epochs, to dazzle the world with its wealth and unsurpassed taste, the spell of its way of life, and a constellation of brilliant stars in every field of art. In defiance of all moralists and moralities, fifty years after the defeat at Sedan, history enacted a scene that reversed Zola's prophecy and negated the symbolism of *Nana*. For the soldiers who had wiped out the disgrace of Sedan marched under the Arch of Triumph and Paris echoed not with mere shouts of unthinking and baseless hope but with a song of victory that restored to France the provinces lost half a century before, and with the names of generals that were to cancel in the national legend the inglorious Marshals of the Second Empire. And at that very moment Proust was concluding his monstrous, magnificent epic, with its description of decay and corruption that was to surpass anything that provincial Zola believed might rouse the conscience of a dying world.

This instance alone should serve as a warning not to seek in corruption of manners, or in comparisons with Byzantium or the Rome of Nero, evidence on which to base death-sentences on cultures, for these, like human beings, have their own secrets, more profound and complicated than moralists on the verge of becoming totalitarians could suspect. Yet it remains certain, as Valéry has said, that cultures die like human beings; they cannot last forever, and death is the inescapable end of their very existence.

---

[16] Oswald Arnold Gotfried Spengler (1880-1936). German mathematician and philosopher. His 1919 title *The Twilight of the West* is considered the leading work of twentieth century catastrophist thought.

Authentic Europeans, not those who, decadent in their sophistication, obstinately defend the most brutal Byzantine diseases of our culture, but those who struggle to rescue its genuine content in monuments of law, masterpieces of art and patriarchal beauty of manner, have no choice but to fight on for the preservation of this culture and for the reconstruction of principles on which its heritage depended, and the denial of which sounded the knell of Europe. Such a struggle must call on the tragic instincts, most rare in Europe today because they are regarded as fatal to material and intellectual comfort — instincts that compel us to witness and survive the spectacle of a new world at hand and the natural death of our own cultural past. This death — though it sets trembling the frightened rabbits, great and small, led by a Mauriac incapable of the tragic approach — need not display the violence of a new Pompeii or Hiroshima; it can arrive merely as a gentle, undramatic underscoring of old and hidden signs of moral and material bankruptcy.

Vienna was not bombed in World War I. Its museums and parks, its enchanting garden restaurants and concert halls remained untouched; its conductors, its Oscar Strauss, Lehar and Kalman remained; the state secretaries and philanderers of Schnitzler and Rittner,[17] the charming "Wiener Schätzchen" and the unique "Gutentagsagers," even the archdukes, imperial counselors and ladies of the Court survived the downfall of the Hapsburgs. All these, untouched by any tragic sense, were ready to go on as a choir of many millions, singing the "Hinreissende Wälzer" without which it seemed Europe could not exist. The end of World War II and the incessant volcanic transformations that then shook the world caused other demises as peaceful as the end of imperial Vienna. Recorded by no seismograph, these were not comprehended by puppets who danced on to the old rhythms as if they were dead inhabitants of dead cities, vestigial specimens of a vanished culture. Today there is no need for a stern professor of the old style or for an unruly, naive anarchist, like the child in Hans Andersen's tale, to disturb in their

---

[17] Arthur Schnitzler (1862-1931), Austrian playwright, and Tadeusz Rittner (1873-1921).

nakedness dancing spectres who believe themselves clad in regal mantles.

Europe is rightly proud of its past cultural achievements, its art treasures, inexhaustible despite the eagerness of American museums, its ever new intellectual lights who can silence their American interlocutors with brilliant quotations from the classics. But in the wish to base its pre-eminence on an established ascendancy in the realms of art and intellectual speculation, Europe forgets an old truth: that not such values alone, and not always such values at all, have determined whether a civilization was strong and viable.

In Rome we find the example of an empire that lived by its Greek inheritance in the realm of art, and lived also by wars, under the merciless contempt of Greek exiles and refugees. But this empire laid the foundations of the modern world. It extended the range of Greek, and later of Christian culture, and it translated into practical terms the code of beliefs, moral principles and manners that without Roman aggressiveness and robust practicality would never have gone beyond the Greek Acropolis and PEN Clubs of Athens.

Some are able to confront the problems raised by the suddenly revealed interdependence of all continents: they are aware of the tragedy of millions of peoples of all races, civilizations and faiths, already victims of cruel wars and bloody internal conflicts or threatened by newly perfected bombs and the horror of so-called social and national liberations. Such persons must consider it foolish and near-sighted to undertake to defend our great Western and Christian culture merely in terms of its more picturesque, refined and hermetic symbols — decorations that serve only a privileged minority and often mask egoisms and spiritual perversions in conflict with that very culture.

The writer recently received from a colleague in Europe a most complimentary letter about one of his recent works. By way of appreciation and friendly solicitude for the spiritual well-being of an author whose writing he found so much to his taste, he concluded with the exclamation, "I can imagine how you must feel, there in America!"

If I may speak of the personal experiences that impelled me to put these reflections on paper, I should like to convey an impression that embraces ten years of toilsome effort of acclimatization by an immigrant unhorsed from the European Pegasus. Perhaps it could serve as a concise summary of the thoughts and observations expressed in these pages. It seems to me that the greatest obstacle to an understanding of America by emigrants from "happier" countries of traditions and habits of thought like those of Poland, is a complete inability to perceive exactly these phenomena which are most significant and favorable in American life — an insensitivity of our retina to the authentic images and a simultaneous sharpening of our awareness of everything that could offend the European eye. The simpler explanations of such misunderstanding, which say merely that there is a basic opposition between essentially European taste and emotional habits and the more typical manifestations of Americanism, are based on criteria too flimsy for such large questions.

In the first place, the very immensity of the American land and life is an obstacle to awareness of their complexity. A European, whose sense of superiority usually colors his observations, is not necessarily struck at once by the size of the phenomena; to him they do not appear gigantic at all. Lost in the turmoil of an enormous, alien world, he does not grasp their dimensions, contradictions and validity. Standing in the depth of the fantastic canyons of lower Manhattan, that modern, outsized Florence, he does not feel the height of the buildings towering above him. Not until he has seen New York from the far bank of one of its two rivers will he be able to measure its power and cruel, unrivalled beauty.

Granted that any search in America for the charms and comforts of European individualism, for the atmosphere that was the breath of our life in Europe, must lead — despite all the attractions of Greenwich Village, of the *far niente*[18] of the South and of the French cuisine in New Orleans — to the conclusion that

---

[18] *Dolce far niente* (Italian), "How sweet to do nothing," a catchword of luxury associated with the South of Europe.

America lacks these charms. Is there then nothing that draws us toward America? As in every profound experience, so in our readjustment from familiarity with the European play of life to a perception of the momentarily invisible attractions of America, a creative effort of the imagination is required.

If we can succeed in overcoming our proud conviction that the only possible culture lies in manners, attitudes, superstitions and achievements that provide the individual exclusively with the greatest scope for aesthetic and intellectual insights, and if we can imagine a civilization whose purpose is to resolve the conflict between individual and collective interests — a discrepancy that persists in the balance-sheet of our own culture — our eyes will open to the real beauty and greatness of America. Then we shall discover the hitherto concealed meanings and charms of American life, not as diminished in comparisons with an entirely different world, but measured in its own being.

This discovery can come as a rich blessing and revelation that had seemed unattainable to the offspring of tired Europe. We shall see a world of contradictions, torn in great convulsions between primitive and brutal force and a nostalgia for moral order. A world impassioned and bloodthirsty in its lust for material gain but reaching at the same time toward a masterful and myth-creating poetry. A world whose spiritual mystery is symbolized by two equally powerful landscapes in glaring conflict: the monotonous, grisly desert and the heavenward soaring metropolis, more populous than many a European country — a world that shares with the old continent all its madness and all the dangers except the one fatal danger of hypnotic enslavement to the past, and the fear that tomorrow may never come.

The certainty that tomorrow exists, recently expressed in the remark of the great tragic writer, Faulkner, that the world has not yet been wholly created, is for America neither a program nor a command issued by totalitarian rulers. Anything but a symptom of spiritual decay or artificial rejuvenation, it is the voice of an instinct so potent that a world-weary newcomer from Europe, whose cloak bears marks of all the battles of the old world, scarcely notices that without having lived to see any of his hopes fulfilled he succumbs to the boon of hope itself. Hope in an unknown, dangerous future that bristles with every imaginable pitfall and defies the claims of moralists and philosophers, but nevertheless a future. And sometimes thanks to the primitive, irrational emotion that America evokes, we forget to care whether it evolves in strict accord with our moral prescriptions, and embrace that disorderly future even as we see it strangely, alas, in the light of our old patterns.

In all this I have no wish to absolve the future of its inevitable crimes, blunders and follies, nor to draw a blank check on the account of the life force, which has justified so many stupidities and crimes within living memory. It is probably true that the final outcome of any historical adventure mocks expectation and almost always bursts the dam erected by its creators. Crusades undertaken for religious ends frequently led to the discovery of new trade routes. At the end of Columbus' voyage to India, unforeseen and incalculable, lay America. Thus we can perhaps rely on that hope of which the profound sense is expressed in the paradox that "humanity has never erred."

Through the twilight of prehistoric caves that shadowed murder and death, amid the delusions of whole epochs, across how many blind quests for the absolute embodiment of this unerring humanity that in its name would even exterminate humanity itself, in the dreams that have enveloped whole continents, burying tribes of countless millions in a narcotic trance and obliterating with dust the great highways of history, at various spots on the planet a light has always penetrated and glowed, to reveal a new path toward the mysterious end that we have given the all-embracing and most deeply enchanting name of human fate.

Today only the thoughtless and irresponsible can doubt that one of these paths is America. Here is no straight highway, built for the convenience of traveling salesmen with slogans, but an authentic path of continual struggle. From this struggle may emerge not an enormous replica of past experiences, but a new moral and social experience. Who could have imagined in the profligate days of Henry VIII or amid the piracies and cruelties of Elizabethan England, the virtuous England of good Queen Victoria? Thus no one could foresee in the America of a hundred years ago — conveniently isolated from old-world epidemics by the Monroe

Doctrine — the America of today, which maintains to the world that the affairs of all continents are of legitimate American concern.

The American experiment was undertaken as a practical embodiment not so much of rationalism as of the humanitarianism of the Great European reformers, and guided — almost like Plato's ideal Republic — by men whose equals Europe has never produced in such an unbroken succession, men like Adams, Jefferson and Monroe, who were true men of thought and quite unlike the incendiaries who led the French Revolution. This experiment was given solid reality by Lincoln in a tragic war that was followed by an extension and enhancement of freedom, and reinforced by the impractical Woodrow Wilson, whose importance is still underestimated. Later it was to dispatch beyond the American borders military forces to rescue the liberty of the world. Whatever deformations its main theme has undergone, whatever its inner contradictions, it cannot be compared with the Marxian experiment, bred in the penumbra of perpetual slavery, which is pathological and, in its so-called rationality, insane.

Against all tradition and almost against its own will, the United States has set out to undertake tasks which Europe can no longer discharge and to achieve aims on which the fate of our civilization depends; in doing so, it must avoid the errors Europe has committed in the failure, or loss, of its basic instinct — a loss that remains the most powerful ally of the totalitarians who threaten it. A country of almost unrestricted liberties, of harbors open to all, the United States must nevertheless, in order to preserve and extend these liberties, compromise and impose the disciplines that go with any great achievement. Such restrictions have their equivalents in the structure and customs of all great nations, even those that profess to be rudely shocked today by so-called American reactionism.

We should of course not blind ourselves to changes that result from some of the restrictions being imposed on American freedom; we should even recognize that the threat to some American liberties is not merely temporary. Legitimate fears have been expressed that restrictions imposed only as a means to higher ends might become ends in themselves. Against these fears, however, we do well to look at the main, enduring fact — the

211

American tradition of liberty, never essentially endangered since it can always compromise with common sense. This tradition has endowed the President with prerogatives so wide that they would be regarded in other countries as almost dictatorial. And yet they in no way infringe on the legislative power, and give full control of the nation to its true rulers, the electorate.

The certainty of the average American that his political system assures him a decisive influence on the activities of the government; his attachment to the two-party system, which the predominantly Anglo-Saxon voters do not intend to abandon; the well-tested possibilities of bloodless and yet revolutionary adjustments in labor relations, and, not least the material wealth that history was good enough to give to America — these factors ensure that the United States will escape the medieval convulsions that have seemed inevitable to those who give in to the fatalism of our times — a fatalism that really arises from such causes as the decline of parliamentary institutions, the continued existence of social ulcers, and revolutionary changes in the world hierarchy of wealth.

In what Europeans see as an emerging new American isolationism, still occasionally expressed as a strong emotional attitude despite the political impossibility of carrying it out, and in certain harsh American security regulations and procedures (though the latter have parallels in Western history and cannot be viewed as unique to our time), they persuade themselves that they also see the special threat of a totalitarianism, terrible and familiar, on the American horizon. We can combat energetically such regulations and procedures, as symptoms of latent but dangerous tendencies released by the demands of the struggle against Communism. Yet in light of American realities we cannot imagine that such impulses and symptoms could ever coalesce into a program able to raise up a national Huey Long, who at the summit of America's historic mission would destroy in one strange adventure the system regarded by all Americans as a permanent guarantee of liberty and prosperity. Now these American realities serve also as a safeguard for Europe and indeed the world, having entered the last phase of their development — though so few yet recognize it — on the day Pershing's armies landed in France.

Old Europe may still rouse from its fatigue and discover unguessed energies; other continents may master their destinies more rapidly than we now expect. But the history of the United States cannot remain what it was for old-world scholars and intellectuals of the past: a footnote to that "universal" history, in which nothing — except perhaps Columbus' discovery, Washington's victory, and Wilson's Fourteen Points — could compare in "world importance" with the intermittent dynastic wars in Europe or the marriages and murders of medieval princes.

In a world threatened with extinction by socialist ills and nationalist excesses, this history of a still new country offers the gift of an instinct that can appease or resolve explosive social conflicts, and without recourse to inherited or mechanical formulas. It also offers the gift of its multi-national foundations, which provide an energy now absent in countries integrated centuries ago. There is boldness in the American design and application of essential and long overdue reforms, from which so many seemingly enlightened Europeans have recoiled in fear of vengeful tutelary gods.

The muse of America, whatever the many Sartres and Mauriacs may say, is fully entitled to assume the shape of the goddess lifting the torch of liberty over New York harbor; for she offers one other gift, on the sole condition that we accept it with our eyes closed.

She has the right to make this demand, for she herself does not know the content of the mysterious casket she places in our hands. The treasure it holds is truly Sibylline: for what can be more ambiguous, or latent with the boldest promise or most frightful menace of disappointment, than "the future"? No one knows how much more time history has allotted to us, time in which yet to determine what we shall extract from that casket — time, like a sentence imposed on the Old World for all its follies and crimes, and then suspended until the day that world shall end. We find this priceless gift neither in the worth nor in the innocence of the goddess who holds up the torch of liberty, but simply in her youth. Only our determination, prudence and vigilance can safeguard and use it in the face of mortal danger.

Whoever would reject this gift because the light of that torch occasionally flickers would negate all the claims of this beneficent muse to the leading role she has won for herself in the great modern historic drama. Whoever imagines that some other fairy godmother may offer the same gifts is a madman entranced by some detail in the great historic canvas but blind to the beauty of the whole picture, unable — in the words of great, ruthless Bismarck — to sense when the Lord is passing and to grasp His mantle.

Not until World War I did England identify its own interests with a greater cause. And England never ceased to be governed by the harshly conceived interests of the British, which were regarded as the only moral principle. France, in its literature if not in its official policy, sustained the cause of freedom everywhere throughout the ages. Today both countries lack strength to support this cause, and almost refuse to have anything to do with it. Until recently Paris was embarrassed and London unmoved by this issue; both apparently hoped that, having signed the death warrant for one half of Europe, they could maintain life in the other, the only half that really mattered in the deepest recesses of British thought. The fact is that the free area of Europe cannot survive without the captive area.

Shallow cynics, unaware that historic transformations are merely a subtle interplay of egoism and altruism, will doubtless hasten to justify this attitude as consistent with a genuinely realistic policy, shorn of the usual rhetoric. The fact is that reluctance or inability to undertake efforts in keeping with the times has reduced the policies of former European powers to mere prestige gestures that lack all sense of reality and border on the delusional.

England still wishes to realize these dreams and to ensure an "Alice in Wonderland" return to the Elizabethan era, through Puritan austerity and laudable though economically dangerous sacrifices on the altar of social equality. France, as if attempting to weather the approaching storm behind a veil of oblivion and to spellbind the clouded future by the splendor of French fashions and the reputedly indestructible sparkle of French wit, acted as if to prove an ill-chosen aphorism of one of its great treasurers — that France was a beautiful ballerina, admired and subsidized by the whole world. Here I refer only to the dominant trend in French policy and to the spiritual climate that shaped it; I neither wish to ignore the examples of heroism and sober political thought (which,

214

as exceptions, alas, confirm our dismal thesis) nor to point to a decline of all the French virtues. I refer only to a weakening of those virtues without which there can be no great power or great politics.

Nothing is more comprehensible than France's wish to avoid dangers that we as Poles know so well. The policy of a country as biologically undermined as France has been in the wars of this century must obviously aim at safeguarding the peace. But the understandable narrowing of its aims and its exclusive nostalgia for security have deprived France of the opportunity to take decisions that range beyond a limited conception of its own interests. The restricted interests then depend on solutions that are attractive because they appear to involve no risk; but they are in any case altogether impossible to achieve. Indeed such solutions hold in their very nature the risk of a complete extinction of Europe and France itself.

The well-known Polish poet, Kazimierz Wierzyński, paraphrased in one of his poems words attributed to Marshal Piłsudski in an address to the Polish nation: "I condemn you to greatness, for without greatness you will perish." There is no doubt that this is applicable to the United States at the present stage of its development. The United States has in truth been condemned to a greatness that it can abandon only at the certain cost of extinction. The material interests of this country are fully consistent with its ideology, its instinct, its nature, which despite all temporary compromises and shifts continue to flow like a subterranean current through the historic declarations and collective achievements of the American nation. And the same complex of interests and ideals binds America to the cause of the nations held in Soviet bondage as well as to the cause of the imperiled freedoms of Europe.

The fulfillment of such a destiny is by no means assured. Those who rightly look to the United States as the only power able to halt the destruction of the free world and to restore its former frontiers, cannot indulge in uncritical optimism. At the risk of seeming to betray European shibboleths, it must be said that great danger threatens the fulfillment of the tasks imposed by history on the United States. The danger is this: American policy could either

215

yield to European pressures or bow before the specter of its own isolationism.

The real enemies of Europe are not the common American people, who pay their taxes to support foreign aid and who shouldered arms to take part in foreign wars. The real if unconscious enemies are Americans who are ashamed of America. With no sense of the strength and possibilities of their country and ever fearful of European opinion, they cannot understand that Europe must now be defended even against its will. A player can of course lose the game even if he holds a fine hand; and when one plays chess for the first time it takes real talent to move successfully against an older, more experienced player. Once again, this time on a world scale, America must recognize the differences between an ideal program and workabilities at hand, and must confront realities in such questions as that of colonialism: for realities mock crude sermonizing and imperious commands.

Santayana,[19] who was more European than American, feared that the American experiment might fail because Americans were wanting to teach everyone; and the facts, so far, seem almost to have confirmed that fine Humanist. Casual American travelers have too often ridiculed the alleged backwardness of European ways — signs and symbols of unique values dating from centuries ago, and of immeasurably deep cultural and educative processes active in Europe. They have derided predilections and faiths that may form the only barrier against totalitarian mysticism and that even the astounding miracles effected by America cannot replace. Thus they have injured the American cause in Europe to a degree that might outweigh all the good achieved by far-sighted and truly great plans for the rescue of the continent, and by American generosity not always tied to political arithmetic. Of course it is difficult to gauge exactly to what extent such local defeats are due to an ingratitude complex — as so obviously, for instance, in French-American relations — and to what extent they stem from the skills with which variously ill-informed Moscow agents play on that complex.

---

[19] George Santayana (1863-1952). American philosopher and writer, an expatriate for most of his adult life.

216

But we might say more truly than Santayana that the Americans, far from teaching too much, do not know what to teach. Europeans who regard themselves and are regarded as leading intellectuals have no idea of the present position of American workers or of changes in the Negro problem; they are not even aware that a Negro is a Borough President in Manhattan.[20] Together with the recent outcries over the Rosenberg case,[21] of which French workers and the President of France knew no more than the Bolsheviks had told them, this suggests that Americans are still pitifully inept at teaching, especially in what concerns America.

Integration of the European cause with America's historical role, however, need not inevitably take the form of a wholehearted union based on mutual comprehension and appreciation. History knows instances when necessity overrules ideological prejudices, overrules even profound religious differences, and without resolving them. Europe, having accepted salvation by America, can quite conceivably remain proud of its past achievements and certain of the superiority of its aristocratic elegance over common American materialism. Until now, however, policies based on such pride have been unable to avoid naive and disastrous negations or to move beyond the slogan *Aut Caesar aut nihil*,[22] not publicly proclaimed but nevertheless their basic theme.

The Caesar in question — though Europe is unaware of this — was not nurtured in the cradle of Western empires during the past two thousand years and miraculously preserved on the patch of earth called Europe. The Borgia of today is the uncouth barbarian of Eurasia, no heir of Pushkin or Tolstoy but rather of the Mongol Khans, from whom he has inherited both their cruelty and cynicism, perfecting the latter to a degree far beyond the drawing-room

---

[20] Hulan Jack (1906-1986). Borough president of Manhattan from 1953-1961.

[21] Ethel (1915-1953) and her husband Julius (1918-1953) were convicted of spying on behalf of the USSR. Although their role in delivering American atomic secrets into the hands of the Soviets may have been exaggerated, they were convicted of espionage and put to death .

[22] Latin: "Either Caesar, or nothing."

217

cynicism of a pseudo- or even a true Talleyrand. This Mongolian Borgia, whether garbed in a Marxist jacket, a Tsarist uniform or an existentialist beret, will not allow himself to be outmaneuvered by the wonders of the French cuisine or moved by the genuine poetry of Aragon or Eluard,[23] nor under such influences to make an exception of the French bourgeoisie in his mission of conquest and enslavement. Such hopes are mere delusions of the likely victims of a Parisian MVD.[24]

More than the *Nihil*, however, remains to Europe as an alternative to this so-called *Caesar*, the Borgia from the Volga. Rescue by America of what still remains of Europe would not in truth be the death of it. The cultural entity of Europe has suffered far-reaching defeats that have dimmed its brilliant past; we might say that the worm of its decay was hatched in the very flower of its splendor. Future historians, who count as minutes what have seemed centuries to us, who link together in a chain of causation events utterly remote and unconnected in our minds, will perhaps discover that what Europe finds it most difficult to discard today — its feudal, hierarchic subtlety and refinement — had begun to collapse with Lincoln's action on the battlefields of the American Civil War, and that *Gone With The Wind* was a factual description of the end of a Europe which, inhuman and at the same time utterly human, saw itself as a living truth long after it had been reduced to its own shadow.

But the inexorable end of the sway of fairy godmothers and cruel witches does not doom what is immortal in the European heritage. The twilight on the Parisian boulevards is not the shadow of a volcanic eruption that will engulf in its ashes Michelangelo, Bach, Shakespeare, the Magna Carta and the Code Napoléon. If Europeans understand that they cannot remain satisfied in the contemplation of their own great past, but must make efforts comparable to that past; if they can pay homage to Shakespeare, not through interpretations but through a return to the tragic sense of

---

[23] Louis Aragon (1897-1982). French Communist essayist and poet. Paul Eluard (Eugène Grindel, 1895-1952). French surrealist poet, also a member of the Communist Party.

[24] I.e. a Soviet-style secret police.

life, and can honor the Rights of Man, not by contrived speeches and commemorative ceremonies but by opposing to the new tyrannies genuine social and economic freedoms; if Jena and Verdun are remembered not in torch parades but in the determination of renewed effort until victory: then in defiance of all laws of historical life and death the miracle of a European renaissance may prove true. For astrology revokes its verdicts when the will of man challenges the stars in their courses.

Even if this fails to occur, if European culture petrifies into grand monuments beneath which flitting wraiths of malcontents curse the present because it is not the past, if Europe cannot find a spell to break the magic ring of its culture that would keep it a land of mandarins and coolies, maharajas and outcasts — even then, destruction cannot threaten the human spirit, that chose to dwell for many centuries in Europe as in a land of learning and enchantment.

One of those all too rare, genuine Europeans, a man who not only understands the intricate puzzles of a new China but who can struggle as the spiritual pioneers of Europe fought long ago, the revolutionary patriot, André Malraux,[25] has said:

> *I think that the most fundamental meaning of America lies in the fact that it is now becoming the heiress of the entire world and that it is aware of this . . . New York is not Byzantium. It is the most powerful industrial city that has ever existed. We are simply living in a new era.*

Only men of little heart and no imagination will fail to draw comfort from this idea.

---

[25] André Malraux (1901-1976), French writer, cultural and art historian.

IV. *Sketches and Articles*

Reminiscences

On Polish Literature

On History and Politics

The Spirit of Our Town[1]

Those Americans who have ever made a prolonged visit in our Capital — diplomats, literary men, members of various permanent or transient commissions, scientists, journalists, businessmen — there made many lasting friendships, and left Warsaw with many memories which they like to recall.

For Warsaw, to those who have had a chance to know it well, that direct charm, so appealing, especially to Americans — the charm of being human and alive, made even deeper and more endearing by the fact that, unlike other magnificent capitals, it was a charm not apparent at the first contact.

Of course, Warsaw had its beautiful landmarks too. Connoisseurs of architecture dwelled with delight on the various specifically Polish subtleties of the Rococo. Even Dresden or Nancy could be proud to own such jewels as the Island Theatre, or the Palace in the Łazienki Park. Our Great Theatre could easily incite the jealousy of any city. Also Warsaw's monuments, those of Prince Joseph[2] and Copernicus by Thorwaldsen, or King Zygmunt[3] on the Zamkowy Square were among the most beautiful in Europe.

However, on the whole there was little to admire in the streets of Warsaw for those who came from Paris or those who knew Italy and Spain. It would have been natural for those people to endure their stay in an indifferent mood and to forget the city as soon as they had left her.

---

[1] First published in the *Tygodnik Polski* , 1943 no 42-44 p. 11.

[2] Prince Józef Poniatowski (1763-1813). Napoléonic soldier, participant in the Kościuszko Rebellion (1794), national hero and model of the self-sacrificial Polish soldier.

[3] Zygmunt III Waza (Vasa, 1566-1632). King of Poland and Sweden. He moved the Polish capital from Kraków to Warsaw in 1611.

But talk about Warsaw with Anthony Drexel Biddle,[4] the most accessible of all Ambassadors, or with Charles Dewey, for a time financial advisor to our government, or with the truly apostolic director of the Polish Y.M.C.A., Paul Super, whom we simply call "Superski" or "Superman." You will detect in their words that same warmth with which Parisians speak of their Paris and with which each of them refer to the city of their birth, warmth as human and alive as Warsaw was vital.

No one would venture to deny the facts known from every text book and guide that it is Kraków the magnificent and monumental, Kraków with her many Renaissance and Gothic churches and one of the most beautiful royal castles in the world that is the most historic city in Poland. But Kraków's great royal past ended with the Renaissance. After that this seat of Polish learning and art, this staid university city, appeared in its historical role only on rare occasions — for instance, royal funerals and coronations. Beginning with the XVIIth century it has been Warsaw that furnished the background and became the stage for the development of all the most important events in Poland's history. Not only was this so in cases when, as the capital, she claimed the distinction, but especially when, martyred and downtrodden by the enemy, she rightfully acquired that leading place.

Though so deeply historic, Warsaw never for a single moment became a city of the past, a museum of relics, a cemetery of history, for the interest of tourists alone. What could be taken for the lack of historic consciousness, for the want of an understanding for tradition was actually an instinctive realization that history was not a cult of the past, but the ability to create on an historic scale, a continuous building of the future.

Warsaw's professors, workers, clergy and businessmen felt instinctively that to make history was simply to live and live

---

[4] Anthony Biddle (1896-1961). He served as U.S. Ambassador to the European governments-in-exile in London during the Second World War.

abundantly. Thus Warsaw became one of the most alive cities in Europe.

Reaching her greatest splendor in the Rococo age, most of her outstanding buildings were built in that period. She was to preserve forever something of the spirit of that age. All that Warsaw did and felt was light and gay and poetic. All that happened in Kraków bore invariably a Renaissance dignity, a scientific solemnity. In Warsaw *tout finit ou tout commence par la chanson.*[5]

Few people know and still fewer would believe that the *Marriage of Figaro*, the match that set off the French Revolution, was staged in Warsaw before it was performed in Paris. This fact could be taken as a symbol of her temperament. Again, in 1794, when Kiliński, the valiant Warsaw cobbler, led an insurrection against the Russians, the Warsaw theatre resounded with the humor of the play *Krakowiacy i Górale* (*Peasants and Mountaineers*) and its gay couplets singing of freedom and brotherhood were the rage of the city.[6]

Warsaw's beloved hero, Marshal of France, Prince Józef Poniatowski, who, in 1813 carried the responsibility of Poland's honor as did Mayor Starzyński[7] in 1939, embodied that spirit of the duty performed with a smile. Songs and poems preserved of him sing not only of a gallant cavalry officer with a menacingly raised saber, but of a charming lover of great ladies and humble

---

[5] French, "Everything ends, or begins, with song."

[6] Jan Kiliński (1760-1819). Shoemaker, town councillor, and one of the leaders of the insurrection in Warsaw in 1794. *Krakowiacy i górale* (complete title: *Cud mniemany, czyli Krakowiacy i górale — The Supposed Miracle. or Cracovians and Highlanders*) was written by actor and sentimentalist poet Wojciech Bogusławski 1757-1829. It is considered the national opera of Poland.

[7] Stefan Starzyński (1893-c. 1943). Mayor of Warsaw. He refused to leave the city during the evacuation of the government, and his heroic radio broadcasts won him an undying fame at home and abroad.. Arrested twice by the Gestapo, the date, place, and manner of his death are unknown.

townswomen. The spark that ignited the revolution of 1831 before it engulfed the entire country, scintillated in the conversations and criticisms of Warsaw's cafés (through which the sparks of all future events were always to pass) — in the incomparable *bon mots* and infallibly pertinent characterizations of people and events.

The soldier of Warsaw goes to fight with a song on his lips. In 1794 it was the couplets of *Krakowiacy i Górale*; in 1831 *Warszawianka*, born in France of the pen of Delavigne[8] and immediately adopted by Warsaw; in 1920 a song of Makuszyński.[9] In our day no historical event was to escape the satirical pencil of Czermański or the humorous pages of the *Barber of Warsaw,*[10] or fail to be recorded in the sketches or poems of Hemar, Słonimski or Tuwim.[11] No wonder that the theatre became Warsaw's passion or that Warsaw's theatre became one of the best theatres in the world.

It is generally known that the greatest stars of the Russian Ballet (Niżyński and Niżyńska, Krzesińska, Wójcikowski, Idzikowski) were Poles born in Warsaw. But it is little known that no other city in the world had as many, as good, and as enthusiastically received performances of Bernard Shaw. In fact, two of his plays, *Applecart* and *Geneva*, were staged in Warsaw before their performance in London.

And another deep though hidden element of Warsaw's temperament: it apparently did not live in its streets. National holidays were not celebrated by the street dancing as in Paris; the city was not addicted to public parades, corner speeches or soap

---

[8] Casimire Delavigne (1793–1843), French poet.

[9] Kornel Makuszyński (1884-1953). In 1920 he published his popular *Piosenki żołnierskie* (*Soldiers' Songs*) including "Pieśń o Ojczyźnie," ("A Song of the Fatherland").

[10] *Cyrulik Warszawski.* Satirical weekly published in Warsaw 1926-1934. Lechoń was its editor from 1930 onwards.

[11] Like Julian Tuwim, Marian Hemar (Hescheles, 1901-1970) and Antoni Słonimski (1895-1976) were Polish poets from assimilated Jewish backgrounds.

box oratory. A casual observer would insist that there was a distinct division between the higher classes and the working population. In reality, every true Varsavian lived, like every true Parisian, the life of the entire city. A strong, though invisible, bond of common national and religious tradition, of identical temperament and way of reacting tied together the rich merchant, the priest and the laborer. This bond was the reason that these people of different birth, education and wealth felt and acted together in a crisis at the siege of Warsaw in 1939.

Newspaper boy, cabby, messenger, bartender, marketwoman, all represented well the soul of Warsaw. Patriotic, religious, tolerant, always gay, exaggeratedly ambitious and very sensitive on the subject of ambition, the people were all proud of their city and considered it their own town, even those things that were materially out of their reach. Each president of the Republic of Poland, Piłsudski or Paderewski,[12] and many others, was to the people of Warsaw, their own and thus subjected to their collective judgment; however, only its most integrally honest and worthy men enjoyed this popularity.

When Gilbert Keith Chesterton, a great friend of Poland, arrived in Warsaw twenty years ago, he experienced two very surprising moments on the first day of his visit. The first was when, on alighting from the train, he was welcomed by the whole staff of officers of the most distinguished cavalry regiment, whose commander happened to be a fervent admirer of the *Napoleon of Notting Hill*; and again when before the dignified Hotel Europejski, a group of newspaper boys overwhelmed him and his escort of the fashionable Polish poets with their lively banter and familiarity.

Warsaw's unique dialect, lively and picturesque, inclining toward exaggeration and biting sarcasm, full of subtle shades and nuances depending on the part of the city, admirably rendered the thought and sentiments of its bellicose, gay, and human

---

[12] Ignacy Jan Paderewski (1860–1941), Polish pianist, composer and statesman.

people. A few years before the war, an obscure director of a suburban theatre was called upon to act as a reporter for the petty court trials. He at once realized the unfathomed well of treasures to be found in the language and drew from the materials for his incomparable short stories. Writing under the pseudonym of Wiech,[13] these stories of the humble people of Warsaw become the rage almost overnight.

The hospitality of the Warsaw salons (though perhaps sometimes too lavish), well known and praised by foreigners, had its excellent counterpart in the birthday receptions of the city's shoemakers and laborers.

Sound judgment, a sense of humor and true respect for hierarchy and justice were inborn in the people. Always ready to stand firm against a stronger opponent, to incur the disfavor of the Germans or Russians, a Warsaw worker would never stoop to condemnation or hatred of a weaker man.

Another comparison to Paris occurs. Just as it was possible for a man born in Warsaw to become a Parisian, so people from other cities often succumbed to the spiritual individuality of Warsaw and made her their own. Her fiction is full of tales of country gentry and the foreign-born who came to the capital and became passionately attached to it.

If the Americans who still remember the description of Mme Curie's childhood in the beautiful biography by her daughter, Eve,[14] would reread that book, they would be able to appreciate the real temperament of the people of Warsaw. Mme Curie's father dedicating his life to educate his children, her sisters stifling their own dreams to give her genius a chance to develop, and above all, she herself worrying about her unpaid debts to her country and to those who were deprived of bread

---

[13] Stefan Wiechecki (1896-1979). Author and journalist. He wrote for the Warsaw *Ekspres wieczorny* (*Evening Express*), among others. His specific style is characterized by the use of the Warsaw dialect.

[14] Ève Curie (born 1904), younger daughter of Maria Skłodowska-Curie (1867-1934) and Pierre Curie (1859-1906); author of the first biography of her mother *Madame Curie* (Paris: Gallimard, 1934).

and education were as typical an illustration of that temperament as the cocky cabby or the old veteran of the Polish insurrection.

During her 100 years of oppression Warsaw lived in circumstances not as terrible as today, but yet as suppressed. This period formed two outstanding types of people immortalized by the drawings of Arthur Grottger[15] and by the pen of the great writers Prus and Żeromski. One type was the conspirator generally illustrated by a student who, with his girl, faced certain death in defense of freedom; the other, a teacher like Mme Curie who sacrificed all to spread knowledge and to relieve misery. Mayor Starzyński who, by his concentrated efforts, did so much to build up and beautify the city was a typical citizen of Warsaw.

When you think of that distant city which was the first to oppose the superior forces that are now being crushed, think of the people, my dear American friends. Look for their face in the portrait of Lincoln, in the yellowed daguerreotypes of others who lived for the people and for freedom. Look for the soul of Warsaw among those friends of yours who still believe that overwhelming force and greed for money and power do not rule the world.

You, who were taught from childhood to fearlessly look all danger in the eyes and who based the pattern of your life on this courage, think of those two small newspaper boys who, in September 1939, stood in the ruin of bombs, with the walls of buildings crumbling around them. One of them had an attack of hiccups.

"Stop!" says one.

And the other one, referring to an age old remedy for hiccups, answered:

"Scare me, and I'll stop!"

Think of that and you will understand Warsaw.

---

[15] Artur Grottger (1837-1867), Polish painter of the Romantic school.

The Charm of Warsaw[1]

When five years ago the word "Warsaw" suddenly appeared and, for three weeks, remained on the editorial pages of all the newspapers of the world; when the name of Stefan Starzyński, until then known only to the people of Warsaw, unexpectedly became as familiar as that of Poland's most illustrious historical personalities; when the names of the streets of Warsaw, its monuments and churches, took on, all of a sudden, a new spiritual meaning, similar to that produced by "Belweder," or "Reduta Ordona" or "Olszynka,"[2] — then, perhaps for the first time since Warsaw had become capital of free Poland, many a Pole spurred by an upsurge of gratitude for the capital's glorious stand under fire, found himself perturbed by several vital questions concerning that heroic city. He wanted to find out, first of all, the city's real, imperishable significance in the history of his country and, also, what kind of people its men and women really were. After all, it was the people of Warsaw, ordinarily so undistinguished in their everyday attitudes, so conspicuous in their human shortcomings, and so harshly criticized for their alleged absorption in affairs of little moment, who suddenly, through their courage and intensity of patriotic devotion, reached the levels heretofore associated only with such national heroes of Warsaw as the shoemaker Kiliński,

---

[1] Published first in the *Bulletin of the Polish Institute of Arts and Sciences of America*, 1944 vol. III no 1 pp. 26-33. The *Bulletin* is the predecessor of today's *The Polish Review*.

[2] Belweder — official residence of the President of the Republic of Poland. As the residence of the Tsarist Viceroy, it was stormed during the first days of the November Uprising of 1830 and entered into national lore. Reduta Ordona [Ordon's Redoubt] — fortifications used by the Poles on the outskirts of Warsaw during the November Uprising, made immortal in a poem by Mickiewicz; Olszynka Grochowska — an heroic battle waged here during the Uprising in February 1831 prevented the Russians from taking the Praga (Grochów) section of Warsaw.

General Sowiński, the dauntless Cadets of the November Insurrection of 1830, and the ardent revolutionaries of the year 1905.[3]

Little wonder, then, that to the thousands of Polish refugees scattered throughout the world, Warsaw's magnificent stand at once became a source of pride and spiritual exaltation. In the dark and tormenting days of what looked like complete defeat, the defense of Warsaw electrified their minds and restored their hopes. Instead of utter despair, their hearts were now filled with tender gratitude for the intrepid city which, misjudged, underestimated and often rebuked for her alleged levity, became rapidly transformed into a living symbol of greatness. Many were overwhelmed with surprise. But those of us who had the privilege of knowing Warsaw most intimately, could not be seized with astonishment. The exciting news of her defense was but a confirmation of our unshaken belief in the capital's moral strength, in its well hidden capacity for intransigent fortitude. We knew that, under fire, that fortitude would blossom out in a variety of forms, and that it would be shared by the people of every walk of life from Mayor Starzyński down to nameless fruit sellers or newspaper boys. . .

And when we read the daily communiqués on the fighting in the city and found in them the names of the streets and places so dear and near to our hearts, we could not but see our beloved city as it had been revealed to us by our mothers, by our childhood memories, and as we knew it from the works of Polish writers and poets. Almost subconsciously we peopled the Warsaw of September 1939 with well-known historical personalities who, in our hungry hearts, got all mixed up with

---

[3] Józef Longin Sowiński (1777-1831). Polish general and participant of many a struggle on behalf of Polish independence since 1794. He died during a Russian charge of the Wola section of Warsaw, and was immortalized in verse by Słowacki. Young Polish Cadets stormed Belweder during the opening days of the Uprising. Warsaw was also one of the neuralgic points of the 1905 Revolution in the then Russian Empire, hence Lechoń's last reference.

Warsaw's present leaders and fighters. Thus through the projection of emotional reminiscences our imagination got the upper hand and almost caused us to identify General Sowiński of 1830 with Mayor Starzyński of 1939, the Cadets of the November Insurrection with the soldiers of General Czuma, Warsaw's intrepid defender in the fateful month of September, while the revolutionaries of 1905 got associated with the underground fighters of Mr. Niedziałkowski, Warsaw's fearless Socialist leader.[4]

Moreover, the burning skies of Warsaw revealed to us, as if in a flash of intuitive insight, those values and virtues of our beloved capital, which, however simple and unpretending, turned out to be capable of generating unsuspected powers of determination, faith and devotion. All of a sudden, our loving imagination rediscovered for us a Warsaw full of carefree gaiety, of elegant and crowded theatres, of spacious, well-kept parks. And something which we always felt to be true, though we never attempted to formulate it intellectually, overflowed our lonely hearts with a sense of the poetry of Warsaw, a poetry so unique and inimitable, yet so delicate, imaginative and impassioned, as to make it comparable perhaps only to the poetry of Paris.

The fact that Warsaw has now become the central theme of our contemporary imaginative writing must be attributed to two main factors: one, that through sheer accident the majority of our refugee poets and writers were either born in Warsaw or had lived there for years. The second, that Warsaw's grand resistance, so humbly and universally recognized by all civilized nations of the world, has given her undisputed priority in our hearts. No wonder, then, that contemporary Polish poetry is so

---

[4] Walerian Czuma (1890-1962), Polish general, defender of Warsaw. After the fall of the city, he spent the remainder of the war in German captivity, and after the war's conclusion, in exile from Poland. Mieczysław Niedziałkowski (1893-1940). Polish Socialist politician, representing the anti-Communist line in the PPS. He helped organize the *Służba Zwycięstwu Polski* [Service for Poland's Victory] during the war, for which he was executed in June of 1940 by the Nazis.

predominantly haunted by the sublime image and vision of Warsaw. Indeed, it is in poetry that Warsaw has now found its clearest and most lucid medium of expression. Almost all of our refugee poets, Kazimierz Wierzyński and Antoni Słonimski in particular, either recreate the Warsaw of the pre-war days, or seek to fathom her broken homes and her ruined historical monuments. They attempt to unravel the mystery of Warsaw's plain, unsophisticated people who, though forced to surrender the capital, have nevertheless succeeded in transforming it into a citadel of ceaseless, grim and determined underground resistance.

Among the poems devoted to Warsaw — some of them of considerable length — one finds exquisite masterpieces bound to hold a permanent place in the history of Polish poetry. Thus, to cite only one example, Baliński's[5] *Poranek warszawski* (*The Dawn in Warsaw*) reaches the very heights of beauty through its happy unity of diverse and seemingly irreconcilable moods. These poems literally recreate and rediscover Warsaw. In a way, they may be said to have attained a fitting synthesis of everything that has so far been written about Warsaw by our poets, novelists, historians, or anonymous song writers. Out of the bewildering complexity of moods and feelings they brought forth a superbly integrated picture of our capital and its original personality.

One cannot but think of Paris, which, though it has its unique architectural and poetic individuality, as well as its own historical and cultural background, still does remind one of Warsaw. It does so mainly through its undercurrent of well concealed emotionalism and its instinct for discovering the deeper meaning of everyday happenings, an instinct through which the real sense of history finds, perhaps, its best expression.

For the last twenty years of Poland's independent existence, Warsaw used to strike its casual visitor as a city of

---

[5] Stanisław Baliński (1899-1984). Polish poet of the Skamander group, to which Lechoń himself belonged. Following the war, he lived in exile in London.

234

cabarets and fleeting political songs. Paris, too, used to make such impression on the tourists who, unable to appreciate the Collège de France, or the Louvre, or the Sorbonne, saw only the Casino de Paris. That Chopin was born near Warsaw, may have been a matter of mere accident, but the fact nevertheless remains that his life-long attachment to the capital was deep, passionate and almost fanatical. To be sure, Słowacki, too, spent only a short time in Warsaw, while Krasiński was associated with it only during his youth. Yet it is no exaggeration to say that, since the middle of the XIXth century, Warsaw has been the real center of Polish literature, particularly of Polish prose. Sienkiewicz, Prus, Świętochowski, Sieroszewski[6] and Żeromski — to mention only the greatest of our prose writers — not only lived and wrote in Warsaw, but were themselves a product of specific phases and periods in our capital's cultural life. Moreover, they, in turn, left such a profound and lasting impression on the city, as to justify us in distinguishing between a Warsaw of Prus and a Warsaw of Żeromski.

It may perhaps be said that these two famous writers present the most striking contrast in the psycho-sociological life of Warsaw. Radically different in their literary techniques and social outlook — Prus, a positivist through and through, Żeromski, on the other hand, a romantic socialist — these two novelists have given us, nevertheless, the supreme embodiment of the elusive, ever-changing spirit of our capital and of its poetic individuality. Again, though the characters of their novels seem to belong to different worlds of values, the similarity of the motives underlying their actions is so striking as to make us believe that, like Madame Curie, they belong to a class of their own, at once romantic and positivist. Thus, one of Prus's most lovable and most exquisitely portrayed characters, Mr. Rzecki,[7] a

---

[6] Aleksander Świętochowski (1849-1938). Journalist and dramatist, also known under the pseudonym of Poseł Prawdy [The Representative of Truth] Wacław Sieroszewski (1858-1945) began his literary career after being deported to Siberia by the Tsarist government in 1879.

[7] Character from Bolesław Prus' novel *Lalka* [The Doll].

typical bourgeois with a clock-like precision and regularity of habits, is at the same time a soldier of General Bem's[8] famous revolutionary army fighting "for our freedom and yours." It is, indeed, this particular type that was destined to become immortalized in Polish letters by a host of our leading writers and poets, all of whom were also great admirers of Warsaw.

Of the Warsaw poets, the one whose works may be said to have most clearly reflected the Warsaw temper, rhythm and color, is perhaps Or-Ot.[9] The felicitous unity of humor and Quixotic fantasy, of boundless physical vitality and yearning for the colorful Napoleonic legend, the touching love for the city and the astounding ease with which he could reach the heights of impeccable lyrical expression — all these qualities have caused his appreciative countrymen to regard him as perhaps the most dependable key with which to unlock the elusive mysteries of the soul of Warsaw.

But why is it, one may ask, that for a rather long period of twenty years, Warsaw, Poland's proud capital, gave almost no signs of being able to do what she did in September 1939, and again in September 1944? When one thinks of the awe-inspiring reverence, with which the people of Kraków have always approached their historical past, and compares it with that nonchalant, unpretentious, almost frivolous disposition of the people of Warsaw and their way of looking at their own past, one cannot escape certain definite conclusions. It is true, of course, that Kraków invariably and almost instinctively makes its visitors actually feel history. For this very reason Poles from other parts of the country used to go on a pilgrimage to that Polish Mecca, to get intoxicated with the healing sense of Poland's great history. Yet, it can hardly be denied, I think, that since the Kościuszko Insurrection, in 1794, Kraków has virtually

---

[8] Józef Zachariasz Bem (1794-1850). Polish general, who also served in the Hungarian and Turkish armies, and others, in the revolutionary struggles of the nineteenth century. Also known as Murat Pasha.

[9] Or-Ot, *nom de plume* of Artur Oppman (1867-1931), journalist, poet, commonly known as "the most Varsavian of poets."

ceased to be a maker of Polish history. It has become Poland's great national museum, a repository of living stones and monuments, a storehouse of priceless historic relics and reminiscences. Warsaw, on the other hand, has for more than a century assumed leadership in every political, social and cultural field of our national life. Beginning with the Constitution of the Third of May, 1791, till the latest epic of General Bór,[10] all of Poland's significant movements have taken place, and have been planned, in Warsaw. If every Warsaw house, every Warsaw street, in which those plans were born, or in which Polish blood was shed, were to be marked with marble tablets or monuments, then Warsaw, no less than Kraków, would have turned into a museum of Polish national history.

That Warsaw did not become such a museum, that the cult of monuments never took roots in its soil, that conservative tendencies never aroused any enthusiasm of its people, can, I believe, be attributed not so much to its people's alleged indifference to history, as rather to their wholesome, unerring instinct. It is this instinct which made the people of Warsaw realize that history is not something that happened in the past, but an ever changing, dynamic reality. They simply had no time to think of Skarga,[11] one of Poland's greatest preachers and political thinkers, who was born near Warsaw and had lived in it for years. Nor had they time, for that matter, to think of Chopin, Słowacki, Krasiński, Lelewel, Mochnacki,[12] and other famous

---

[10] Tadeusz Komorowski (1895-1966). Polish general who had previously served in the Austrian army before Poland's independence following the First World War. In World War II, he served in the Home Army (AK) under the pseudonym of "Bór." After the war in exile (England). See Lechoń's article included in this book.

[11] Piotr Skarga (Powęski, 1536-1612). Jesuit priest and court preacher to Polish kings.

[12] Joachim Lelewel (1786-1861) is generally thought of as the first modern Polish historian. He taught in both Wilno and Warsaw, participating in political activism during the period of the partitions. Maurycy Mochnacki (1803-1834). literary critic. He was one of the

men. Never would it occur to them to organize nationwide pilgrimages to places of historical importance, however intimately they may have been connected with Warsaw's past. Deeply appreciative of history, the people of Warsaw refused to be overwhelmed by it. Somehow or other, they could not help feeling that Warsaw's great men, Kiliński, Piotr Wysocki, Traugutt, Okrzeja,[13] have never really become mere shadows or mere historical memories.

On the contrary, the average men and women of Warsaw looked upon their great historical personalities in a peculiarly intimate manner and considered them part and parcel of their own lives, of their own everyday experiences. One might almost say that they fully expected them to descend from their marble pedestals and resume their activities under new conditions. None of us who had had the privilege of knowing Stefan Starzyński in person, and who otherwise sincerely admired his urbanistic genius, would ever have suspected that that unostentatious, plain and forthright little man was soon to gain for himself one of the most honorable and sacred places in Poland's national history. And it is perhaps no mere accident that two dramatic masterpieces glorifying Warsaw, Wyspiański's two poetic monuments of Warsaw's historical leadership, should have been written by a poet who was forever linked not with Warsaw, but with Kraków, and who, owing to his typical Kraków-inspired cult of the past, was so superbly able to sense and express the ethos of the Warsaw November Revolution.[14]

The all-pervading romantic atmosphere of Warsaw, so perfectly symbolized by its lovely Łazienki Palace, was by no means limited to its architectural monuments alone. One could sense it in the capital's enchanting mood of its autumns, when

---

moving spirits behind the November Uprising, and later chronicled it for posterity.

[13] Piotr Wysocki (1797-1874). Polish army officer, hero of the November Uprising. Stefan Okrzeja (1886-1905). Polish conspirator during 1905 revolution. Executed by the Russians.

[14] Stanisław Wyspiański.

the parks were bestrewn with leaves noiselessly falling from the trees, and in the equally dramatic mood of its winters when, crunching its crisp and glittering snow, one instinctively looked for traces of those who had fought in the fateful insurrection of 1863. This peculiar though indefinable mood was further symbolized by the small and austere mansions, witnesses of so many historical events, and by the steep banks of the Vistula, that beheld so many acts of national martyrdom. He who was born in Warsaw, or who lived there for some time, remembers only too well how these impressions used to sink gradually into his soul, and how his heart was overflowed with that peculiar melancholy, for which the world knows neither name nor remedy.

If today we again turn to those unforgettable memories, we do so not only because we realize our irreparable loss, but also because it is only now that we are able to appreciate fully Warsaw as it really was, the Warsaw of plain and lighthearted people who, in times of great historical crisis, rose to unprecedented heights of greatness, and did so in a manner so unassuming and so natural, as to make them doubly dear to our grateful and penitent hearts. . .

No one knows how much of that unique poetry has been left, not in our own memories or in books, but in the buildings and monuments of Warsaw, and above all in the souls of its people heretofore so proud and so confident. No one knows whether the men who now steal through its desolate streets, will not forever retain in their eyes that heart-breaking look, which we have recently found in a picture of General Bór-Komorowski riding to the German commander to surrender Warsaw. . .

Some of the poems reaching us from the Polish Underground prove that new literary talents have been born in our country. They seem to be exceptionally strong and sturdy. Two of these poems in particular, different as they are in artistic qualities, may well be taken as indicative of the Warsaw of today, or rather of what she used to be until a few weeks ago. One, composed during the last Warsaw uprising, is a crisp and trenchant satire upon our émigré hysteria, our tearful sentimentalism toward Warsaw, a grand and splendid city, which welcomed the possibility of an open fight as a supreme blessing, and which looked not for sympathy but for ammunition. The other poem, written at a much earlier period, superb in structure and powerful in expression, is called simply a *Psalm*. Indeed, its truly biblical intensity of feeling and prophetic vision mark it as a masterpiece. It portrays the Last Judgment as already descending upon our world and administering to it a terrific punishment for the betrayal of Warsaw in her grand and tragic days of September, 1939. In the astounding simplicity of its language, as well as in its penetrating analysis of Warsaw's moral experiences, the poem reminds one of a classical tragedy.

These two poems, indicative of new trends and attitudes of the people of Warsaw, affirm at the same time those elements of our national life, which are constant and perennial — a joyous determination to fight for Poland's sacred rights to freedom and independence. They also emphasize our own moral duties, as yet unfulfilled, and outline the road, along which our total unity can best be achieved. We thus learn from them, if any additional lesson was needed, that our supreme duty today, a duty of which neither our own conscience nor our country's verdict will ever relieve us, is to utilize all our available resources, intellectual as well as moral, to see to it that the blood which flowed through the streets of Warsaw, and the agony of despair experienced by the capital's unflinching defenders, so confident and so hopeful until recently, but now again forced to surrender, broken-hearted and smeared by Poland's foes — that all these great sacrifices shall not have been made in vain. And that the imperishable moral and national values, for the preservation of which the people of Warsaw fought so bravely and died so calmly, shall not be taken away from us either by our enemies, or through the indifference of the outside world, or even through our own unpreparedness and weakness. Only Poland which is really free, territorially intact, and truly independent politically, can be regarded as satisfactory recompensation for the blood shed by

240

the Polish people in general, and the heroic people of Warsaw, in particular.

The Forces of Faith, Hope and Spirit in Polish Literature[1]

One might say of Polish literature that it experienced, all alone, one hundred years ago, the catastrophe which is convulsing the world today; it invested the sufferings of Poland with truly Dantesque dimensions, it elevated them to a symbol embracing humanity in its entirety, so that everyone may read in the prophetic books of our poets the destiny and sorrows of his own country.

In no other literature, before or since, has the sentiment of patriotism been defined so clearly, developed with such ardor, embellished by such poetic opulence — nowhere else has the national spirit, awakened by Romanticism, found expression in such masterpieces or been transformed into so noble and pure an art. Throughout a period of 100 years, the majority of our romanticists, as well as all the great Polish novelists and poets speak of Poland, finding a source of inspiration for their themes in her history, in the events of her political life; a consequence of this was that their works were mistakenly regarded as hermetically Polish, incapable of being deciphered and therefore unreadable.

A few Polish names of letters became known through legend, history, and hearsay, a case in point being that of Mickiewicz, who enjoyed prestige among the intellectual elite of Western Europe. Others, like Sienkiewicz and Reymont,[2] won glory on an international scale. Here and there a novelist became appreciated in one country or another; but all these are exceptions.

---

[1] First published in *The Polish Review*, 1943 no XXXIII pp. 4-5; 11, 14.

[2] Władysław Stanisław Reymont (Rejment,1867-1925). Polish novelist. He won the Nobel Prize in Literature in 1924 for his novel *Chłopi* [The Peasants]. Sienkiewicz won the same award in 1905 for his lifetime achievement in literature, and not especially for the novel *Quo vadis?* as commonly assumed.

National tendencies are timidly in evidence already in the early Polish writings and they dominate our literature up to this day. During the course of the 15th — 18th centuries, while the Italians sing of celestial ecstasy and of terrestrial passions, while the French construct admirable monuments of psychology and human thought, while Shakespeare makes his great discovery, that of man, whom he places in the presence of divine truths — our honest writers hardly touch upon inner life in their works; speaking of love, they find but lukewarm and bucolic words to describe it: they themselves are original and eloquent only when they treat of public matters, bad laws, the perils of war, when they teach, when they reprove the weak and extol the valiant and the good.

Jan Kochanowski, the Polish Ronsard, dreamy and thoroughly human, and the nostalgic Sęp Szarzyński,[3] who knew how to invest his erotic meditations with funereal accents of genuine originality and rare profundity, are approximately the only great lyric poets of our Renaissance.

In the 18th century Karpiński and Kniaźnin[4] alone wrote about sentiments, mainly religious at that. The most impassioned words ever recorded by the literature of independent Poland, the most burning images ever evoked by it, are those of our Savonarola, our Jeremiah, the Jesuit Father Piotr Skarga Powęski, a great tragic preacher who is often erroneously compared to the classic and rational Bossuet; he was a visionary but it was always his imperiled country that he saw in his moments of inspiration, it was always the fate of Poland that lent

---

[3] Jan Kochanowski (1530-1584). the only truly great Slavic poet of the Renaissance; a widely read humanist who composed in both Polish and Latin. Mikołaj Sęp-Szarzyński (1550-1581). Mystical poet who looks toward the Baroque and shows affinities to the Metaphysical style.

[4] Franciszek Karpiński (1741-1825). Chief representative of sentimental poetry in Poland, he also authored the popular Baroque carol "Bóg się rodzi" [God is Born]. Franciszek Dionizy Kniaźnin (1749/50-1807), a poet known for his sentimental-erotic lyrics and as a forerunner of pre-Romanticism.

fire to his words, worthy of the great Biblical prophets. With a lucidity bordering on the metaphysical, he foresaw the misfortunes which were to beset Poland; two centuries later these prophecies became reality; Poland, dismembered and enslaved, descends into the kingdom of dreams and lives only in the hearts of her children.

It was in the midst of sufferings, remorse, the fire of battle, surrounded by the atmosphere of proud memories and seemingly mad hopes, that the great Polish literature was born. For the Europe of his day, Adam Mickiewicz became a living symbol of the freedom and brotherhood of peoples. At the same time, he symbolized the moral values and the prophetic spirit of literature — its educational, trail-blazing role, its political and social importance. Out of this period came the creation of an imaginary personality who represents the Polish soul just as Faust represented the German soul, as Alocha Karamazoff represented the Russian soul, and as the historical heroes of Shakespeare stood for the English soul. This personality, Gustaw-Konrad, is in the drama by Mickiewicz, *The Forefathers.*[5]

The story of this hero, half-real, half-phantom, whom Mickiewicz endowed with his own personal experiences and his own psychological traits, concerns the transformation of an individual, one might say of a Nietzschean individualist, into a public man, into an apostle of ideals.

"My name is Million," Gustaw-Konrad says in his famous soliloquy, "because I love and I suffer for millions."

Konrad expresses an inner moral attitude that did not need immediate victories, that counted on the future, that held to a belief in justice, that taught love and sacrifice. To Mickiewicz, patriotism did not mean a duty, an ideal; to him it was as it was to the Polish nation, a fervent, intense sentiment, an inner state of being, abounding in all the nuances characteristic of personal feeling.

---

[5] More commonly spelled Alyosha Karamazov, the innocent hero of Dostoevsky's novel *The Brothers Karamazov,* Mickiewicz's monumental drama *Dziady* is more often translated *Forefathers' Eve.*

To this day, Mickiewicz, in the eyes of all the Slavs, symbolizes not only the Polish soul, but also the aspirations of all Slav peoples. His attitude toward Russia was one of uncompromising severity, yet Russian poetry contains some magnificent translations of his works. His influence upon the foremost Russian thinkers and poets has provided ample material for the scholarly research of numerous specialists.

Among the great liberals of Europe who gathered around Mickiewicz and who assisted him in editing the *Tribune des Peuples*, there were many who had read but a few badly translated pages of his poetry — nonetheless they considered him one of the greatest poets of their epoch and the magnificent statue of Bourdelle, erected some fifteen years ago in Paris, immortalized the admiration which liberal Europe bore for him who was simultaneously the Polish Homer and Dante.

These enthusiasts, these dreamers, these revolutionaries sensed that the poetry of Mickiewicz measured up to his political dreams, to his powerful oratorical talent; they divined from his magnificent lectures at the Collège de France, from his impassioned and stinging articles, the literary genius of a man consumed by an inner fire.

Every great and generous artistic creation, whatever its subject may be, contains within itself that priceless gift of consoling us, of warming us by that inner warmth that is characteristic of greatness. It transports us into another world where everything is noble, pure, and true, where all our misfortunes and sufferings rise to the heroic and the sublime.

Still, neither the tragic contradictions of Hamlet, nor the experience and the deceptions of Faust, nor the bottomless and perverse anxiety of the heroes of Dostoyevsky, nor even the loneliness of Oedipus brought face to face with eternal cruelty, can recall to the poor contemporary what he himself feels, deprived of his country, evicted from his home, outraged in his most sacred feelings.

Konrad, shut up in the Wilno prison; Słowacki and his Anhelli dying on the snowy steppes of Siberia; Krasiński[6] and his Last One,[7] the last insurrectionist, forgotten in a distant dungeon by his finally triumphant comrades, these can understand us today and comfort us — Frenchmen, Dutchmen, Czechoslovaks, Belgians, Greeks, Yugoslavs, Poles, and that whole panoply of the twentieth century's multitude of the *misérables*.

These poets, these seers, speaking of somber events in the brightness of eternal verity, with prophetic force which is sometimes Biblical, guiding us, directing us through the labyrinth of our destinies, all probed the depths of our miseries. They not only took stock of their own country's martyrdom, but also of their mistakes; and they extracted invincible consolation and hope from them.

Zygmunt Kasiński, the least artistic of the pleiade known as the Great Romantic Trinity, perhaps underestimated by the Poles because of the absence in his works of purely national elements, is, nonetheless, the one who best permits the non-Pole to grasp the clairvoyance, the prophetic gift, the social spirit, and the intellectual qualities of Polish Romanticism.

His drama, *The Undivine Comedy*, the work of a twenty-year-old adolescent, written one hundred years ago, antedates both the theory of Marx and the utopias of Nietzsche (a formula suggested to me by Daniel Halévy).[8] It is a vision of class warfare in all its horror, with all the convulsions and paradoxes that we have been witnessing. It is a great, dramatic, and powerful vision, surprisingly objective for a young aristocrat attached to the traditions of his noble and proud family. *The Undivine Comedy* expresses the social spirit which is so much a part of our

---

[6] Zygmunt Krasiński (1812-1859). Polish poet and dramatist. Often spoken of in one breath with Mickiewicz and Słowacki, he is the most conservative, politically, of the three great Polish Romantics.

[7] References to the heroes of Słowacki's poem *Anhelli* and Krasiński's *Nie-boska komedia* [Undivine Comedy].

[8] Daniel Halévy (1872-1962). French historian and essayist.

literature, a social spirit which prompted the inscribing on Polish banners of the phrase "For Our Liberty And For Yours."

In attempting to select the most characteristic element of our letters, in attempting to determine which problem our literature has posed and developed better than have other literatures, by which discovery it enriched our individual or collective conscience — we are led to the realization that this problem is the struggle between the personal and the collective and the search for happiness in the ideal.

The heroes of the dramas and poems of Mickiewicz, Słowacki, Kasiński, Wyspiański, and the heroes of the novels of Żeromski and Sienkiewicz are virtually all engaged in the conflict between sensual love and love for country, between personal feeling and civic duty; and although at first glance there seems to be nothing in common between the hieratic and hermetic Konrad of Mickiewicz and the intrepid but very realistic and jovial soldiers of Sienkiewicz, they nevertheless all belong to the same family of soldiers of duty and lovers of great causes.

Fate has willed the Polish character in its absolute purity, cleansed of everything that is passing and folkloristic, and the Polish attitude towards the great problems of life to be immortalized in the work of a novelist of Polish birth who wrote in a foreign language and became one of the giants of English letters — I mean, of course, Joseph Conrad. The heroes of his novels, almost without exception English, are engaged in conflicts which have nothing Polish in them, but react exactly as our soldiers and our romantic heroes reacted in fighting for Poland; they always behave as Poles, just as the characters of Dostoyevsky behave as Russians, and the proud and fearless heroes of Kipling behave as Englishmen. In order to understand why the Poles always battle until death for liberty, in order to learn what sentiment impels them to become attached to apparently futile causes, one must read Joseph Conrad, who, like no other, and with greater virility than the others, has depicted what lies at the bottom of the Polish soul: a sense of honor and fidelity to its dreams.

The novels of Henryk Sienkiewicz are, in effect, a magnificent lesson in optimism and vitality. Greeted by the West as if they were historical tales of adventure, rich in coloring, well-written but not going beyond the genre in which Alexander Dumas excelled, these novels shook the Polish nation to its core.

What the great poetry imparted to us in Sibylline parables, Sienkiewicz succeeded in translating into daily life. He transformed the heroes of Mickiewicz into average Poles, provided with all the faults peculiar to us, but capable of great deeds, knowing how to fight heroically and blessed with indomitable optimism. Polish youth learned from Sienkiewicz that courage is a virtue accessible to each one of us.

It is understandable that our writers of the 19th century — a century so cruel to us — were all in search of strength. They followed the collective instinct of the nation in seeking it in the life of the peasant, in immersing themselves in their primitive and hard life, in which love for the soil retained its religious character and developed into mysticism. Out of this spirit were also born the two masterpieces of our contemporary literature, the subject matter for which came from country life: the cycle of mountain tales by Kazimierz Przerwa-Tetmajer[9] and a prose epic by Władysław Reymont, for which the Nobel prize was awarded, *The Peasants*.

These writers had no aim other than to give voice to powerful and primitive feelings, to paint their native landscape, to soothe their nostalgia for open spaces. And yet, their works growing out of such pure artistic tendencies have continued and fortified the educational work of Sienkiewicz; this vitality whose apotheosis Sienkiewicz saw in the noble past of Poland, is exalted by Tetmajer and Reymont in their descriptions of the

---

[9] Kazimierz Przerwa-Tetmajer (1865-1940). Polish poet and dramatist. Mention here is of his cycle of works written in the Góralski dialect of southern Poland, *Na skalnym Podhalu* [On the Granite Cliffs of Podhale].

struggles and labors of the peasant; they discuss no social problems but in these narratives, permeated with a hieratic dignity and a rude, refreshing humor, is heard the voice of the Polish nation, whose social layers succeed one another, transmitting the secret of this biological force that fashioned our history.

The fraternity sealed between the historical strata and the peasants on the day of the battle of Racławice,[10] where these peasants appear as conscientious and heroic citizens for the first time in our history — has become one of the guiding principles of our literature; our poets appoint themselves guardians of this fraternity, they devote themselves to the misery of the peasants, they extol the peasant-soldier, stubborn defender of his land, they recall to the forgetful gentry their duty to their brothers.

The great Polish writers might have been democrats or conservatives, but they were all enamored of peasant life, of peasant strength, some because of their social outlook, others because of the tradition of Kościuszko, which, in a way, became national — but all because of a taste for the country and a humanitarian concern, innate in the Polish character.

The democratic tradition, reflected in so many of Poland's masterpieces, is based upon spontaneous humanism, on an instinctively and well applied Christian spirit.

It is thanks to these tendencies of our character that the march of social progress was not followed by bloodshed in Poland and that the laboring classes did not need to resort to force to obtain their rights. The great novelist who, as no other, influenced the pre-1914 generation and held it under the magic of his style and his ardent sensitivity, Stefan Żeromski, linked, once and for all, the cause of national freedom with the memory of heroic workers who gave their lives for their country's independence. Continuing the democratic and humanitarian tradition, Żeromski paused over each human unhappiness,

---

[10] On April 4, 1794, a group of poorly-armed peasants under the leadership of Tadeusz Kościuszko stormed and took Russian artillery positions in this southern Polish locality.

denounced injustices, went out of his way to support any initiative which sought to alleviate this misery. He never stinted in defending the dispossessed, to demand the boon of work for everyone. Incidentally, he was the only one of our great spiritual leaders to see his country's independence realized. To his death, he never ceased teaching, censuring laziness and injustice, and demanding greater efforts of will power and conscience.

Żeromski was the last in our long line of writers and poets who during 100 years actually took the place of the beneficial political power of which their country was denied. More than the majority of our political and military leaders, with the exception of Kościuszko and Piłsudski, they influenced our thinking and the course of events, drew from the bottom of the national temperament hidden instincts which could not normally develop and formed the national character — courage, altruism, mysticism, optimism, and action.

The world of generosity, of love of neighbor, of the Christian spirit, of a creative and optimistic force, the world that breathes the air of collective feelings and the refreshing atmosphere of history, the world of the future which will provide justice for all — this is the world of which these poets and novelists spoke.

In the vaults of the Royal Castle in Kraków, where lie the remains of Polish kings — the ancient Piasts, who brought Poland out of the Middle Ages, the wise Jagiellonians who fashioned Poland, Lithuania, and Ruthenia into one republic dedicated to culture and liberty, Sobieski who saved Christendom[11] — there also lie the remains of two great romantic poets — Adam Mickiewicz and Juliusz Słowacki.

The Castle has now been pillaged, the famous libraries of Kraków have been despoiled, the old parchments which spoke of our glorious victories and of our just and human laws have been

---

[11] On September 12, 1683, King Jan III Sobieski (1629-1696), at the head of a Polish army, delivered Vienna from a siege by Turkish forces under Kara Mustafa. Muslim armies never again threatened Central Europe.

destroyed and burned; it is in Kraków that the German hordes have perpetrated the particularly odious crime of throwing all the professors of the old University of the Jagiellons into prison and inflicting barbaric tortures upon them.[12]

But it is from the vaults of the Wawel that hope comes to us. The tombs of Mickiewicz and Słowacki who, poverty stricken and exiled, dreamed the resurrection of Poland and who now rest among kings, speak to us of forces that no others will ever equal: the forces of hope, faith, and spirit.

---

[12] On November 6, 1939, the Nazi occupiers invited the professors of Jagiellonian University to a "meeting" in the great hall of Collegium Novum, at which they were ostensibly to hear a lecture on the attitude of the German government to education. They were summarily arrested and carted off to the Sachsenhausen concentration camp. This event is known as the *Sonderaktion Krakau* [Exceptional Measure Kraków].

Polish Literature[1]

Accepting the invitation of my friend Lednicki who asked me to speak to you about universal ideas in Polish literature I immediately and perfectly realized the difficulties that I shall encounter in the accomplishment of this task. All the distinguished scholars and critics who have preceded me at this table and who spoke of the literatures of their respective countries: Mr. Nock as well as Mr. Bonfante, Mr. Cohen as well as Mr. Castro, Mr. Nicoll in the same measure as Mr. Foerster, had only to appeal to your memory, your recollections from school, your favorite reading in order to evoke before you those worlds of thoughts, sentiment, passions and images that are contained in the names of Shakespeare, Pascal, Goethe, Cervantes and Dante.

In a few weeks it will not be difficult for Wacław Lednicki, who will speak of Russian literature, to be understood by you, and later for the great writer Madame Sigrid Undset to establish contact with this audience by simply reminding you of what we all owe to Ibsen and to Madame Undset herself.[2]

I am certain, on the contrary, that almost all of our foreign friends who are present in this hall know almost nothing about the literature of my country. They have perhaps read, very long ago, *Quo vadis?* and some of them perhaps also *The Peasants* of Reymont who also won the Nobel prize. They know from hearsay who was Mickiewicz and because they saw at Paris his magnificent statue by Bourdelle. I am sure, however, that all these names seem to them to be well-meaning but entirely local

---

[1] Published first in the *Bulletin* of the Polish Institute of Arts and Sciences in America, 1943 vol. I no 4 pp. 884-903, originally delivered as a talk at PIASA headquarters on 12 March 1943. Wacław Lednicki was at the time president of the Literature Section of PIASA; Lechoń was vice-president.

[2] Sigrid Undset (1882-1949). Norwegian Catholic novelist. She was awarded the Nobel Prize for Literature in 1928.

celebrities. Of the whole of our literary works they have doubtlessly the same idea.

I am by no means indignant at this ignorance of which I know the causes. I wish, on the contrary, to excuse before you my audacity of speaking on a special subject by endeavoring to demonstrate that it is really thrilling and of a general interest. Reminding you that the history of Poland is almost to the same extent as our literature unknown abroad I shall perhaps touch the truth that will explain to you why the world knows Goethe's *Faust* and very few people are familiar with Mickiewicz's *Forefathers' Eve,* why it is the same with Corneille's *Cid* and Krasiński's *Undivine Comedy,* with the theatre of Calderon and that of Słowacki, with *La Chanson de Roland* and *Pan Tadeusz,* with the works of Emerson and the poetry of Norwid, with the novels of Alexiei Tolstoy and those of Madame Kossak-Szczucka.[3]

It is so because behind each great work of literature extends the country that gave it birth, the native country of the author; if that country is great and powerful, if it has interests that go beyond its frontiers, if its history was intermingled with that of other peoples, if, above all, its language has the privilege of being known abroad, it is almost certain that all the great literary creations of such a people will one day form part of the spiritual patrimony of humanity and that they shall be appreciated according to their real values.

It is obvious that neither Pascal nor Balzac, Goethe and Shakespeare do not need any propaganda, that we have read them in order to come nearer to truth, to find there the guiding thread in the maze of our doubts and anguish. It is difficult for us to imagine that Shakespeare, Tolstoy or Goethe should be unknown in the United States. It is impossible for us to imagine a serious gentleman in London or Rome who would reply to the

---

[3] Zofia Kossak-Szczucka (1890-1968). Polish novelist of historical works. A Catholic author, she fought in the Polish underground during the war, initiated the Committee for Jewish Relief (Żegota) and survived imprisonment in Auschwitz.

sound of the name of Balzac with the words: "Who was that fellow?"

Yet I dare to express the hypothesis that if Dante were not Italian or if his country were not what it was in the period of the Renaissance, if thousands of travelers, students, scholars, adventurers traversing the whole world would not have spread everywhere the knowledge of Italian, the snobbery of Italian, the scandals of the Italian courts, if all the sad adventures of Ugolino, all the misfortunes of Paolo and Francesca, all the complicated intrigues of papal Rome and feudal Italy, and, finally, the hieroglyphics of the *Divine Comedy* could not have been the subject of conversation for every self-respecting person in London, Paris, Nuremberg, Kraków, Prague — Dante would have certainly remained what he was, but few people outside Italy would have known what he really was.

And it would have sufficed for Czarist Russia not to be a great empire exercising his known influence on the affairs of Europe, for Alexander I not to be the victor of Napoléon, for Nicholas II not to be the object of the sighs of Quai d'Orsay, and for the ambassador of the Czar of all the Russias not to be the most influential personality in the diplomatic corps of Paris. And had Dostoevsky not been Russian but Bulgarian or Serbian, he would have in vain looked for translations to make himself known in Paris, and once known he would certainly be less so than he was.

By these hypotheses I do not want to tell you, Ladies and Gentlemen, and it is not at all a Polish habit to tell that we did not experience epochs of splendor, that Poland did not live through great hours when the whole world admired and even gave its blessing to our achievements.

During the hours through which we live at present it is consoling for us Poles to think that five hundred years ago the Order of the Teutonic Knights, the ancestors of the present day Nazis, was reduced to ashes by the Poles and the Lithuanians who in that period formed a kind of first United States of Europe.

255

At a time when Poland suffers persecutions the account of which makes the world tremble, when we see Czechoslovakia under the Nazi yoke, when the Hungarians learn through a bitter lesson what it means to be a weak neighbor of a big imperialist state, it is impossible not to think with pride and emotion of our Golden Age, the Golden Age of Central Europe, when all these states enjoyed happiness and when our Casimir the Jagiellon, King of Poland and Grand Duke of Lithuania and Ruthenia, was at the same time the father of the King of Bohemia and Hungary.[4] It is above all impossible not to think of that scene that the brush of our great Matejko,[5] the Polish Rubens, has rendered immortal, when in the market place of Kraków prince Albert Hohenzollern of Prussia kneeling before Sigismund I, King of Poland, took the oath of allegiance that was to be renewed by his heirs for a century. Three hundred years ago our great and noble general, hetman Stanisław Żółkiewski, received in the Kremlin on behalf of King Sigismund III the homage of the Russian boyars and a few months later these boyars came to Warsaw and prostrate before the King requested the favor of having his son Władysław for the throne of Moscow. And in 1683, a fact already generally known, in the face of the mortal danger threatening Vienna, count Waldstein, ambassador of the emperor, came accompanied by the Papal nuncio Pallavicini to the residence of King John Sobieski in the environs of Warsaw, threw himself on his knees before the king and implored his succour for besieged Vienna. And it was a beautiful day, that of September 12, 1683 when the bells of all the churches of the world rang out the glory of John Sobieski and when Pope Innocent XI, the famous Innocent of Velasquez, gave the name of the king to a constellation of stars.

---

[4] Kazimierz IV Jagiellończyk (1427-1492). His son Władysław II Jagiellończyk (1456-1516) ascended the Czech throne in 1471 and that of Hungary in 1490.

[5] Jan Matejko (1838-1893). Polish painter of Czech extraction, noted for his sweeping historical canvases.

I do not evoke before you, Ladies and Gentlemen, these glorious deeds of arms in order to praise, *à la polonaise,* my country; I only wanted to explain to you why, in spite of the fact that we had a powerful state that played a primordial role in the history of Europe, Europe does not know our literature while, after what I tried to demonstrate, a powerful state is always by its very nature a magnificent instrument of propaganda for its literature.

Moreover, in the periods of our political greatness of which we have spoken, during the epoch of the Jagiellonians, of the capture of Moscow, of the battle of Vienna, we have had famous universities, magnificent lordly residences, palaces at Kraków, Wilno and Warsaw, built by masters of Italian architecture, our great lords and scholars undertook long journeys and amazed foreigners by the extent of their culture, we have had the most powerful parliament in Europe, most liberal political institutions, we had our national dances with inimitable rhythms that expressed our pride, our solemnity, something incomparably optimistic and at the same time pathetic in the Polish character. These rhythms, especially that of the *Polonaise,* inspired all the great musicians of the world including Johann Sebastian Bach.

It suffices to mention the name Copernicus, a Pole born at Toruń, who owed his education to the University of Kraków, to have an idea of the level of Polish culture already, in the XVth century.

It is therefore clear that we must have had a national literature, writers and poets, and we had them indeed: the noble, wise, melodious Kochanowski, friend of Ronsard; the pensive and tragic Szarzyński whose grave mournful stanzas of a Valeryan classicism would be the envy of many a modern poet; we had Rej of Nagłowice, jovial and philosophic, the true Sarmatic Rabelais; Andrzej Morstin, chauncellor of the Commonwealth, great lord and great poet, impassioned, perverse and baroque; Wacław Potocki,[6] grandiloquent, oratorical and yet impulsive and inspired, and many others among whom one of true greatness, the Jesuit Father Piotr Skarga Powęski, a tragic preacher, sublime as the biblical prophets, solemn like Bossuet, who illumines our prose with the mystical lights of El Greco.

And yet, in spite of all those names, of all those important works, all those monuments of culture, the noble literature of great independent Poland certainly lacks something essential that creates the importance of the artistic work, something personal, inimitable, new, truly national.

All that is well said by Kochanowski in Polish was certainly better expressed in French by Ronsard. Morstin, though a magnificent poet of the Baroque, took his inspiration from Marini;[7] to our national Rabelais, Rej of Nagłowice, we shall always prefer the real Rabelais.

Indeed Poland of the XVth, XVIth, and XVIIth centuries was the Rome of Central Europe. Like ancient Rome spread Greek culture, Poland spread Latinity in the regions of her political influence.

But with all due respect to Virgil and Horace we may nevertheless say that they only imitated the Greeks and that if Roman literature had never existed almost nothing would be changed in the spiritual and esthetic development of humanity.

We can repeat the same when speaking of the literature of ancient Poland before the XIXth century. We say this without false modesty, because we are convinced that the Romantic period has given us brilliant proofs of the originality of the Polish genius in the domain of literature, that it has given us masterpieces of burning timeliness whose universal character

---

[6] Mikołaj Rej (1505-1569). Polish nobleman and poet, second only to Jan Kochanowski in the Renaissance period. A Calvinist, he wrote only in Polish. Jan Andrzej Morsztyn (*vel* Morstin 1621-1693) was a poet of the Baroque age and a courtier, as was the magnate Wacław Potocki (1621-1696), who immortalized Jan III Sobieski in his Sarmatian epic *Wojna chocimska* [*The Chocim War*].

[7] Giambattista Marino (*vel* Marini, 1569-1625). Italian Baroque poet.

and importance should be particularly revealed at the present time.

Our great, truly national literature, that is our great Romantic poetry, was born of suffering, remorse, obsessing memories of the great past, oaths of vengeance, mad hopes, prayers of despair, prophetic visions of the future.

It was the literature of a great people which, after having witnessed the capture of Moscow, the victory of Vienna, after having attained the heights of political power, had to suffer the most atrocious martyrdom, and the cruelest humiliations, which was enslaved and partitioned, which was among nations what the biblical Job was among men.

Poland was crucified at the end of the XVIIIth century, in a period that seems to us to be the dawn of all liberties, of all prosperities, of the greatest human initiatives. It is at that time that are born the rights of man and the rights of nations to liberty, the epic of Napoléon, the imperial apotheosis of England, the great French prose, industrialism, bourgeois prosperity, Socialism, individualism, great music, Romanticism. Everywhere there are revolutions and wars, but at the same time everywhere congresses amuse themselves, everywhere songs reverberate no matter whether of love or of vengeance and the gods are no more thirsty because they drink blood.

What the entire world then experiences in that period is certainly not commonplace prosperity, it is the fullness of life.

France, England, Russia, engaged in continuous wars, nevertheless breathe the grand air of history. The German states, the Italian kingdoms prepare themselves for a new life; Poland alone is condemned to what misfortune can teach her. And misfortune teaches her to be herself and to sing.

The great Polish poetry that is then born does not resemble any known spiritual phenomenon in importance for its people, influence on its life, riches and variety of forms. In the literary history of the world there is nothing comparable to the union of that poetry with the nation, except the divine dialogue between the Hebrew poets and the people of Israel. Born of suffering it brings to its people the strength, the hope that alone will enable it to survive.

We shall see that everywhere peoples suffer: in the Balkans, among the Czechs, the Slovaks, one hears the stanzas of our Romanticists, particularly of Mickiewicz, as the voice of all oppressed countries. Everywhere where Polish is understood, among the Russians first of all, Mickiewicz is recognized as the greatest poetic genius of the time, the prophet who speaks in Polish to all mankind.

He becomes the prophet of exiles and those who have revolted, of revolted souls and revolted peoples. The Jacobins, the Democrats, the Socialists of all peoples listen to him and acclaim him. The Italians, Russians, Roumanians, Czechs, Hungarians crowd the auditoriums of the Collège de France to listen to his prophetic lectures, and the noble spiritual union of the great idealists Michelet, Quinet[8] and Mickiewicz bound their names forever.

But acclaimed, adored, discussed, apotheosized, Mickiewicz remains as a poet unknown not only by the West but by the very Paris that acclaims him. He was known through his impassioned lectures and inspired courses at the Collège de France, through his brilliant articles in the *Tribune des Peuples,* finally thanks to Montalembert's translation of his political writings; nevertheless it is not the great poet whom Paris adores, but the great revolutionary, the orator of genius, the prophet of liberty. It may be said that *Forefathers' Eve* is for the Poles what the *Divine Comedy* is for the Italians, that *Pan Tadeusz* written by Mickiewicz at the age of 36 is an epic as serene, limpid and divine as the *Iliad*, that as an artist Mickiewicz is indeed at once the Polish Dante and Homer, not their imitator but their equal. Yet all the most extraordinary things that the Poles can say about Mickiewicz leaves the French completely indifferent because they were unable to read him.

---

[8] Jules Michelet (1798-1874). French historian and essaist. Author, among others, of *La Pologne martyre.* Edgar Quinet (1803-1875). French historian, author of *Pologne et Rome.*

The translation of *Pan Tadeusz* and of *Forefathers' Eve* made during the poet's life by honest artisans could only turn the French away from that poetry, however precise, clear and human, but which like that of Racine is all music, all harmony of unique and irreplaceable words. These are the reasons why our great literature is almost unknown by the West.

When we contemplate the history of our literature until our days we must admit that we have fully expressed ourselves only in poetry. We have great prose writers, but we have geniuses only among the poets.

We are certainly the only great modern people that has preserved the instinct of giving poetic expression to all its joys and all its misfortunes, for which poetry is not an amusement, a spiritual pastime or a thrilling esthetic problem, but a kind of ceremony, ritual or sacrament, that which according to Paul Valéry is the *raison d'être* of all poetry.

It is certainly not by accident that we have buried Mickiewicz and Słowacki in the crypt of Wawel Cathedral beside our kings and our great military heroes Kościuszko and Prince Joseph Poniatowski. They repose there because our poetry is an integral part of our national myth, because it always has been for our national consciousness what great historical events and great battles were for it.

It is certain that our poetry is above all national and it is easy to say, as it has been often said, that consequently it is of a purely national interest, that it cannot teach anything to the Americans, French or British, that it should therefore remain forever an anachronism of an ancient myth in the modern world that has lost the taste for it.

We are convinced that what was defendable three years ago is not only a prejudice today, that the hour has come when our Romantic poetry to which we owe the heroism of the defenders of Warsaw and our aviators, which taught us for a century how one should live with honor and die for liberty, that this poetry, so human, enthusiastic, confident and Christian has at this particular time a great message to offer to all the oppressed peoples, to all nations who fight, and to all martyrs who suffer.

The subjects of that poetry, the atmosphere that it emanates, its perfume, its music, are certainly those of Poland. It breathes the air of our forests and fields, it recites our old legends, it speaks of the graves of our fathers, it reminds us of the naive songs sung of yore by our mothers leaning over our cradles.

That poetry is an incomparable picture of our country, our landscape, our history, of the noble virtues and charming faults of our ancestors. Reciting the stanzas of Mickiewicz that are of marble smelling of roses, we seem to return home, we see our relatives and friends, and thanks to these stanzas full of pride and pity we are able to hope and live.

This poetry is for us "music above all;" we hear its words as one hears the *Polonaises* and *Mazurkas* of Chopin, and it is certain that even in the best translation the charm and the harmony of its cadences, the unique concordance of words, and finally that which is in it "pure poetry" must escape foreign readers. But we are also sure that the dramatic power, the psychological truth, the clairvoyance, the prophetic spirit, and the intellectual greatness of *Forefathers' Eve, Anhelli, The Undivine Comedy*[9] will always reveal themselves, even through imperfect translations of these masterpieces, eternally human and astonishingly new.

If we are asked what our literature, though unknown in the West, has given and can still give to the world, we can answer pure conscience, having in mind *Forefathers' Eve, The Undivine Comedy, Anhelli, Samuel Zborowski, Deliverance,*[10] that we have given expression, like no other literature, to collective sentiments, and that we have better than others

---

[9] *Anhelli*, mystical prose poem by Juliusz Słowacki. *Nieboska komedia*, drama by Zygmunt Krasiński.
[10] *Samuel Zborowski*, drama by Słowacki; *Wyzwolenie*, drama by Stanisław Wyspiański.

fathomed the problem of the struggle between the personal and collective elements, between happiness and duty.

This tendency that was to express itself by unique masterpieces during the period of Romanticism, is manifested throughout our literary history since the earliest writings. On the whole lacking originality, each time when our courageous writers of the XVIth, XVIIth and XVIIIth centuries speak of collective feelings, when they appeal to the social spirit, when they teach civic duties and exalt heroism they find true, strong, and new accents.

The underground soldiers of France, Yugoslavia, Norway, Belgium, Holland, the martyrs locked in dungeons, the noble vanquished soldiers, the intellectuals deceived by evidence, betrayed by learning, who see, terrified, the abyss of the human soul whose horrors even the most audacious psychology did not suspect, young people whose youth founders in the thickest darkness that mankind has ever known, our entire poor Europe, enslaved, martyred to which nothing remained of its middle class happiness, its nonchalant prosperity, which cannot expect anything from its old idol, its skeptical and opportunist intelligence, for so many years an accomplice of barbarism, that Europe which is hungry, threatened by death, ashamed by its past — can it be consoled, fortified, cured by fine psychology, beauty of style, and beautiful cadences?

We know well that in one country, the most intellectual of the world, in a country with perfect and even perverted taste, where the finesse of the literary language was the object of a real cult, where the anatomic observation of the soul became a kind of national sport, we know that in the unfortunate France of today the most advanced poets are inspired by Victor Hugo and that the grave stanzas of a majestic mournful monotony, the great words bare like the walls of Romanesque churches — the poems of Charles Péguy[11] are recited by everybody and listened to as the words of the Bible.

---

[11] Charles Péguy (1873–1914), French Catholic poet and dramatist.

Péguy's spirit astonishingly resembles the leading ideas, the pathetic quality, and the heroic character of our literature. We shall certainly astonish the French when we tell them that Péguy seems to us a particle of that great moral and artistic universe that is our national poetry. His art of a peasant Debussy, his patriotic and Catholic litanies, like real litanies thanks to the ritualistic repetitions, important and mysterious, his spirit born of the spirit of the saint apostles of France unites through the underground ways with that of Mickiewicz and Słowacki that one hundred years ago revealed to us the truths preached by Péguy to the French and confirmed by their misfortune.

We fully realize that we have given nothing to the world that as the knowledge of the individual can be compared with the discoveries of Balzac or Tolstoy. We did not have a single Stendhal, Proust or Meredith. However, we shall not at all exaggerate if, having in mind the immense work of Mickiewicz, Słowacki and Wyspiański, we say that in the domain of feelings that were those of Péguy, our literature is unequalled by any other.

In the XVIIIth century when the spirit of ancient Poland, a spirit truly patriarchally Roman, countrylike, faithful and heroic, combined with the spirit of the enlightened West, what we call the true Polonism was born, and we witness a veritable flowering of political literature that, remaining an applied literature, uses high literary forms and produces sarcastic pamphlets, exquisite satires, charming comedies and mock-heroic poems of ethereal lightness. The great prose of Kołłątaj and the crystalline poetry of the princebishop Krasicki,[12] the Polish Jean de la Fontaine, are certainly equal to the best didactic writings of the West.

The literature of our Age of Enlightenment, intelligent, clear, noble, highly artistic, does however appeal only to our spirit, and charms only our taste. It is born of a pure and

---

[12] Hugo Kołłątaj (1750-1812). Polish philosopher, writer, and educational reformer. Ignacy Krasicki (1735-1801). Bishop of Warmia and intimate of Frederick the Great of Prussia, poet especially known for his fables and satires.

clairvoyant patriotism that is rather an idea and a duty than a sentiment. The Romantics will transform this sentiment into a powerful passion that knows all the delights and all the despairs peculiar to personal feelings.

The martyred homeland, lost Poland became for the Poles that which are for us our most loved ones who are threatened by death, of whose cruel sufferings we know, who are far from us and who implore our assistance.

Polish poetry, until then so colorless and conventional in the expression of personal sentiments, that appeared to be only bucolic, didactic and jovial — when hearing the laments of enslaved Poland, the cries of women and children tortured by the soldiers of Suvorov,[13] felt for the first time the beating of its heart, like Racine's heart beat when he heard the wailing of Phèdre, like Shakespeare's heart beat when the ghost of Hamlet's father entrusted to him his lugubrious secret.   .

This is a strange thing and a profound phenomenon that should make all the Freudians of the world ponder.

The first words of love in our poetry that betray passion, the first true and profound accents expressing terrestrial love are spoken by Mickiewicz's Gustaw who was soon to abandon them in order to serve a great cause. The tender, burning words that we have never heard from our poets we hear at the very moment when everything egoistical was to be banished from the heart of every Pole. It may be said that hurt in the collective feelings, the Pole became truly human and at last understood the whole profundity of love. It could be therefore said that groups like individuals have their sentimental secrets and that peoples can like men have their Oedipus complexes.

The fictitious character who then appeared in our poetry, Mickiewicz's Gustaw-Konrad whose imaginary destinies were forever united with the fate of our entire nation, embodies like nobody else all sublimations of the Polish soul and symbolizes

---

[13] Aleksandr V. Suvorov (1729-1800). Russian general. During the Kościuszko Uprising, he was responsible for the butchery of the civilian populace of the Praga section of Warsaw.

265

that which is essential in that soul: the search for happiness in the ideal.

The pretended realists and skeptics may be made to smile when one tells them his history.

Those who have never read *Forefathers' Eve* can easily imagine that its subject is a noble idealistic fable invented for the edification of grown-up children, a fable that, though well rhymed, put into splendid verse, only reflects the noble illusions of a dreamer whose feet have never touched the ground. If the history of a man who without complaining dies for a great cause is an edifying fable, we have transformed it into a living reality and Mickiewicz has made out of this reality pure poetry.

This Gustaw-Konrad of Mickiewicz, this Polish Werther who is transformed into a Polish Cid, into a Polish Constant Prince, was certainly only a fictitious and symbolic character. But every time he spoke we heard thousands of Poles speaking who thought and acted like he. When he lamented he expressed the sorrow of thousands of soldiers, insurrectionists and prisoners. When he cursed the tyrants he did so on behalf of millions of Poles who entrusted to him "the thread of their thoughts and the flowers of their feelings." He appeared on the scene dressed, like a typical Romantic hero, in a black cape, with upturned collar. Of his past we know only a few details which he reveals to us in his famous monologue in the house of the village parson.

But we have known the names, the misfortunes, the sacrifices, the heroism of thousands of Poles who during a hundred years lived possessed by the single idea of liberty and who unlike the imaginary Konrad were not Romantic spectres but living beings of flesh and bone.

From the pyramids of Egypt to the snowy steppes of Siberia they followed the phantom of the homeland, from the tropical islands to the Kremlin, wounded, barefoot, in torn uniforms, starving, they marched indefatigably and hummed the song, gay as everything that is Polish, and yet born of misfortune:

Poland is not yet lost
As long as we live. . .[14]

All our great-grandfathers, all our grandfathers and even the fathers of some of us were Mickiewicz's Konrads who were unable to speak in verse.

As young boys they took before the shadows of the past the oath to live dangerously at each hour of their lives threatened by death. With a heavy heart they would leave their families and their enslaved country, and everywhere where enchained peoples were breaking their bonds there were seen our pilgrims of liberty and our banners inscribed with the truly Polish motto "For your liberty and ours."

Others trampled by the enemy went underground into catacombs where arms were forged, while still others subterraneously taught the religion of freedom and imparted the lesson of honor and sacrifice.

Even in the XVIIIth century, before the *Marseillaise* is born, in the hieratic poem of our prince-bishop Krasicki there appear the words so similar to those that in a few years were to make Europe tremble:

"Sacred love of the beloved homeland". . .[15]

For every Pole, for all the anonymous Konrads, love of country has always been a religious sentiment, a sacred love that like religion ruled all the activities of their lives. At the same time when any Pole thought of his country and of liberty he would recall some familiar landscapes, a carefree childhood, and a pair of blue eyes he had loved and which he would never

---

[14] *Jeszcze Polska nie zginęła, / Póki mi żyjemy*. The first line of the "Mazurek Dąbrowskiego" [Gen. Dąbrowski's Mazurek], a song composed by the soldier-poet Józef Wybicki (1747-1822) during the early Romantic period, which was to become recognized as the national anthem of Poland.

[15] *Święta miłości kochanej ojczyzny*, from the short poem "Hymn do miłości Ojczyzny" ("A Hymn to Love of the Fatherland").

forget. Like all love this religious love was for us at once simply love, almost physical love and the dreamed-of liberty was for us really "beloved liberty."

Mickiewicz appears to have been born to celebrate this love in song. His genius lay in his realism, it may be said in his clairvoyance of reality, that enabled him to penetrate to the core of characters, events and problems, but had in it nothing learnedly intellectual, that was all intuition, like that of Shakespeare sensual and virile. He could speak as naturally of the secrets of the Lithuanian cuisine, the sentimental vicissitudes of an old pretentious coquette and the most sublime moments of the lives of great heroes.

He did not seem to change his tone when he was passing from a sarcastic account of a banal worldly conversation to hermetic ecstasies. Everything in him was true and human; he understood all weakness and by the divine smile of his poetry he accorded them the grace of forgiveness and raised himself to true sanctity. He spoke to God as only the Biblical prophets had spoken. "Behold the man" exclaimed Balzac when he saw him for the first time.

He gave to humanity, which by the way is unaware of it until now, a general expression of a sentiment that was as new for his epoch as love of one's neighbor was for the pagan epoch. His Gustaw-Konrad said: "My name is Million, because I love for millions and suffer torment for them."[16] He expressed what he really felt and that was not felt by any other great literary personality. King Oedipus, the characters of Dante, Hamlet and King Lear, Faust, Phèdre and Alyosha Karamazoff have all suffered like ourselves. We admire them because we see in their fate the symbol of our fate, in their suffering the refined variety of our misfortunes.

However, suffering like ourselves, rising to the heights of human dignity they have never suffered for us. They were all

---

[16] *Nazywam się Milijon — bo za milijony / Kocham i cierpię katusze.* (*Forefathers' Eve,* Part III, Scene ii ["The Great Improvisation"], 260-61.

like Ugolino and Berenice forever enclosed in the magic circle that separates the individual from his neighbors and the universe. Konrad was the first and only one among the great literary personalities to leave this circle by a Christian sortilege that enables us to forget our sufferings by identifying ourselves with those of others.

Proclaiming this ideal and giving it shape Mickiewicz revealed the innate instinct of our race.

He found and affirmed himself in the sublime myth, in Konrad who did not seek the truth like Faust or Raskolnikov, who did not try, like Hamlet, to reconcile the tragic contradictions of our sentiments, who was not, like Phèdre and Lady Macbeth, tormented by unsatiated passions, but who aspired to the only happiness that is accessible to us, poor mortals, that of good works which no gratitude will ever reward. It may be said of our literature that it is merely a continuous development of those tendencies, that it merely shows the conflicts between happiness and the ideal, between the selfish and heroic elements.

From Słowacki's *Anhelli,* that angelic poem, purer than all the Shelleys of the world, where everything is filled with snow and moonlight, from that moonlit poem which tells us in subdued tones of a mystical sacrifice of unreal beings, through the enchanting melodrama of Sienkiewicz's *Trilogy* where we find the taste for sacrifice in the simple and savage hearts of adventurer soldiers, to the last idealist comedy of the great novelist Żeromski who expressed the necessity of sacrifices in accents of a rare psychological finesse — our great writers lead an uninterrupted procession of idealist heroes, soldiers of duty, modeled or styled after living heroes and give evidence of the incurable idealism of which we were so often accused. Our great poets and our prose writers who follow them are only rarely concerned with the individual as an isolated being. The individual psychology is even often somewhat summary with our great prose writers. What interests them is man as a social being, his attitude towards his country, the great collective conflicts.

269

They know particularly well how to paint great historical pictures and great group scenes.

As a general expression of that collective spirit as a series of historical and social frescoes our letters equal or even surpass the greatest literatures. There are indeed few peoples that could boast of having created two great rural epics, one of them the ingenious *Pan Tadeusz* and the other the artistically important *Peasants* of Reymont. Both show another typical feature of our letters that is certainly the basis of the difficulties encountered by a foreigner when he tries to know and understand us. That foreigner, after having overcome the obstacles caused by the poetic element of our literature, finds himself in a world charming perhaps but anachronistic, the majority of whose problems do not interest him at all, in a world apparently not linked by anything with what is called modern social life.

It must be recognized that we are peasants: this is not only a social fact or an economic condition; this is above all the moral fact, the spiritual condition, the destiny and the leading idea of our culture. We are all, however scandalous that may appear to certain industrialized spirits, peasants and soldiers.

To this character of our culture, to this destiny we owe all that is the most original, the most Polish, the most incomprehensible and perhaps the most unbearable in our daily life. We also owe to it everything sublime that great events will always reveal in the Polish soul.

We are accused of not being democratic enough and it is true that we all consider ourselves great lords. But we all believe ourselves to be lords, the Radziwiłłs and the Czartoryskis as well as the Michalaks and Pietrzaks, the braided diplomats as well as the Warsaw shoemakers. "The small gentleman on his farm is equal to the Palatine" said the old proverb which was the motto of our social life of long ago but which well explains what is most profound in Polonism, in our culture and in our history.

The Polish middle class, the Polish workers are in their character, their tastes and their temperament but émigrés from the countryside. Attached to their cities as only peasants are attached to their soil, they preserve and will preserve forever the taste for big spaces, love of freedom and the pride of proprietors common to peasants and noblemen.

It may seem ridiculous when a poor and badly dressed man assumes the airs of the rich, but it is sublime when this poor man makes sacrifices that one demands only from great lords. This is our democracy, these are our workers and the poor devils who defended Warsaw.

We are by no means democrats in the banal sense of the word. We are a patriarchal, proud, military, ceremonious, poetic, instinctively poetic, and, I believe, in the main a monarchist people. But we are human people like no other in the world. We have the instinct of quality and hierarchy in our blood; we have no respect, and it has to be often deplored, for purely material values, but we have a mystic admiration for heroism and for disinterestedness. The great Colbert could only be for us, as was the great prince Lubecki,[17] a functionary who knew how to extricate himself from terribly complicated and tedious matters. But our great poets rest at the side of kings in the crypts of Wawel Cathedral. We did not have St. Thomas Aquinas, St. Augustine, St. Francis de Sales, Pascal, Cardinal Newman, Maritain, we have no liking whatsoever for religious disputes and we completely lack understanding for any kind of dogma or apologetic finesse. By contrast we did not have either a St. Bartholomew's Night or Torquemada, and we accepted the Jews expelled from England and Spain.

There are obsolete forms of respect that some of our peasants observe towards noblemen, but the same forms are obligatory with us in the relations between the master shoemaker and his pupil.

We do not pat the President of the Republic on the back but I have myself written frivolous songs that were sung by

---

[17] Jean Baptiste Colbert (1619-1683). Minister of French king Louis XIV, propagator of mercantilism. Franciszek Ksawery Drucki-Lubecki (1778-1846). Treasurer of the Russian-controlled Kingdom of Poland, initiator of the Tariff War with Prussia.

puppets about Mr. Wojciechowski and Mr. Mościcki because the President of the Republic had become a traditional character of satirical revues.[18]

The newsboys of Warsaw adored our capital not only because they loved our parks, the boulevards on the banks of the Vistula, the popular kermesses at Bielany, but also because they considered that everything in Warsaw even that which is inaccessible to the poor belongs morally to the whole world. They knew all the gossip and the behind the scenes of all political intrigues.

These newsboys were also great lords. We are not democrats. We are brothers.

We are above all, as has been said, peasants, and if our literature is inferior to many others in everything that touches city life, it surpasses all others, even Russian literature, in everything that pertains to the countryside, peasants and rural life.

Almost everything that is great and original in our literature takes place in the country or is derived from the rural spirit. Mickiewicz's *Pan Tadeusz,* Reymont's *Peasants,* Fredro's *Vengeance,* Tetmajer's *In the Rocky Highlands,* Weysenhoff's *The Sable and the Girl,* Maria Konopnicka's *Mr. Balcer in Brazil,* Kasprowicz's *Book of the Poor* and Wyspiański's *Wedding,* not to mention innumerable lyrical poems.[19]

It is certain that the purely poetic character of our literature and its mystical significance are due to its rural spirit. It is also clear that we owe to this spirit the love for the peasant which characterizes our literature and which in some of our writers reaches the heights of mysticism. One could speak of a

---

[18] Stanisław Wojciechowski (1869–1953), President of the Republic of Poland 1922-26 Ignacy Mościcki (1867–1946), President of the Republic of Poland 1926–1939.

[19] *Chłopi* (Reymont), *Zemsta* (Fredro), *Na skalnym Podhalu* (Tetmajer), *Soból i Panna* (Józef Weyssenhoff), *Pan Balcer w Brazylii* (Konopnicka) *Księga ubogich* (Kasprowicz), *Wesele* (Wyspiański).

272

veritable peasant myth in our literature, a myth that corresponds to the events of our historical life and reflects the fraternal spirit of our culture.

This myth that could be called the myth of Racławice was born on the day of the famous battle between the Russians and the forces of Kościuszko that was won thanks to the heroism of the Kraków peasants. They threw themselves, almost without arms, on the guns of Suvorov and forced them into silence.

The next day Kościuszko donned the peasant garb; after the fashion of the Kraków peasants he attached a peacock feather to his hat, and it is in that costume of a peasant general that he appears in legend. It is this Kościuszko of Racławice whom the poets have sung and who was adopted by popular sentiment.

The Polish peasants entered Poland's history at a time when mortal danger threatened the country's existence. They appeared as conscious citizens and patriots attached to their land as the privileged classes. Their heroic appearance revealed to the nation the existence of unsuspected forces that are at its disposal.

The Polish élite, all those who were thinking of the future, received this revelation with enthusiasm: noble reformers and great idealists saw already a future Poland in which the heroism of the nobility would be supported by peasant strength and the faults of the past redeemed by the hard and young virtues of the conquerors of Racławice.

Poland remained always faithful to this noble myth and dreams. Noblemen, great idealists, coming from ancestral castles and small gentry manors became the upholders of that myth. The white and red of the Kraków costume were welded in our dreams with the colors of our flag, and during a hundred years free Poland had for all of us the face of Kościuszko who marched at the head of his brave Cracovians and who took the oath that he would give bread and land to every Pole.

The Poland that our great poets, the great prophets of our people, saw in their visions was always the Poland of Kościuszko, and of the freedom of all peoples and of all men.

The Polish state of which they dreamed was not a state like any others, it was not a contract signed between the government and the citizens. It was a Promised Land of freedom, a Christian community that was to give to all people an example of justice, magnanimity, love of one's neighbor, of the greatest revolution of the world whose command would not be hatred and destruction but creation and love. This utopia has taken, in the writings of some of our Romanticists, Mickiewicz above all, the exalted forms of a mystical heresy, a Messianism that saw in Poland's sufferings the signs of a divine choice. We well understand that these were only the feverish dreams of impassioned minds who with these visions consoled their poor compatriots whom nothing realistic could console. Bur we also believe that these dreams testify to a profound, a true, a militant Polish Christian spirit, and that nowhere, since the Jewish prophets, St. Theresa and the dreams of Calderon, this fiery Christian spirit has expressed itself in such celestial cascades of poetry as the great soliloquy of Konrad called the "Great Improvisation," the "Vision of Brother Peter,"[20] "Samuel Zborowski" and "Anhelli."

These dreams of ideal Poland clothed by our great poets in mystical forms were transformed by our prose writers into a constructive program, social criticism and idealist climate that made of Bolesław Prus, Mme Eliza Orzeszkowa,[21] and Stefan Żeromski, true enough unwitting inheritors of our Romanticism.

They embraced with their pity all the social injustices, all the miseries, all those who suffer, who are hungry, all unemployed and disinherited. They were all great writers, capable like Prus of painting with exquisite irony portraits of an astonishing psychological truth. By the majestic grandeur and the unparalleled musical quality of his prose Stefan Żeromski creates an era in the history of our literature.

---

[20] Both from Mickiewicz's *Forefathers' Eve,* Part III. The following two titles are by Słowacki.

[21] Eliza Orzeszkowa (1841–1910), important author of the Positivist period.

They did not believe, however, that to be a great writer it is sufficient to chisel words and to observe under the microscope human microbes. They were less concerned with what man is than with what he can do and what he should be. There were thousands of Poles whose destiny was changed by reading Prus and Mme Orzeszkowa, who thanks to them forgot their insignificant troubles in order to serve others, who fascinated by the magic words of Żeromski sacrificed their lives and perished on the scaffold exclaiming "Poland is not yet lost."

Among our Romantic masterpieces we have one of indisputable universal value which, little known by the general public, has for a long time been appreciated by learned critics. This astonishing work entitled the *Undivine Comedy,* written a century ago by a young man — we would say today by a young boy — of 20 years of age, Count Sigismund Krasiński, is a drama whose subject is a social revolution that opposes the aristocracy against the people and their chiefs, Count Henri and Pancrace, against each other.

No other work reveals to the foreigner as powerfully as this prophetic drama with its Dantesque accents the true spirit of Polish literature. It is a masterpiece of a literature which is profoundly peasant, and yet its author, alone among the many great writers of the XIXth century foresaw the drama that was preparing in the misery of great cities.

Krasiński was a great aristocrat attached to the proud traditions of his family and yet no other work of the epoch accused the privileged classes more severely. No one saw more clearly than he the faults, the sins and the vileness of those classes.

Our literature — the *Undivine Comedy* demonstrates it forcefully — is a great idealist art, it is a literature of great collective problems that even if it does not speak of them, draws from the profound sources of Christianity. Inspired by the collective spirit it has a tendency to create myths and build epics. For the same reasons it orients itself towards history and it examines contemporary events under their historical aspect. Its educational role and its social significance have no didactic elements; they correspond to the most intimate tendencies of the Polish race, to the pure artistic inspirations and are expressed in lofty and original literary forms.

It is at once active, mystical and optimist, it is a literature of heroism, of sacrifice and instinctive love of one's neighbor. Although unknown abroad it is certainly the literature of the present and of the future, of exceptional universalist value, capable of consoling those who suffer and of pointing the way to uneasy and erring minds.

And now, coming to the end of my lecture I would like to go back to my personal memories to give you, Ladies and Gentlemen, an idea of what is most important and significant in our literature.

It was in 1927. Reborn Poland in the full flowering of her young forces and her old culture enjoyed peace and marched confidently towards the future.

Marshal Piłsudski who was then the chief of government ordered one day that a grave in the Montmartre cemetery in Paris be opened, that the ashes of a great Polish poet be removed from it and taken to Kraków in order that he may rest at the side of the great kings of Poland. This poet, Juliusz Słowacki, was during his life an exile, poor and unknown, a solitary, an incurable dreamer who wrote angelic poems in which he predicted the resurrection of Poland and his posthumous fame. When he died only a few persons accompanied his poor casket to the cemetery. From his youth Marshal Piłsudski admired the works of that poet. He found in them a sublime apotheosis of the sentiment of honor which of all human virtues was dearest to him, he knew by heart whole pages of that noble and proud poetry that told us of the heroism of our brothers and divine justice.

I had the honor, never to be surpassed by any other, to be designated to be present at the exhumation of the poet's ashes and to accompany them on their posthumous journey.

On a beautiful spring morning in Paris I saw how the grave diggers opened the grave and I saw the brown earth, all that remained of the great man.

I spent ten days on the battleship that transported Słowacki from Cherbourg to Gdynia and I was alone with the casket on the captain's deck when the Polish earth appeared in the distance.

The days that I subsequently experienced were the most sublime of my life: I witnessed an ancient apotheosis that united and fraternized a whole people in a religious admiration of the beautiful; I saw how along the banks of the Vistula an uninterrupted procession of peoples of all social classes waited the whole day in the pouring rain for the appearance of the funeral ship.

I saw how old generals wept, how great ladies fell on their knees, how the greatest writers remained standing all night as a guard of honor before the casket of the man who, poor, ill, and exiled dreamed of this fame and this posthumous return.

I still see under the colonnade of Wawel Castle at Kraków Marshal Piłsudski, the liberator foretold by the poet, and I hear his voice giving to the generals the order to carry the casket to the tomb of the kings.

And when I recall these improbable days, I really think that in the world there are no forces more powerful than those of the Spirit, Hope and Faith and that indeed our literature, our poetry have given striking proof of that truth.

The Elderly Gentleman with the Rose[1]

The anniversary that we observe today, though being a national holiday of the Poles, is above all a holiday of Polish literature conceived not only as the sum total of ideas, but also and simply as the writer's trade. And it should be said just today that Henryk Sienkiewicz dubbed by the Polish nation, infinitely grateful to him, its spiritual leader, a man of almost national greatness, was first of all a writer, that he considered this his noblest task and honor, that he was a consoler of hearts and awakener of faith. He was a writer first of all because his word had the power of reaching the Poles, because his imagination, his pictorial sense resurrected old Poland in a dazzling splendor of color, in an intensity of movement, in a fire of passion that bewitched and carried away the nation.

In Sienkiewicz's contemporary generation, in the great pleiade of prose writers of the second half of the XIXth century, we had writers who really lived for the nation, who shared all its cares, who wept and laughed with the poor Poles of Warsaw, then a provincial city, with the students from the attics, the workers from the basements, with the destitute peasants. Maria Konopnicka, Bolesław Prus and Eliza Orzeszkowa did not always strengthen the hearts, often they hurt them painfully, but their literary intentions were always guided by the Polish and human concern of alleviating the nation's misery, of helping the poor and suffering. In their writings you will time and again find some literary negligence, but never negligence of man, of the poor and abandoned.

---

[1] English version first published in *The Bulletin of the Polish Institute of Arts and Sciences of America*, 1945-1946 vol. IV pp. 79-82. The title is taken from a photograph of Sienkiewicz that graced the cover of the 1946/19 edition of the *Tygodnik Polski*, celebrating the hundredth anniversary of the writer's birth. Lechoń's article was first given as a talk organized by PIASA and the Stowarzyszenie Pisarzy Polskich [Union of Polish Writers].

After Sienkiewicz had become for the Polish public not only the greatest writer, but simply the highest ranking Polish person, after almost royal tributes were paid to him, after the nation that then had to take care of so many primary necessities had presented him with the Oblęgorek estate and after his unparalleled world success had consoled and strengthened Polish pride so terribly oppressed since many years, not only invidious pettiness, but also criticism resulting from profound national anxiety, loudly proclaimed that Sienkiewicz did not seem to perceive that contemporary Polish life was not a breath-taking adventure *à la* Kmicic,[2] that it was difficult for the nation to keep consoling itself by the fact that it once was a great state, that once there was a magnificent Polish army, when now there was neither state nor army.

It was then that Stefan Żeromski became the love of his generation because he accomplished that very thing that Sienkiewicz did not express, did not see or did not want to see. Żeromski saw and penetrated to the depth of the misery of Polish enslavement, extended his hand and lent his words to the fighters in students' uniforms, to the homeless people, to the strong women wrestling with Polish poverty. Żeromski thought not only of the Polish army that was, but also of the one that in the Warsaw attics was preparing weapons for a new struggle.

Sienkiewicz had in his life only a short, youthful period when he shared the constant anxiety of the heart that made Prus, Konopnicka and Orzeszkowa fraternize with the simple man, look into the face of the apparent drabness of Polish life and beneath that very drabness discover the wonderful luster of humanity. With the selfishness of a great artist Sienkiewicz turned away from this drabness, from this Polish misery. His pictorial sense did not see Rembrandtian, let alone Daumierian, shadows, it was enamored of Rubens' splendor, of Veronese's banquets profuse with color, and Sienkiewicz, like Conrad to the distant seas, escaped where his eyes could enjoy this

---

[2] Character in Sienkiewicz's *Potop* [Deluge].

magnificence to the full, where his ears could delight in the din of battle, where his shame of drabness could bask in the richness and luxury of life. In his *Deliverance* Wyspiański said in a pathetical, tragic-ironical tone that he did not feel the nation's enslavement, that he was a free man. Thrusting himself into Poland's past Sienkiewicz, perhaps less consciously, desired the same deliverance, protested in his own way against slavery; not over the cloudy pinnacles of thought like Wyspiański's Konrad, but through the ravines of Podolia and the steppes of the Ukraine did Sienkiewicz lead simple, healthy Poles to freedom.

Though he wrote *Without Dogma, The Polaniecki Family* and *Whirlpools,*[3] Sienkiewicz did not participate as a writer in Polish contemporary life, for this contemporary life was not created either in Płoszów or Krzemień, but in the very places into which Sienkiewicz did not look, in the attics from which Piłsudski's fighters descended into the streets of Warsaw. Sienkiewicz the man quickly became a great lord, feted by great lords, adorning with his presence the most exclusive hunting parties, at great dinners seated between princes and bishops.

Whenever some noble initiative asks for his name or help, Sienkiewicz always eagerly complies; whenever there is the need of speaking in behalf of the nation, Sienkiewicz always does it splendidly, with unparalleled dignity and tact. But he always fulfils these duties like a king, infallibly, with monarchal splendor that does not permit emotion; he does perhaps more than any other Polish writer could have done in his place, but we do not know whether Sienkiewicz could have said: "I live, suffer and weep with you."[4]

Having escaped from the Polish drabness into the past, having settled on the Olympus of comfort and luxury, having assumed that monarchal pose and feeling excellently in it,

---

[3] Titles in Polish: *Bez dogmatu* ; *Rodzina Połanieckich* ; *Wiry.*

[4] *Żyłem z wami, cierpiałem i płakałem z wami.* From Juliusz Słowacki's "Testament mój" [My Testament]. Lechoń plays with this well-known citation from the great Romantic in his poem "Cytat," which can be found among the poems in the first part of this anthology.

Sienkiewicz is then nevertheless the most read, the best understood writer of the Poles, not only of his hunting party associates, not only of his fellow club members, but of all Poles, also and even of those who suffered, fought poverty, starved, those whose fate Prus, Orzeszkowa and Konopnicka regretted and tried to improve.

The little poor Polish man then needed bread, work, a warm and light home, but for the very reason that he did not have them, he above all needed that which Sienkiewicz gave him — a fairy tale of a different, better, more exuberant life. The little man felt his powerlessness in the face of misery like many a Piłsudski fighter, and wrung his hands over the weakness of his civilian army in the face of Russian power. This dreamed-of strength, this better tomorrow were conjured up in Sienkiewicz's work, the secret of that strength was held by Skrzetuski, Wołodyjowski and Kmicic. And as Sienkiewicz turned away from everyday Polish life and weakness, Polish everyday life and weakness turned away from themselves and with enchanted eyes, with heart filled with hope they followed Sienkiewicz. Prus, Orzeszkowa and Konopnicka wrote about the fate of the little man but they were read especially by people like themselves, by the moving suffragettes, by heroic social workers, self-sacrificing teachers, biblical philanthropists. The simple man, if he chose between that literature, so profoundly human but reminding him of his own misery, and the dazzling gallop of marvelousness that the adventure of the *Trilogy* was, chose without hesitation Sienkiewicz; he placed the indifferent great lord of Oblęgorek above his friends who lived for him and thought of him. And therefore what one says of Sienkiewicz's national service the day before yesterday, today and tomorrow is not an empty phrase. Sienkiewicz gave the joy of life, the hope of life, to all Poles and opinions will always be divided as to whether the underground men, whether the heroes of Żeromski and Strug[5] owed more to these writers or to Sienkiewicz,

---

[5] Andrzej Strug (Tadeusz Gałecki, 1871-1937). Polish writer of Socialist leanings.

whether they preferred to read the *Homeless People*[6] or the *Trilogy.*

However, the public imagined this national service differently than it was in reality. Sienkiewicz was a different man than the lord that he was regarded to be, the "consoler of hearts" venerated by the nation, the banal, ritual figure of hagiography. He was an artist, above all and perhaps as no one at that time in Poland, exclusively an artist. A sentence of perfect cadence, a word of ideal accuracy, a period of classical composition were the world of his thoughts, of his cares, of his struggle. Sienkiewicz consoled the hearts with his *Trilogy,* but he certainly did not console them with *Without Dogma.* We know, however, that he thought of the latter, and rightly so, as a very important work, and he wondered and complained that he was not understood, that the human soul seemed to the Polish reader less important than Wołodyjowski's duel with Bohun. Critics and connoisseurs will always debate the percentage of real greatness in Sienkiewicz's art. They will always say that it is only melodrama: as if almost the entire Victor Hugo, many poems of Słowacki, and many of Żeromski's most famous pages were not melodrama. These details and doubts will never in the least diminish the enthusiasm that every Pole feels when reading the *Trilogy,* or the admiration of the most outstanding connoisseurs of Rome for *Quo vadis;* and above all they will never lessen the truth that Sienkiewicz's language is one of the most beautiful treasures of Polish art. Even if history would want to dig out a hundred times an old Poland different from the one of Sienkiewicz we shall always see her such as he saw her in his vision and painted her with his magnificent colors.

The triumph of Sienkiewicz will forever remain an example of the triumph of art, its salutary influence on the soul not only through the heart, but through the art itself, through the magic of words, through colors, sounds and, though we speak about literature, one might say, even through scents, through the

---

[6] *Ludzie bezdomni*, a novel by Stefan Żeromski.

medicines that a good physician sometimes applies unemotionally, and that act like the gift of a most tender heart, bringing recovery and happiness.

Some time after Sienkiewicz had died far from Poland, causing general regret and mourning, there came to Warsaw his photograph, one of the last ones, representing an old gentleman, clearly tired by life, but dressed with exquisite smartness, with a rose stuck in his buttonhole. This photograph could symbolize what was in Sienkiewicz most important, what he served all his life and to which he remained faithful until his death. Sienkiewicz believed that beauty is the supreme good, that art is a consolation and escape. He also had escaped to art. He escaped from the drabness of life to luxury, from its misery to exuberance, from its weakness to strength. And the nation led by this instinct of life, followed as if spellbound his ideal, the ideal of beauty, the ideal of the fairy tale bringing happiness and deliverance. And therefore Sienkiewicz's ideal symbolic portrait must not necessarily have as a background the white eagle, arms and banners. It may also simply be his last photograph showing an elderly gentleman with a rose in his buttonhole.

Stefan Żeromski
(1864-1925)[1]

The concept of "national character," or, as the Slavs prefer to call it, the "national soul" has given rise to an untold amount of nonsense, but its everlasting vitality in the face of incessant attack and ridicule is, in the last analysis, evidence of its indispensability. In the case of Poland, there really are certain distinctive features of Polish culture and Polish sensibility which can be singled out as a common heritage of the Poles as such; thus the "Polish character" is ultimately not a mere poetic phrase, but a demonstrable moral fact. It stems, at least in part, from the influence of literature, and especially poetry, on the national life, the mutual interaction of historical reality and poetic myth. Or at any rate a study of a nation's literature is one of the best means for arriving at an adequate definition of its collective spirit. This mutual interaction should not be identified with the cult of the word, the beautiful image, the precisely expressed thought — in other words, with that high literary culture in which the French lead the world. Basically phenomena of the same order of aesthetic sensibility are involved here, but at bottom they are utterly different. Polish literature, and above all Romantic poetry, has been a very real psychological determinant for several generations of Poles. The artistic values of this literature, the suggestiveness of its words, sounds, and images explain, perhaps, its initial appeal, but the real function of this influence has not been to provide artistic enjoyment or to refine aesthetic taste, but primarily to equip the Polish people with the spiritual resources necessary to enable them to survive their enslavement and to fight for their freedom.

In its use of art — true, genuine art — for performing historical tasks and in its fusion of history and poetry to create a national mythology, Polish literature, although in many other respects unable to stand comparison with the highest

---

[1] First published in *Harvard Slavic Studies*, 1954 vol. II pp. 323-342.

achievements of the West and of Russia, is perhaps unique in modern times. In this it has a significance and value which the rest of the world has yet to discover.

This messianism — the word is inescapable — of Polish literature, this continuous dialogue of the great Polish poets with their people, is a phenomenon hardly paralleled since the times of biblical Judea. It arises at the beginning of the nineteenth century, soon after Poland's political subjugation and the almost simultaneous flowering of Romanticism, with the appearance of the eminent writers who were to fill the new literary forms with the tempestuous themes which suited them so well, drawn from the depths of the national consciousness. Before this time there was no lack in Polish literature of noble moralists, wise teachers, foresighted reformers, merciless scoffers. They were particularly numerous toward the end of Polish political independence, when a pleiade of writers — Krasicki, Kołłątaj, Niemcewicz, Staszic[2] — saturated with Western ideas, led the work of political reform and social progress. Yet in spite of its high artistic quality and even, frequently, its brilliance, and in spite of the importance and timeliness of the problems it dealt with, the literature of that period was primarily a literature of the schoolroom. Though it often, as in Krasicki, attained a dazzling lightness and grace worthy of Voltaire or La Fontaine, its appeal was predominantly intellectual and, like all instruction, incapable of reaching the deepest — or, as we would say today, subconscious — layers of the human spirit.

It was the great Romantics, Mickiewicz, Słowacki and Krasiński, who penetrated and stirred the Polish spirit to its innermost depths. They brought the Polish people to an awareness of their spiritual individuality, provided them with a

---

[2] Julian Ursyn Niemcewicz (1758-1841). Polish statesman and man of letters. A poet whose work stretches through Neoclassicism and pre-Romanticism, he served with Kościuszko, and became an American citizen, for a while living as a farmer in New Jersey. Stanisław Staszic (1755-1826) was a Polish philosopher and political writer who played a key role in the Four Yearrs' Sejm.

revelation and definition of their national identity, and summoned them from political enslavement to a spiritual life richer than they had ever experienced in the times of their greatest national power. By the force of their poetic vision, their prophetic sense of the future and, one might say, their miraculous intuitive grasp of the present, these poets made the national cause the personal concern of every Pole.

The revolution they produced, not only in Polish literature, but in Polish life as a whole, cannot be understood or fully appreciated without a realization of the purely artistic brilliance of Mickiewicz and Słowacki, and, if one takes into account his great poetic prose, of Krasiński as well. To employ a comparison which, as always, has only relative validity, the great Romantics were for the Poles what Shakespeare would have been for his English contemporaries if his heroes had been taken, not from antiquity or from remote English history, but from the great living figures of his own day, the foes and favorites of Elizabeth. As the author of *Forefathers' Eve* [Dziady] Mickiewicz might also be compared with Dante, who descended into the Inferno only to encounter there the most famous personalities of his own contemporary Italy and then wove their names into the most beautiful poem yet created in the Italian language.

The great Romantic poetry — Mickiewicz's *Forefathers' Eve*, Słowacki's *Kordian, Lilla Weneda* and *Samuel Zborowski,* Krasiński's *Irydion* — revealed to the Poles completely new perspectives of moral responsibility resulting from the nation's political situation. Through these works the Poles learned to regard as their personal affair the great questions of honor and dedication, truth and falsehood, nobility of ends and legitimacy of means for attaining them. The national cause thus became, as it were, an autochthonous idea, the ultimate moral criterion around which the entire spiritual life of the nation was crystallized.

In its impact on the Polish spirit, an influence which has lasted almost to the present day through the poetry and prose derived from it, Polish Romantic poetry may be said to have

287

created an actual mythology by consecrating, symbolizing, and personifying the beliefs. instincts and spiritual experiences of the Polish people. It drew spiritual treasures from the national subconscious and then returned them to their sources magnified many times by the magic of art. The principal figure of this Polish myth, its supreme artistic realization, is Gustaw-Konrad, the hero of Mickiewicz's *Forefathers' Eve*. In his imaginary destinies Mickiewicz expressed his own spiritual transformations with a power of artistic suggestiveness possessing at the same time something of the mystical reality of the sacraments and the fullblooded truth of a Shakespearean drama. He pronounced the supreme adjuration and the most important commandment of this new Polish religion: the obligation to sacrifice one's personal happiness for the sake of a higher end, or rather to seek one's happiness in that sacrifice.

It is true, there arose various deformations of that religion, to whose psychopathological tensions Mickiewicz himself succumbed: for a long time he was addicted to the heresy which interpreted Poland's gloomy fate as a sign of its messianic mission. These disfigurations were overcome, not without difficulty and not without painful vestiges in Polish psychology and creativity, by other trends of thought opposed to Romanticism and by actual experience in the effort to rebuild, in captivity, a Polish army. But the commandment of self-sacrifice and the tradition of placing duty above personal happiness instituted by the Romantics became permanent values of Polish culture. Together with the sense of a community of existence and feeling between Polish poetry on the one hand and the Polish people on the other, these moral imperatives were inherited from Romantic poetry by Polish prose as well. The writings of Stefan Żeromski are deeply rooted in this heritage, and he himself is the last representative in Polish literature of the writer's mission so conceived.

Żeromski was born in 1864 — the year after the suppression of the last Polish uprising — to an impoverished, though well-connected gentry family living in a village situated in one of the southern *gubernii,* as they were then called, of the "Polish Kingdom," i.e. the part of Poland incorporated into Russia. Memories of the recent rising and the persecutions to which its participants and their families had been subjected dominated the spiritual climate of this social sphere and of that part of Poland for many years afterwards. It was in this atmosphere that Żeromski grew up, and to a large extent it determined the character of his work. There is a striking similarity between the great Romantic poets and Żeromski both in their historical situations and in their influence on Polish life. Mickiewicz, Słowacki, and Krasiński appeared after the loss of the Polish-Russian war of 1830, while Żeromski was to give battle for the soul of a people crushed by their defeat in a second armed conflict, the insurrection of 1863. And not he alone. In other artistic forms and on different levels other writers also undertook this recuperative mission: above all, the hedonistic, colorful Sienkiewicz, who appealed to the primitive national biology, and the hermetic, mystic poet Wyspiański, who penetrated to the inner reaches of consciousness by means of the most refined artistic associations of Polish themes and rose to the summit of magnificent satirical metaphor. Nevertheless, of these three writers it was Żeromski whose work was most directly bound up with the calamity of 1863. With its rapturous lyricism and its emotional responsiveness to the real life of the new generation it had a profound appeal, primarily an appeal to the heart, where it left indelible traces.

In the period between the defeat of 1831 and the catastrophe of the insurrection of 1863, only thirty years apart, the Poles who remained at home were fully occupied with their efforts to rise from the material ruin into which particularly the gentry, Żeromski's own class, had been plunged by persecutions and confiscations. Everything in their life seemed uncertain and provisional, lacking leadership and those broader ideas which the debilitated national organism, recovering with difficulty from its wounds, was unable to produce. Leadership, ideas, and everything that was best in the nation were in exile, mostly in

Paris. From there it was a long and arduous process for the creative products of the exiles to reach the apartments of Warsaw and such manor houses as the one where Żeromski was born. But somehow they did — the masterpieces of Romantic poetry, the manifestos of the Democratic Society, and even the names of the heralds of socialism, like Stanisław Worcell,[3] which were to reappear so often in the pages of Żeromski.

The Democratic Society, founded in Paris by radical participants in the uprising of 1831, called for social progress and especially for improvements in the lot of the unfortunate and exploited peasants, the most numerous class in Poland, which was still primarily an agrarian country, dominated by its provincial nobility. In the minds of the majority of the democratic leaders this program of reforms was based as much on political as on humanitarian motives. After emancipating the peasant they planned to enlist him at last in the national cause and thus provide future revolutionary armies with numerous new soldiers.

The insurrection of 1863 gave tragic proof of the correctness of that policy of the émigré Left and its advocates at home. The Polish peasant had been kept in bondage not only by the partitions, but equally by the selfishness and passivity of most of the gentry, who had postponed and blocked emancipation for as long as they could. Now, in 1863, the peasants not only failed to support the rising, but in many cases actually abetted the Russian troops in pursuing the insurgents or helped the police authorities to track down survivors. This national drama, which was certainly enacted in Żeromski's immediate surroundings, affected him, as it had the Romantics, with the force of a profound personal experience. It was to develop into one of the basic complexes of his work.

Among the secrets of his youth which Żeromski guarded so jealously and did not confide to any of his biographers, there doubtless were happenings not only capable of satisfying the

---

[3] Stanisław Worcell (1799-1857). Polish revolutionary and Utopian Socialist.

perverse curiosity of the psychoanalysis maniacs, the professional gossips and the expert debunkers of greatness, but also of shedding light on the sources of his unusual creativity. For all his works are centered in a few experiences and represent a constant development of and variation on the same few ideological and emotional motifs. As a child Żeromski no doubt heard tales of wounded insurgents crawling through the snow, afraid of falling into Russian hands and uncertain of receiving help from the peasants. This connection between the national catastrophe and the tragedy of the peasant problem is the ideological theme of his first work, the short story "Ravens and Crows Will Peck Us to Pieces" [Rozdziobią nas kruki, wrony]. It remains one of the main themes of his work from *Ashes* [Popioły] to the two dramas written at the end of his life, *I Shall Become Whiter Than Snow* [Ponad śnieg bielszym się stanę] and *Turoń.*

A closer scrutiny of the process of transmutation of these elements in Żeromski's work, supported by my memories of personal conversations with him, justifies me, I believe, in the hypothesis that this general theme both of peasant grievances and peasant revenge had been reinforced by some entirely personal current unknown to us. It was probably some humiliation arising from the poverty suffered by Żeromski in his youth, perhaps further aggravated by the contrast with the wealth of his neighbors and distant relatives. Literary echoes of such an experience may be detected in the romance of Raphael and the Princess in *Ashes,* and they ring forth with truly youthful vigor in the love scenes between Cezary Baryka and Laura Kamieniecka in Żeromski's last novel, *Before Spring* [Przedwiośnie]. They may indicate that the real source of this complex was a humiliation inflicted on the poor youth by a girl of exalted rank. We advance this hypothesis by no means as a mere tidbit for the curious, but to support a view basic for the understanding of Żeromski's work, namely that his general ideas were always reinforced by personal experiences. Because of this, his ideas are expressed both with unusual realism and with an ecstatic poetic

291

lyricism. Żeromski was a nobleman enamored of the beauty of the Polish past, but as a result of these personal experiences he also adopted as his own the cause of social justice. Thus there developed in his mind a state of constant dramatic discord. He felt an heir to the gentry's past, but at certain times he also regarded himself as an underdog wronged by Poland's history with difficulty restraining himself from revolting against it, just as Baryka raised his riding crop against Laura in *Before Spring*.

However, Żeromski was above all a reviver and defender of the ideas which had, it seemed, suffered final defeat with the collapse of the January uprising of 1863. He was the exponent of the great ideological thesis which held that armed struggle for freedom was both the only means of regaining that freedom, and the only moral discipline capable of maintaining the national spirit at the height of its mission. The Revolution of 1863 was a new confrontation of that idea with reality; it was at the same time a critical test of the Romantic literature which had proclaimed that idea and had nurtured a new generation to resume the struggle lost in 1831 and to do so under conditions a hundred times less favorable. It was a tragic confrontation, resulting in thousands of victims killed and deported to Siberia, in material ruin, in the abrogation of all the concessions which Aleksander Wielopolski,[4] that great statesman and great opponent of Romantic thinking, had succeeded in wresting for Poland from its oppressors. History seemed to have sided with him and to have branded forever the folly of the Poles' repeated armed revolts against an enemy many times more powerful, their hopes of foreign aid always disappointed, always rewarded in the worthless coin of Western "sympathy." The same history, however, was soon to prove that the so-called realists who

---

[4] Aleksander Wielopolski (1803-1877). Conservative Polish politician who advocated collaboration with the Tsarist government. He strove to introduce Polish into the official and educational use of the Tsarist Kingdom of Poland, but also initiated a program of forcible military conscription in an effort to stave off the January Uprising of 1863, to which he was opposed.

thought they alone perceived reality, had grasped only the fragment of it contained in the period they had lived through, while another reality, hidden in the future, was the one which had glimmered through the Sibylline prophecies of *Forefathers' Eve,* the archangelic incantations of Słowacki, and the lofty naiveté of Krasiński's *Pre-Dawn* [Przedświt].

The great war which broke out at the beginning of our century, for which Mickiewicz had prayed, at last severed the alliance of the three great empires which had seemed to be united forever by their joint dismemberment of Poland and their joint supervision of her enslavement. It was to end in the successive defeat of them all. This had not been foreseen by any of the alleged "realists," by any of the so-called "sober statesmen." However, this very sequence of events seemed inevitable to Józef Piłsudski, the creator of a new underground Polish army, who based his seemingly insane policies on just this calculation. The writings of Stefan Żeromski, with their echoes of the tragedy of 1863 or, as in *Ashes,* their exploration of the history of the Polish legions under Napoléon in the search for guidance in the new struggle, lent powerful support and in fact contributed to the very inception of the movement originally formed by Piłsudski within the Polish Socialist Party. This movement proved itself in the revolution of 1905, which, though quelled in blood, revived the idea of a Polish army and gave to the young men new examples of self-sacrifice and courage. The Polish Legions of 1914, the first military force in more than a hundred years to see Poland united and independent, were the direct heirs of this revolution.

Żeromski's influence on the young men who joined the ranks of the Polish Socialist Party's Fighting Organization and on those who sympathized with its deeds would astonish all the literary schoolmasters and authors of lively edifying slogans. For the picture Żeromski unfolded both of the uprising of 1863 and of the earlier effort at liberation was far removed from any consoling optimism of any tempting analogies promising easy victory. Żeromski's innate pessimism and the lessons he had

293

learned from his study of the past would have seemed rather to discourage him from advocating further attempts to continue the struggle: their tragic result was epitomized in the title of masterpiece — *Ashes*. And yet from the pictures of struggles and suffering which he drew, from the descriptions of the Polish landscape, in which he is still unrivaled, from the portraits of the leaders and soldiers which he brought to life in his work there emanated such a power of suffering love, so mighty an instinct of unity with the nation's past, with the native soil, such fervent worship of Polish heroes and martyrs, that all young and noble-hearted people in Poland suddenly felt that the bonds with the past of sacrifice and struggle, which seemed already severed, could never be broken, that they were a destiny from which no true Pole could escape.

Among the intellectual outcasts of Poland Żeromski met those who were to dig up from the ashes of the past the weapons of revolt, and without ever entering directly into any partisan activities he nevertheless became the voice of this new armed movement in Polish literature. To the pages of Romantic poetry glorifying the Napoléonic heroes and the conspirators of 1830 he added new and powerful stanzas; though not couched in rhymes, they were full of poetic inspiration, and in such pages as his drama *The Rose* [Róża] he recorded for the nation's memory the exploits and martyrdoms of students and workers dying on the gallows with the words of the national hymn of hope on their lips.

The young men who in 1905 went into the streets of Warsaw with revolutionary pistols in their hands, which symbolized the military weapons then unobtainable, and to a considerable extent also the Legionnaires of 1914 regarded Piłsudski and Żeromski equally as their masters and leaders. That last revolutionary upsurge before victory drew both on the teachings of history and the transports of poetry to an extent perhaps never achieved before. Indeed, Piłsudski regarded himself as a disciple of Słowacki, and Żeromski's apostrophes were derived not only from the great Romantic poems but also from the revolutionary thought of Sułkowski and Worcell and from the manifestos of émigré democracy.

Allegedly as a result of a dispute over the orientation of Polish policy during the First World War, the two men later drifted apart. The only literary traces of this rift are the painful and incomprehensible pages of *Struggle with Satan* [Walka z szatanem]. It was never repaired and only deepened more and more with the years. It might be interpreted as the inevitable tragic dissonance between the dream of a free state and the actual exigencies of that state, almost as the eternal discord between poetry and historical reality. With no intention of belittling either of these two unusual figures, it is worth dwelling on this dispute, which has so far been passed over in silence by biographers and critics. In the utterances and allusions of both Żeromski and Piłsudski there are echoes of their struggle for the soul of the nation, for what Mickiewicz called the "rule of souls." In Żeromski's resentment against Piłsudski in which he was quite alone among his friends at certain times, we can witness, as it were, the last scene in a magnificent drama, in which Polish poetry acts out the denouement of its role as the nation's spiritual mentor, rendered superfluous by the very fulfillment of its prophecies.

With his first volume, *Ravens and Crows Will Peck Us to Pieces*, Żeromski became the voice of the conscience for the Polish people, and he remained so, notwithstanding all the errors of his diagnosis of reality and his artistic lapses, until his last work, *Before Spring*. The rapturous erotic lyricism and ideological passion of this book seemed to be the creation not of a master withdrawing from love, but of a young man never reconciled with injustice.

His career was, of course, attended not only by the adoration of his admirers, but also by the open or secret enmity of the defenders of old, privileges and the sensualists, principled or immoral, who did not feel the disgrace of enslavement and did not care to rise from under it. In his work, which is an impassioned hymn of love for the Polish land, an exalted apotheosis of national heroes, imbued with an infallible instinct and cult of the Polish language, his detractors tried to find a foreign spirit, and especially an imitation of Russian models. Żeromski defended himself against this, maintaining that his masters were not the great Russians, but Flaubert and Stendhal. Proof of this allegedly pernicious foreign influence was sought in Żeromski's pessimism; his cruel, relentless pursuit of truth was contrasted with the serene biology of Sienkiewicz and the mild didacticism of many other writers, so aptly characterized in Mickiewicz's phrase, "We Slavs love idylls" [*Słowiane, my lubim sielanki*].

Żeromski was particularly sensitive to such attacks, but he proudly concealed his weakness and continued the struggle he had begun in the belief that it was the loftiest task a writer could undertake. He became the conscience of the people because continuous moral vigilance was a natural function of his mind and had become an irresistible emotional need. His morality, notwithstanding the title of his cycle *Struggle with Satan,* had nothing in common with the theological demonism of Dostoevskij or his Catholic successors François Mauriac and Graham Greene; it was guided by a primitive instinct of charity, which was its highest standard of judgment. On this, and it may be said on this alone, Żeromski's Christianity was based. His Catholicism was reduced to the two commandments: love God and thy neighbor. In love of one's neighbor and in communion with nature he saw the only secure foundations for faith. Because of this uncompromising attitude Żeromski obviously had to resist any compromise between the projected ideal and the concrete possibilities for achieving it. Therefore his idealism often sought expression in Utopias, in wonderful inventions which would give the weak preponderance over the strong in the struggle for freedom, and transform life in cellars and garrets into Arcadias of flowers and sunlight. Like so many idealists of his generation, he failed to recognize that the restoration of Polish independence had transferred responsibility for social life, laws, and morals from men of letters to the state, and he persisted to the end of his life in demanding reforms of men and institutions. He never accepted the morality of the so-called "necessities" of the state, refusing to understand its tragic compulsions, but also never demeaning his calling by defending moral compromises. In the last period of his life his views on Polish foreign policy brought him close to the nationalists of the extreme Right. But in social matters, while resisting the internationalism, cruelty, and tyranny of Communism and opposing to them the ideal of voluntary surrender of land, he nevertheless proclaimed very radical principles of social transformation. He could repeat after Victor Hugo that he was for the good in all parties and against all of them in their aberrations. Indeed, this individualism, which from the standpoint of party orthodoxies has been interpreted by many political bigots as an ideological contradiction in his work, actually was an expression of his monolithic moral structure. And because of these same apparent contradictions, every Pole could discover himself in Żeromski and find in this rich, tempestuous body of literature unconstrained by any canons, his own thoughts and unconfessed secrets, or emanations of the Polish spirit particularly dear to him.

The life of Żeromski, though in many manifestations of his personality it was obviously very far from the average, nevertheless remains reasonably typical of a Polish intellectual of the second half of the nineteenth century, and particularly a Warsaw intellectual, since the creative clash of ideas after the Insurrection of 1863 was confined primarily, if not exclusively, to the Russian-dominated part of Poland, and more precisely to Warsaw, the focal point of the intellectual life of that sector.

It was there that the movement known in the history of Polish culture as "Warsaw Positivism" originated, as a protest against the fruitless waste of lives and fortune in quixotic attempts at armed revolt. The positivists claimed to be followers of Comte and wanted to be regarded as a passionless philosophical school. As a matter of fact, however, they adopted this philosophy with typical Polish passion, and sought remedies in it for Polish misfortunes. With polemic fury they demanded an end to pernicious illusions and advocated a program of preserving Polish nationality by spreading education and developing industry and trade to enrich the country. The soldiers of this crusade first gathered around Adam Wiślicki's *Weekly Review* [Przegląd Tygodniowy] and later under the banner of *Truth* [Prawda], whose editor, Aleksander Świętochowski, supported their anti-Romantic slogans with his magnificent style and the seemingly irrefutable logic of his arguments. The impossibility of undertaking new armed uprisings seemed at that time so obvious that even the most devoted young men professed allegiance to Positivism, but they soon transformed Comte's teachings into a Polish religion which was not only alien to the intentions of the master but even to those of Comte's Polish lieutenant, Świętochowski.

It may be considered a proof of the Pole's hopeless incapacity to adjust to modern life, the anachronism of Polish culture, its lack of any economic instinct, yet it is a fact that of all the Positivist watchwords, the one which proclaimed *"Enrichissez-vous"* as a patriotic duty found the least adherents. On the other hand among the younger generation there was a great increase in the desire for knowledge and particularly an enthusiasm for the natural sciences. University studies were regarded not only as an obligation of the wealthy but became the object of the dreams of indigent young men who acquired their education at the cost of great sacrifices, paying for a university diploma with years of starving and living in crowded and stuffy garrets. In this fanatical cult of learning we may discern the influence not only of Positivism but of the discredited Polish Romanticism. And this double inspiration also underlies the impulse to go down among the peasantry and later among the workers, which seized the post-Insurrection young generation, producing the type of evangelistic women teachers and physicians who buried themselves in remote provinces to fight against disease and ignorance. The youth of Marie Skłodowska-Curie, and her sisters, the atmosphere of the Skłodowski home in Warsaw, is an excellent example of the state of mind and

298

morality of the generation to which Żeromski belonged. Heroism on the battlefield was replaced in that generation not by cold calculation of ends and means, but by a new heroism of learning and trying to raise the underprivileged classes to a higher material and cultural level. Indeed, it was not the Olympian, icy Świętochowski who became the interpreter of the thoughts and feelings of that generation, but the Polish Dickens, Bolesław Prus. Disillusioned and skeptical about armed uprisings, he called for an end of idle dreaming, but he himself was no less a dreamer and always followed the promptings of his heart. From the information available on Żeromski, it is difficult to ascertain whether it was an early tendency to consumption, later completely cured, or merely poverty that prevented him from continuing his education after graduating from the secondary school in Kielce. It is certain, however, that his lack of higher education gave rise to a complex in Żeromski which obsessed him to the end of his life. It is evident not only in his cult of learning, but also in his naive sense of inferiority towards professional scholars, who, after all, are not always creative. Though not a university student himself, Żeromski nevertheless led a life similar to theirs. He studied independently, attended debates at student meetings, and for many years earned his living like a student by tutoring, mainly in the homes of the landowning nobility. He also taught peasants and workers and gradually joined the circles which were to revive the ideas seemingly crushed forever on the battlefields of the Insurrection of 1863. The collapse of the Rising had not only brought about a momentary triumph of its opponents, but among the majority of its survivors it had also shattered all faith in the efficacy of armed resistance. The survivors of 1863, witnesses of the defeat, could more easily discourse on the hopelessness of Polish destiny than pass on the shredded remnants of the insurgent tradition to the new generation. Yet those few who remained faithful to the ideals of the uprising were able to find impassioned listeners and through them to reach wider groups of young people.

Such links between the generation of 1863 and the renascent liberation movement were above all Benedykt Dybowski and Bronisław Szwarce,[5] both of whom lived in Lwów. Szwarce, whom Piłsudski had met in Siberia, became the first inspirer of his political career. In Warsaw it was Stanisław Krzemiński,[6] a critic, publicist, and member of the National Government of 1863, who by his writings, personal influence, and the noble example of his private life kept intact the ideals of the liberation movement. At one time he was certainly close to Żeromski, and in *Before Spring* his name appears in an impassioned apotheosis. All of Żeromski's work up to *Before Spring* was determined by the intellectual, moral, and spiritual influences of his youth — the seemingly contradictory combination of the romantic positivism of Prus and families like the Skłodowskis on the one hand and, on the other, the insurrectionary tradition preserved by people like Dybowski and Krzemiński, a tradition later revived by Józef Piłsudski and the fighting organization of the Polish Socialist Party. Men of these two groups were Żeromski's closest associates during his sojourns in Warsaw and summers at Nałęczów, a resort in the Lublin region, which was also the permanent summer residence of Bolesław Prus. Żeromski's first wife, Oktavia Radziwiłowicz, a sister of a well-known doctor and one of the most influential members of the Polish liberal camp, linked him very closely to that group. She was probably the model for the principal character in Prus's novel *The Suffragettes* [Emancypantki], a type also immortalized in Żeromski's earlier works.

This marriage of a young and promising writer to a woman older than himself was the result less of emotional attachment than of spiritual affinity and identity of intellectual interests. It was broken when Żeromski met the young and beautiful painter

---

[5] Benedykt Dybowski (1833-1930). Polish scientist and patriot, famed Siberian explorer (whence he was exiled following the January Uprising). He popularized Darwinism in Poland. Bronisław Szwarce (1834-1904). Engineer, like Dybowski a post-1863 Siberian exile.
[6] Stanisław Krzemiński (1839–1912).

Anna Zawadzka. For him she became the embodiment of personal happiness, the ecstasy of love, and the whole realm of joyful feelings which he himself defined in the title of one of his novels and the *Beauty of Life* [Uroda Życia]. For a man with such a sense of moral responsibility and such a sensitive conscience, a sharp conflict inevitably arose between his feeling of obligation toward a woman to whom he undoubtedly owed much and who was moreover the mother of his beloved and gifted son, and the elemental passion by which he was seized and which provided him with experiences that proved extremely fruitful for his writing. This conflict gave rise to a drama which found expression both in the themes and the atmosphere of many of his books, and therefore cannot be passed over in silence. The death of his son and his difficulties in legalizing his second marriage, which dragged on throughout his life, were doubtless felt by Żeromski as tragic stigmata, or, to use the language of the ancients, as signs of the "wrath of the gods." These are the main autobiographical incidents which Żeromski drew upon for his fiction. The allusions, mentioned above, to some insult suffered in his youth keep recurring to the end of his life. The drama in his immediate family was probably the basis for his *History of a Sin* [Dzieje grzechu] and *The Beauty of Life.* But most of all it is the conflict between duty and love and the conviction that the attainment of happiness always calls down the vengeance of fate which constitute the hidden but always potent inner themes of Żeromski's work and maintain its tone of high lyricism.

Żeromski's connections with the revolutionary movement of 1905 and the crisis in his personal life forced him to leave Russian Poland. He first settled in Paris and later at Zakopane in Austrian Galicia, from where he returned in 1919 to Warsaw, then already liberated.

In the beginning of his literary career Żeromski had to contend with dire poverty; he lived not only on royalties but on his salary as a librarian at the Zamoyski Library in Warsaw and the Polish Library at Rapperswil in Switzerland. Later, thanks to the large editions of his books, he became sufficiently well off to

301

enable him to devote himself exclusively to writing, without anxiety about the future. His material wealth and, ultimately, his unquestioned position of leadership in Polish literature and life, did not change Żeromski's style of life nor induce him to assume any pose. He remained unshaken in his loyalty to the moral code he had imposed on himself as a poor writer; he retained the image of himself he had expressed in his famous novel, the *Homeless People* [Ludzie bezdomni]. Even after being honored by all dignities and decorations at the disposal of the Polish state and Polish literature, when living in the Royal Castle at Warsaw as an honored guest of the Republic, and, like a rich industrialist, owning a villa in the most fashionable summer resort, Żeromski to the end of his life still felt himself a part of the environment of his youth, that world of teachers, social workers, and writers, hostile to all ceremony and pomposity, which the intellectuals of his time called the "artistic fraternity."

Żeromski was unable, except with those closest to him, to emerge from his gloomy loneliness. The magic of his talent, the weight, beauty, and elevation of his work as well as the force of his powerful personality created in all those who approached him a sense of distance which excluded any intimacy. Throughout his life he had no close friends, but he had a warm, living, and responsive attitude toward the people he respected and toward those people, especially the young ones, who offered him their genuine admiration.

In his choice of those to whom he showed admiration and respect as if they were his masters — at a time when he himself was recognized as a supreme master and was surrounded with a halo of legend — he was guided above all by his cult of moral values and, as we remarked above, by his touching, though in some respects abnormal veneration of learning. As a young writer hardly twenty years old, I was fortunate enough to be admitted to Żeromski's circle and to a degree of intimacy which the great writer magnanimously called friendship. In our numerous conversations during several years of close intercourse he exhibited a human solicitude, tactfulness, and respect for

302

others' opinions rare in human relations in general, let alone in the relationship of so great a writer to a young literary novice. By acting thus Żeromski was paying what he regarded as his debt to himself, to his moral ideal, and to the spiritual magnanimity which dominated both his work and life, between which there was no discrepancy whatever. In the last play he wrote, the comedy *My Little Quail Has Fled* [Uciekła mi przepióreczka], the hero, having made a great sacrifice which dishonored him personally but saved the life of another and furthered a noble cause, says that he has made his sacrifice because "such is his custom." This proud principle was the motto of Żeromski's entire life.

I often had occasion to be amazed when I saw the great novelist, whose standing in public opinion almost put him above any criticism, trying by ceaseless efforts to master the secrets of literary forms he found difficult. He read play after play with the obstinate determination of an industrious student, he held endless discussions with stage directors and actors — all in an effort to reach the essence of that feeling for the stage which he lacked, as his previous works seemed to demonstrate.

For all those who experienced it, the premiere of his last play was an unforgettable moment, which had something of the quality of a family festival, a beloved father's graduation with honors. After so many defective plays this one at last was perfectly constructed. The sixty year old writer appeared on the stage, wearing evening clothes for the first time in his life, and received the tribute not only of the spectators but of his readers, who by their prolonged, standing ovation expressed their joy at his victory and thanked him for everything that he had written and also for what he was as a man.

When he died a year later, Poles of all classes and convictions, from the President of the Republic to the workers and unemployed from the Warsaw suburbs, passed before his coffin where it rested in a hall of the castle. In his person, in this figure of the homeless man who yet gave his all for others, they bade farewell not only to the great author who could stir Polish hearts like no other writer of his time, but also to the whole epoch of underground struggle and nameless sacrifice in which Polish idealism had reached its most beautiful expression and the greatest beauty of its style.

Żeromski occupies a unique position in Polish literature, for, as has previously been stated, his work, though written in the forms of prose, casts its spell above all by its poetic qualities. It is a charm so irresistible for the Poles that it enabled thousands of enraptured readers, if not purist critics, to overlook the basic and otherwise unforgivable shortcomings of his prose. This growing and finally overpowering admiration for Żeromski's literary art and his influence on several Polish generations makes it impossible to apply recognized criteria to him. His work must be considered as a phenomenon outside established forms and ruled by its own autonomous laws.

Żeromski's novels, which constitute the majority of his work, as well as most of his plays, doubtless lack logical, coherent structure; it is broken by outbursts of unbridled lyricism, innumerable descriptions, and publicistic intrusions. This lyrical and didactic aspect of his works overshadows the plot and action, preventing them from appearing sharply and clearly in accordance with the best models.

However, these objections cannot be raised with regard to the entirety of his work. His *Homeless People,* for example, is a novel written according to classical rules, while *The Faithful River* [Wierna rzeka] is a model of a long novella with concentrated action and strong, rigid structure. If in some of his works, as in the second volume of *The Beauty of Life,* the author seems to be lacking ideas for the development of the plot, from others we get the impression of an almost cinematographic excess of this inventiveness. *The History of a Sin,* an uneven novel, which time and again stoops to vulgar effects, reads like a detective story with sustained melodramatic intensity. In the play *A White Glove* [Biała rękawiczka], a failure from the intellectual and artistic standpoint, there are scenes of theatrical bravura for which many master craftsmen could envy Żeromski. Finally, in his last novel, *Before Spring,* the parallelism of several plots interwoven with political disquisitions and apostrophes, lofty lyricism and brutal melodrama, seems to be the perfect expression of the author's individuality, his conscious literary method applied with the skill of a true master.

Żeromski's style, too, was bitterly criticized for its departure from the conventional language of prose, in which Sienkiewicz had scored such triumphs just before Żeromski appeared on the scene. This type subordinated syntax to musical phrasing, it affected the idiom of everyday speech and dialect, it garnered forgotten expressions from old Polish dictionaries, it strove above all for a choice of emotionally suggestive words and powerfully dramatic metaphors that would create in the reader a spiritual tension no less heartfelt than the author's own.

This was, of course, the type of the period, the Impressionist style, but above all it was the style of Żeromski's own passionate and lyrical soul, which could never have found adequate expression in the narrative form of the conventional novel.

Indeed, all his departures from established rules, including his neologisms, were not merely consonant with the true spirit of the Polish language, but a positive enrichment of it — creative discoveries penetrating to its core. Żeromski's phrase was a musical instrument of unexampled resonance and mysterious overtones — but only in the hands of its creator. The imitators who followed him did not have his infallible instinct for what was truly Polish, did not possess his marvelous musical sensibility, the sense of measure which controlled even his most far-fetched metaphors and original expressions. They tried to achieve by ratiocination and aesthetic theory what Żeromski had done quite simply, with the perfect tact of genius. And so they shattered all sentence structure, let the language run to seed and landed in the blind alley of theoretic innovation from which Polish prose had barely emerged only by the Second World War

— notably in Maria Dąbrowska's[7] magnificent cycle *Nights and Days* [Noce i dnie], which preserved some of Żeromski's musical cadences and some of his linguistic conquests, but in general reverted to the quiet narrative of his predecessors.

As I have already remarked, ordinary aesthetic standards are inapplicable to Żeromski's art, which developed its own forms corresponding to the uncommon and complex personality of its creator, who was at once a journalist, a poet, and a realistic storyteller. *Ashes,* the most ambitious of all Żeromski's works and at one time the most influential, is not so much a novel of the Napoléonic wars as an epic poem whose landscapes, love scenes, and patriotic invocations affected the readers as pure poetry. At other times, as in his *Lay of the Hetman* [Duma o Hetmanie], Żeromski actually tried to create a form of prose poetry or to revive the art of the folk tale, as in his *Story of Walter, the Goodly Wight* [Powieść o wdałym Walgierzu], while his *Wind from the Sea* [Wiatr od morza], written a couple of years before his death, is a brilliant display of archaic diction and poetic stylization.

He was a realist precisely in those works which seem to us today to have the greatest poetic value, for example *Homeless People, Andrzej Radek,*[8] and *The Beauty of Life,* works in which he dealt with men of his own time and gave an authentic picture of Polish life, but as seen by an eye which could scan its heights as well as its depths, which perceived not only its grayness and gloom but also its beauty, the secret radiance of human souls.

The principal characters of these novels, Judym, Piotr Rozłucki, Joasia, Andrzej Radek, Krzysztof Nienaski, are all dedicated souls, tempered by self-sacrifice and living only for others, but they are no less real than Vautrin, the Karamazov brothers, Anna Karenina and Vronskij. Poland's tragic destiny compelled thousands of Poles to live as selflessly as monks or

---

[7] Maria Dąbrowska (1889–1965), leading realist novelist of the XXth century.

[8] A mistake by Lechoń. Andrzej Radek is a hero in the novel *Szyzfowe Prace* [A Sisyphian Task].

soldiers and multiplied in everyday life that human type which Balzac tried so hard to discover by the light of his own genius, which Dostoevskij, yearning for sainthood, was able to find only in the monastery or the madhouse. Foreign readers who believe that psychological truth is to be found mainly in descriptions of the quest for riches and amorous conquests, may regard the plot of *Homeless People* as a mere edifying fairy tale and dismiss Judym and Joasia as the figments of a visionary pedagogue. Such incomprehension will always be one of the greatest misfortunes of Polish literature and at the same time a source of silent pride for all Poles.

The fate of the various translations of *Ashes* showed how difficult it is to present to the foreign reader those spiritual and aesthetic values which are Żeromski's greatest attraction for the Polish reader. The magic of his style depends largely on a unique collocation of words beyond the power of a faithful translator and on musical cadences inseparable from native sounds. For an example capable of giving the foreign reader a comparative idea of Żeromski's spiritual world, we must turn to Joseph Conrad. Despite the very different expression each gave to his essential lyricism — unbridled, eruptive and passionate in Żeromski, discreet and proudly restrained in Conrad — there is an unquestionable similarity in the moral physiognomy of the two writers, especially in their common "taste for lost causes," to use the words of Conrad's biographer G. Jean-Aubry.[9] Because of the remote but indubitable similarity between the fate of the Polish gentry after the Partitions and the Southern planters after the American Civil War, there is also a subtle affinity between the work of Żeromski and Faulkner's novels of the Civil War. Especially in their feminine characters and in their evocation of families shattered by the national calamity, the two writers show an amazing similarity of feeling and expression, a poetic vision common to them both. May these comparisons help to give the

---

[9] Gérard Jean-Aubry (Jean Aubry, 1882-1950), French poet and critic. Translator and friend of Joseph Conrad. He wrote the first biography of the writer, and published an edition of his selected letters.

American reader some idea of a great foreign writer otherwise completely unknown to him.

Mickiewicz Yesterday and Today[1]

Several weeks after the September catastrophe, one of my Warsaw acquaintances came to my room in the Paris Embassy. He was not a friend, nor even close to me, but simply an acquaintance from the days of our journalistic and cafe activity — a former writer who in his quest for success in life, had abandoned his nobler ambitions and become a so-called connoisseur of living, or an indulgent observer of human frailty, compromises and struggle for success at all cost. I will not say that I expected this very man to let me feel the essence of an experience I had been spared. I might even say that this man in particular seemed to me incapable of having been changed by anything in those days which had told so many Poles they knew neither their country nor themselves. And then, no sooner had I exchanged the first few words with him than I realized I had been completely mistaken. This man, habitually affected, covering up with constant irony his hidden grudges against the world and himself, always preoccupied with the foibles of his neighbors — impressed me by his quiet cordiality, almost deep joy, and by a tenderness, masked and yet reflected in every word he uttered, toward all those of whom he was speaking. At one point in our conversation, which several months earlier I should certainly have regarded as the height of sentimentality and naiveté, he said to me quickly: "Do you know that the day after Warsaw capitulated, people rushed to the bookshops to buy poetry and find some escape from despair? That day I began reading *Pan Tadeusz* and read it through at one sitting. You've no idea how much it gave me! What a wonderful book!" His lips

---

[1] First published in *The Bulletin of the Polish Institute of Arts and Sciences of America*, 1945 vol. III no 3/4 pp. 472-479. Originally a talk given at a May 3rd celebration at PIASA in 1945, which also marked the publication of an English edition of Mickiewicz's works (A. Mickiewicz: *Poems.* Translated by various hands and edited by George Rapall Noyes. New York: PIASA 1944).

trembled and he turned away so that I might not see he was crying.

In the posthumous life of Mickiewicz, and surely we all agree that the greatness of men like Mickiewicz lies in the fact that they live on after they die, experiencing varying vicissitudes in this life — in the history of these changes to which Mickiewicz is subjected in our mind and heart, the deep consolation he has given to the Polish nation, in bondage and martyrdom, will certainly constitute one of the most beautiful and most important pages. For of course, my journalist-acquaintance was no exception or rarity. It suffices to read the poems of all the more prominent poets of the present emigration — their best poems at that — to perceive that they have all found themselves within the radius of Mickiewicz's spell, that they have rediscovered in Mickiewicz our times, our feelings, the measure of happening things. Virtually all of them have succumbed to his influence in no lesser degree than one hundred years earlier the so-called lesser Romantics had succumbed to his moral influence and to the suggestion of his poetic form, which by its inspired simplicity came forth of itself to express those painful yet simple emotions. Baliński in his *Great Journey*[2] has charmingly stylized not only Mickiewicz's motifs but even his landscapes, with which he feels a family bond, the romantic heritage of great-grandfather Odyniec and great-grandmother Ludwika Śniadecka.[3] This entire volume is, if one may express himself so fancifully, something like a transcription into poetry of Moniuszko's[4] music for Mickiewicz's *Forefathers' Eve;* various good influences may be detected here, that of Słowacki is also very strong, but the fragrance suggested by this poetry is essentially the fragrance of herbs from the shores of Lake Świteź

---

[2] *Wielka podróż*, (London, 1941).
[3] Antoni Edward Odyniec (1804-1885). Romantic poet and author, friend of Mickiewicz. Ludwika Śniadecka (1802-1866). Youthful love of Juliusz Słowacki, later wife of Michał Czajkowski (Sadyk Pasha), at whose side she fought for Polish independence in Turkey.
[4] Stanisław Moniuszko (1819–72), Polish operatic composer.

and of blossoming trees in the park at Tuhanowicze; one gleam of the spell which these verses cast over us is that of the evening lamp under which a sublime and melancholy Mickiewicz sits in a stained frock coat in his Paris room.

Baliński is perhaps the most eloquent example, but future dabblers in influence-tracing will some day find a beautiful occupation for themselves, hunting for Mickiewicz themes, reminiscences, versification, and most important of all, his spiritual influence, in the best as well as in the weaker poets, in the emigration poetry of Wierzyński, Słonimski, Rostworowski,[5] Hemar, and in the soldier-poets of the Second Corps. This spiritual influence, strongest in the morally strongest poets, has found only formal, rather superficial expression among the less original poets, but both types of manifestation of his influence show to what great degree Mickiewicz has become for Polish literature in exile a consolation, escape and refuge.

In this, however, the writers have merely mirrored the reflex of the entire nation, they have only expressed the feelings of every reading Pole, who after the calamity of September 1939 sought in Polish books solace for his despair and a confidant for his tears and lonely prayers. And just as in their personal life, through the purifying fire of horrible experience, they all suddenly recovered the imperceptible meaning of such forgotten but all-important words as: country, brethren, sacrifice, heroism — so the mind and the imagination, shocked by the national misfortune, instinctively and unfalteringly selected from Polish art what is most human, most Polish in it, and they saw this above all in Mickiewicz, above all in *Pan Tadeusz*.

For, in our literature Mickiewicz is what these simple words are in life, and if his work, revolutionary for a century ago, immediately became the possession of the whole nation, this happened because he touched that collective instinct, that deepest humanness in people and that deepest "Polishness" in Poles. The Polish nation had been reading books for several

---

[5] Jan Rostworowski (1919-1975). Polish soldier-poet, brother of Emanuel and Marek and son of Karol Hubert Rostworowski.

centuries before Mickiewicz, it had had such fine poets as Kochanowski and Krasicki, but it was Mickiewicz who made literature and poetry so important to Poles that they could not imagine life without them. "A nostalgic poem" was how *Pan Tadeusz* was described at the Sorbonne by the transcriber of *Tristan and Isolde,* Bédier,[6] upon the occasion of its centenary. And to be sure, it might appear that the reason why the first emigration reacted to this poetry was because it longed to return to Poland, and that the same thing has happened again now. But *Pan Tadeusz* has become the Polish Bible not only of the Emigration, but also in Poland itself during the period of partition, while at present it is not only the confidant of the refugees, but also comforts those who are in Poland and who despite their frightful tortures, can still listen to the whispering of the birches and gaze at the meadows yellow with buttercups.

To say that *Pan Tadeusz* is a national *épopée* is to use a professional hieroglyph that tells little. One should say rather, that it is a literary symbol of Poland, simultaneously of its language, history, people, customs, that being the greatest masterpiece of Polish literature, it is something infinitely more important in that literature than is *Faust* in German literature or *Hamlet* in English literature — because it is at the same time a social fact, an inseparable part of the nation's life, one of the cornerstones of its spiritual existence and individuality. Of course, longing forms the spiritual atmosphere of *Pan Tadeusz.* Słowacki expressed this beautifully when he said: "A poem seemingly gay, but sometimes in the seemingly gayest spots a strange sadness takes hold of a person." Only, this longing is a state of mind which is not caused by geographical distance from the beloved object, but by the barrier between the Platonic world and ourselves; this longing is simply the permanent emotional state of true creators and one might presume that had he remained in Wilno, Mickiewicz would have longed for it just as he did when he was in Paris. Thus, it is not the longing for

---

[6] Joseph Bédier (1864-1938). French medievalist.

Poland but its ubiquity which is the reason for the acceptance of *Pan Tadeusz* by the whole nation and for our very real feeling of closeness to it today. It has been said that the great Romantic poets had taken the place of Poland's independence. Piłsudski stated at the burial of Słowacki in Kraków that he had taken the place of a Polish army. Undoubtedly, *Pan Tadeusz* has, for the second time, replaced Poland for the enslaved Poles. To each of us the question has occurred whether there could ever appear in Poland a poet greater than Mickiewicz and I am convinced none of us thought this possible. Wyspiański was a genius, in a certain sense unique in the world; his magnificent intellectualism, which expressed itself so plastically, so theatrically, the absorption by him of the entire Western culture and then the expression of this culture so dramatically, are a phenomenon in world literature. Had Norwid been a Frenchman, he would have lowered the poetic rank of Mallarmé and Paul Valéry, who would then have been recognized as his followers. Słowacki's *Samuel Zborowski* is a masterpiece without parallel, the height of esoteric poetry. And yet we feel that the case of Mickiewicz is utterly different, that here it is a question of another world of phenomena, another classification, that nothing higher than *Pan Tadeusz* can ever be born, because the Polish nation, having ripened to full cultural and spiritual maturity, found complete expression in it. And since neither the Polish landscape nor the Polish character will ever change, nothing more perfect than *Pan Tadeusz* can ever come into being.

Various critics, harboring purely rational conceptions, attempted several years ago to revive the old charges of professional democrats dating from the period of the great emigration, to the effect that Mickiewicz described only the gentry, that he apotheosized the country squire's mode of living and that therefore *Pan Tadeusz* is not democratic and its significance will end as soon as a truly people's Poland will arise. After the Russian experience, which hopelessly confirmed Trotzky's wise opinions regarding the non-existence of proletarian poetry and Lenin's dislike of Majakowski

313

accompanied by his admiration of Pushkin, we may foresee all the more boldly that regardless of Poland's future character, *Pan Tadeusz* will be for every Pole a national poem, symbol of the nation. The peasant *sukmana* is after all only a costume worn by the same man, a Pole with the same reactions and feelings, who at one time wore a gentleman's *kontusz*. When Wyspiański presented Bolesław the Bold in a *sukmana* he expressed with genius the truth about the peasant origin of the gentry.

Shortsighted or rather unseeing critics to the contrary, *Pan Tadeusz,* which is called a realistic poem, is — in spite of all its realism, in spite of its countless details of everyday life and of astronomy and gastronomy, — a symbolic poem because that wealth of details is not lost in a chaos but furnishes a complete picture of the Polish land, the Polish soul and Polish life and because the poetry of Mickiewicz elevates this seemingly commonplace world into Platonic regions and after every seemingly trifling occurrence, opens the horizon of deep meaning and eternity.

Everyone understands full well that the *mazur* and the *polonaise* are not Polish rhythm by accident, but that they conform to the deepest truths and laws of the Polish temperament and feeling; in a certain sense the same is true of Mickiewicz's poetry. We are not even concerned at present with what that poetry expresses, but with its sound, its cadence and music.

Słowacki wrote poetry that is as meaningful, as melodious as the poetry of Mickiewicz, and yet in the music — we must call it that — of Mickiewicz there is something else, something which makes *Pan Tadeusz* a symbol of the Polish nation: a rhythm in harmony with which every Pole feels and acts. That is precisely why the unimportant events at Soplicowo, set to this divine music, have become the great song of the Polish nation. Just as Gustaw changed into Konrad, so Mickiewicz too changed in his life and creative work from the lover of Maryla[7]

---

[7] Maryla Wereszczakówna (1799–1863), a youthful love of Mickiewicz's, reflected in some of his poetry.

314

into the lover of his Country. He really loved Poland as one loves a beloved woman. That is why his love was so alive, so passionate and could penetrate the nation.

In spite of everything that has already been said about the role played by Mickiewicz's poetry in Polish history and the struggle for independence, we probably do not fully realize how much the Polish nation, out of whose soul, suffering and virtues Mickiewicz was born, owes to him; we do not stop to reflect that our frenzied Polish patriotism, our devoutness, our faith even in moments when there seems to be no hope — that all this is the spirit of Mickiewicz. It was Mickiewicz who, having transformed the Basilian cell in Wilno into an interplanetary space between heaven and earth, welded us into a nation, which in every great historical crisis, is guided by the instinct of a higher morality and looks far beyond momentary advantages.

Wyspiański saw perfectly that the whole Polish nation is under the sway of Mickiewicz, and as is the privilege of a great poet, he challenged this power. However, it was not a contest with Mickiewicz himself, but with one of the forms of his posthumous life, with one of his distortions in the Polish soul, with the erroneous picture entertained by the nation about him — a picture which bore the same relation to the truth that pietism bears to real faith. Therefore, Wyspiański did not oppose any other poet to Mickiewicz, nor any other idea, but only that real Mickiewicz or Konrad, who in *Deliverance* thinks and wishes to fight as at one time Mickiewicz thought and wanted to fight.

When *Deliverance* was presented in the Polish Theatre several weeks after Piłsudski's death, Boy-Żeleński, who was then virtually living Mickiewicz, wrote that Wyspiański's Konrad created the impression of Piłsudski's spirit materializing at a séance — to such an extent did everything he said coincide with the great and seemingly contradictory thoughts of Piłsudski.

Here we have still another proof of Mickiewicz's eternal posthumous life and of his importance to our nation. Mickiewicz is without question the poet of the Polish nation, in a sense in which no other poet — with the sole exception of Dante, to

315

whom Mickiewicz could best be compared — ever was to his people.

For, what Mickiewicz has accomplished by himself has elsewhere been the result of centuries of literature and history. He simultaneously gave expression to the nation's real life and created or recorded its mythology. *Pan Tadeusz* is the Polish *Iliad*. But all of us still do not realize that Polish mythology is not concerned with pagan gods like Światowid and Darzbóg,[8] but with the fortunes of Mickiewicz's Konrad, of his manifestations in literature and in ourselves. This mythology is no less important to us than the life of Olympus is the Greeks.

Mickiewicz appeared at a moment constituting one of the paradoxes of history, at a moment when on the one hand, the Polish state was being suppressed, while on the other the Polish soul was being crystallized, changing from a jovial and domestic Mazovian soul into the soul of the Polish Republic, shaped by the common life of all its nations; the passion, ardor and mysticism of Mickiewicz are the contribution of the Ruthenian and Lithuanian provinces to the Polish soul. Mickiewicz never was in Warsaw or Kraków. He visited Poznania only by chance and briefly. Wilno was his capital. To him Litwa was the symbol of all Poland. Those who think Eastern Poland can be severed from the whole without mortally wounding its body and its soul — would do well to ponder this.

Thousands of good political, economic, ethnographical considerations defend our rights to this land. But what defends them in our soul, in our instinct — and after all this is the most important — is Mickiewicz. Just as he can never stop being the greatest Polish poet, just as no one can ever appear who will be greater than he was — so his posthumous and immortal life in the Polish soul, in Polish history and in Polish poetry can never

---

[8] Światowid was a pagan Slavic god — steles of him displaying a god of four faces, looking at the cardinal directions at one and the same time, exemplify his omniscience. Darzbóg (or Dadźbóg) was considered a god of the sun, or a chief god — at the root of his name is the Slavic word for "to give."

come to an end. Millions of Poles do not think of Mickiewicz day after day, living as if he never existed and never reading his poetry, just as they do not think about what the Polish language is, about the meaning of sacrifice, death and the word "brother." And then in one moment such as it has been given us to live through — they suddenly comprehend that for them there is nothing more important in the world than the courtyard of a Warsaw house in which they lived at one time with a mother and brothers and that they desire nothing more ardently than to do something for some humble Pole.

And then without quite knowing why, they reach for one book chosen from among a thousand other beautiful and wise Polish books and discover in it everything that is really important to them, without which life has no meaning. And they cannot read with calm those simple words that seem so trite to us on weekdays: "Lithuania, my country, thou art like health; how much thou should be prized only he can learn who has lost thee."[9]

---

[9] The first lines of *Pan Tadeusz*, which most Poles know by heart. *Litwo! Ojczyzno moja! Ty jesteś jak zdrowie. / Ile Cię trzeba cenić, ten tylko się dowie, / Kto Cię stracił.*

Mickiewicz in Polish Poetry[1]

Mickiewicz's influence on Polish poetry — nay, on Polish literature — is obviously a theme of very large dimensions. Much has been written about that influence, and scholars will long continue to investigate it. A theme so large is beyond the possibility of detailed treatment within the framework of an anniversary volume; nevertheless, it seems to me that in just such a book as this it is both possible and necessary to voice certain basic truths concerning the unusual character and exceptional quality of Mickiewicz's role, not in the history of Polish poetry alone, but also in the history of Poland itself. And in order that his influence may be rightly emphasized, certain perspectives must be made clear. I shall address myself to these problems in the pages which follow.

Mickiewicz, as a writer, is a unique phenomenon in the history of world literature. It would appear that he voiced and embodied in his work the soul of his people. By means of his work he symbolized their land, its history, its customs, and its character. At the same time, he drew forth from the national subconscious the desires which were dormant there, and brought to development latent possibilities which previously were unrecognized and unexpressed. In so doing he stepped beyond the enchanted circle of art and became one of the creators of history — one of the true fathers of his people. Such a destiny, as we know, has by no means been the lot of all the great writers of the past. Even the greatest did not necessarily identify themselves with their people as Mickiewicz did. Moreover, they did not become figures — and leading ones at that — of the national myth as he did. This is not at all to imply that the mission which Mickiewicz took upon himself, and in the pursuit of which he himself, his work, and the fate of his people became identified, is the highest task and measure of greatness of a

---

[1] From Wacław Lednicki, ed. *Adam Mickiewicz in World Literature: a Symposium* (Berkeley and Los Angeles: University of California Press, 1956), pp. 1-12.

writer. After all, Shakespeare, the greatest English poet and, after the Greek tragedians, the greatest discoverer of man for the very reason that he expressed all humanity, gave his people only one voice in humanity's symphony. One cannot even say of him, as one can of Goethe, that he presented humanity in the costume of his people; one can only say that, in its name, he spoke in the most beautiful language of his people. Pushkin, the just pride of Russia, who alone filled out two centuries of Russian culture (until there came the oversubtleties of the decadence), could pass rather for the antithesis of his society than for its expression. Montaigne, Pascal, Descartes, Molière, Balzac, Victor Hugo, each in a manner wholly his own and perfectly realized, represent only certain spiritual tendencies, only certain aspects, of the French genius. No one of them, but rather all of them together, may be taken to represent that indivisibility of a nation and its literature which is so markedly achieved in French culture. Can we say of Mickiewicz that he expressed, at one and the same time, all the affirmations and contradictions of the Polish soul? I believe we can.

At once a classicist and a romanticist, he expressed his people's everyday life, the objective, structured reality of their existence, and at the same time he gave voice to nightmares, visions, and prophecies. He also gave expression to spiritual forces which were first awakened, perhaps even created, by him, and thus mapped out for his people the paths of their spiritual future. He was at once the Homer and the Dante of the Polish nation. It is here that we have his uniqueness among all the writers of the world. If it is a question of his national significance as a poet, it is with Homer and Dante or with the Judaic prophets that he must, be compared. But to get a glimpse of the full measure of his influence it is probably necessary to go beyond the limits of literature and recognize Mickiewicz's spiritual significance for the Polish people, as well as the myth which he created, as being equivalent to that posthumous influence which Abraham Lincoln constantly exerts upon the American soul: one must compare, with the legend of the great poet who was also a political leader, the legend of the great statesman who in the Gettysburg Address produced a literary masterpiece. Zygmunt Krasiński, who even in the fullness of an exalted moment retained the judgment of a tragic skeptic, said after Mickiewicz's death: "We all are of him." And now, a hundred years later, every Pole who takes a part in the spiritual life of his people could repeat these words, each speaking for himself.

It suffices to compare the image of Polish life as it has been transmitted to us by the literature of the epoch which preceded Mickiewicz or even the image which he himself painted in *Pan Tadeusz,* with the world of his other masterpiece *Forefathers' Eve,* to see that a change occurred in the Polish soul. It suffices to compare the reactions, deeds, words, and attitudes toward life and toward civic affairs of the heroes of *Pan Tadeusz* and of *Forefathers' Eve.* One need only align Pan Tadeusz himself and — not Gustaw-Konrad, a mystical and symbolical figure, but, rather — Jan Sobolewski, a child of a court like that of Soplica, to see the change. And this change makes it possible to divide the spiritual history of the nation between the pre-Mickiewicz Poland and the Polish poetry and Polish life which date from the November Uprising and *Forefathers' Eve,* placing on the one side several hundred years of a "Pan Tadeusz" Poland, and measuring the other from the moment when Gustaw is transformed into Konrad in the cell of the Basilian Fathers. Of course this does not mean that the Poland of *Pan Tadeusz,* rural Poland, which lived, so to speak, biologically, and was almost entirely restricted to that biological existence, was swept from the earth by the November tornado and the romantic storm which accompanied it. Nor does it mean that Pan Tadeusz was transformed into Konrad. Rural Poland's often tragic flaws as well as its undervalued virtues, which assured to the Polish people precisely their biological endurance amidst so many adversities and Dantesque torture (as in the last war), will still often be met with. In literature we shall find them presented not only with the epic calm of Mickiewicz, but also with the splendors of the hazardous and stunningly magnificent apotheosis of Sienkiewicz. I believe that it is thanks to Mickiewicz that a new stratum has overlaid this basic component, as it were, of Polish geology, this salt of the Polish earth which exists to this very day in the all too carefree churl (who is also, be it noted, unusually valiant). This new stratum has made possible a completely new spiritual shaping of the Polish nation. In this shaping, the forces which Mickiewicz extracted from the depths of the national soul from that moment got the upper hand over the blind biology of the Pan Tadeuszes and the subsequent heroes of Sienkiewicz. The Polish nation accepted a new hierarchy of spiritual values. They were those values at the summit of which Mickiewicz placed the ideal of Konrad, who renounced personal happiness for the good of his people, or, rather, found his own happiness in that of the whole.

If we say that Mickiewicz accomplished this change we are, of course, well aware that he was not its only creator. We know that the transformation of the Polish soul took place under the burden of national misfortune. We know that the medicine of salutary revolts and anaesthetic sublimations was brought to us by the Romantic Movement, which was, after all, passing through all Europe at that time. We remember that that same ideal which Mickiewicz was propounding was celebrated enchantingly in Słowacki's verses and adorned with the glitter of Krasiński's dazzling rhetoric. We recall that a veneration of this ideal informed Sułkowski's[2] life and the proud, pessimistic heroism of Prince Józef Poniatowski, as well as the anonymous sacrifices of Dąbrowski's legionnaires and those of the soldiers who took part in the war of 1830. But although Mickiewicz did not bring about the change by himself alone, he so identified himself with it, both as a man and as a writer, he gave expression to it with such emotional power, such force of poetic suggestion, he created a figure that was so perfect a poetic embodiment of the spiritual ideal, that the Polish nation saw him not as one of

---

[2] Paweł Antoni Sułkowski (1785-1836). Polish officer who assumed command of the Polish army after the death of Józef Poniatowski.

the creators of the change but as its only creator. The Polish people elevated his life and work to the position of a national myth; it converted them into one of its historical legends. To speak of Mickiewicz's influence on individual contemporary or subsequent authors would mean a restriction of the sphere of that influence to the forms of a caricature. Although his influence was, indubitably, exercised directly upon literary creativity in selection of themes, selection of verse forms, and the formation of literary views, it nonetheless, and to no less a degree, penetrated to the depths of the national soul. This occurred not just because of Mickiewicz's poetry. It happened, in part, because of the action of the legend, in which participated the poems themselves, Mickiewicz's political, all too often unhappy, and prophetic activity, historical events connected with the poems and sometimes issuing from them, and the life and deeds of people who often without knowing it were Mickiewicz's pupils and sometimes were sacrifices of Konrad's. All these things created an indivisible unity which was the spiritual climate of several generations of Poles.

However, it was Mickiewicz above all who shook the nation with his works and it was he above all who excited the literature and altered it. Even if one were to admit that he, Słowacki, and Krasiński were "equals," he was nonetheless "first" among them. That which Krasiński said after his death could have been said, and with even more justice, by Słowacki. Inasmuch as Słowacki truly dedicated his life to the nightmares of the imagination and the demons of literary fame, and inasmuch as he attained to magnificent originality, there would be no point in searching for the influences which he formerly absorbed. But Mickiewicz made Słowacki conscious of the gravity, and later of the holiness, of a vow of life-and-death dedication to art which Słowacki made as a child and often renewed in later life. For Słowacki, it was also a resolve to achieve equality with the cruel giant of poetry who was first observed by the child's sparkling eyes in his mother's salon. It was Mickiewicz's unknowing indifference and misunderstanding that henceforth (with such blessed results for Polish poetry) incited the inspired envy of the admirer and rival who coexisted in Słowacki. As we all know, Kordian was Słowacki's Konrad. He arose out of Słowacki's dreams about himself — undergoing the same Mickiewiczian metamorphosis as Gustaw. But Słowacki was never a Gustaw. He never loved with body and soul, and therefore could never transform himself into a Konrad. That work of so much beauty, one of the brightest jewels of Polish Romanticism, proved the impossibility of Słowacki's comparing himself to Mickiewicz when the latter was depicting his nation — when, as if by a poetic sacrament, he transformed the martyrdom of prisoners, the tears of mothers, and the death of soldiers into his own words. In this respect Mickiewicz could without poetic exaggeration say, "I and my fatherland are one," as if he were speaking of a psychic and almost a biological fact.

Słowacki wished to say this of himself, but it was precisely what he could not say even though, while casting the gauntlet before Mickiewicz in *Beniowski,* he almost ascribed to himself such a mystic union with the nation. Słowacki was enchanted by the unworldly realism of *Forefathers' Eve.* He was immediately aware of the apparently easy but actually very difficult beauty of *Pan Tadeusz.* Although he paid homage to it in his letters and in an attempt at a poetic continuation, he understood that he had to express other beauties in a different manner and that he had other secrets to disclose. He wished to be Mickiewicz's equal — but a different man and a different poet. In his heart of hearts he could not envy Mickiewicz his works any more than another genuine creative artist could have done so. He had too good and too just an opinion of his own work. And he believed too deeply in his own posthumous victory — purchased at the price of an ascetic life. But there was something in Mickiewicz which no one could quite rival. There was something which Słowacki could not achieve even though he equaled Mickiewicz in beauty of language and exceeded him in richness of language. There was something to which he could not attain even though with his fine intellect he apprehended various traps and shadows in the Polish psyche sometimes even more quickly than Mickiewicz. He could not compare with him, even though he too made the national cause the universe of his poetry, and Polonism one of its most profound charms. No one, neither Słowacki nor Krasiński, possessed that elementary power which acts beyond reason, and sometimes in spite of reason, to such a degree as Mickiewicz. No one possessed it, not even Stefan Żeromski, who so captivated and stirred our nation but who committed so many artistic and psychological transgressions. That elementary power converted aesthetic experiences and poetic rapture into a vital event equal to the intoxication of love. No one equaled Mickiewicz in that genius for simplicity which conceals evangelical depths and the experiences of humanity's aeons beneath ordinary words accessible to every child. No other man but this one (whose letters breathe an inhuman coldness) was at one and the same time a wise man, a great artist, and a simple soul. No one expressed himself with such intellectual power, which exerted, as it were, a magnetic force upon those who read or heard his poetry. No one could take as much from the national depths, and therefore return as much, as Mickiewicz.

Mickiewicz made the calling of a poet in Poland a prophetic mission. Through his work as a poet, publicist, and political actor he became the leader of the nation. In depth and breadth of influence he exceeded great and honored leaders and statesmen. One may confidently assert that Poland recognized only two uncontested spiritual leaders in all of post-Partition history: Mickiewicz and Kościuszko. Słowacki wished to become just such a leader. Keenly aware of the beauty of Mickiewicz's work, he struggled with him all his life for the possession of this very "rule of souls," this prophetic cloak — which Mickiewicz had metamorphosed into the royal purple and ermine of the Polish nation. Mickiewicz, who appeared in the *Preparation to Kordian* (introduced by the most beautiful verses ever written about him), actually was never absent from Słowacki's poetry. He was either challenged to battle in the genial tirades of *Beniowski* or else was ever-present in

Słowacki's great designs — in his constant efforts of soul and ailing body to equal that unique master of Polish souls who, it would seem, had been freely granted that for which Słowacki had to struggle. A contemporary psychoanalysis would have had fertile ground for its labors. In going through Słowacki's creation, following the traces of that ever-tempting competition, it would have no need to exaggerate anything in Słowacki's work (in favor of its own theories) in order to discover in Słowacki's relationship to Mickiewicz a genuine complex — a complex which culminated in the posthumous debate between Zamoyski and Samuel and was almost resolved by it. This debate gave Słowacki the illusion that he had at last overtaken and drawn into dispute the rival who had rid himself of Słowacki with so offensive a silence and so inconceivable lack of understanding.

As I have said before, Mickiewicz placed the calling of a Polish poet alongside of, or rather above, political leadership. In creating a Polish legion, and later a Turkish one, he assumed, too, a military leadership. This helped to erase, in the mind of the public, the differences between a "rule of souls" and rule *per se*. Mickiewicz — a poet who was both prophet and leader — could wield such control in a time of national bondage, whatever one may think of his political temperance. Krasiński and Słowacki, in accepting the idea of this calling from Mickiewicz also became leaders in their posthumous activity. They became leaders through the great spiritual style of their poetry, through their mutual religious attitude toward it, and through their moral feeling of responsibility for the people. The pathos of their poetry is never merely the unforced expression of a pathetic spirit; it is a natural attitude generated by the tragedy of the lot of the Poland of their time, which placed Polish poets face to face with the world as Greek tragedy had seen the world, and bade them turn to God as the sole refuge. This mission could only rest upon truly prophetic shoulders; it could not burden every Polish poet, irrespective of his inclinations or the measure of his powers. Unfortunately, many of them strove for this spiritual control thereby deforming their own talent and contributing to that catastrophic devaluation of pathos that has taken place in our literature.

The same sort of thing occurred with the idea of the moral mission of the Polish people set forth in the parables and commandments of Mickiewicz's *Books of the Polish Nation and of the Polish Pilgrimage*. If it was genuinely a spiritual deliverance, or, if less than that, at any rate a charitable narcotic for a people paralyzed by a lost war of liberation, divested of the fire of Mickiewicz's genius, and fallen into the hands of shamans, quacks, and intellectual swindlers, it passed into the service of the forces of inertia — the camp of national self-praise. From an instrument of struggle and spiritual effort it became an obstacle in the path of that struggle. The *Books* were only drawn upon for journalistic catchwords with which to stupefy the will. To the degree that our Mickiewicz was sundered from life, to the degree that his work was instinctively falsified and he, together with his creative legend, was whittled down to the needs of secret political propaganda, a pernicious legend of him began to take shape. Mickiewicz — if one may use the words of the poet — from "the wing of strong men" seemed to become, time after time, "the stone of weak men." Moreover, the charm of his poetry, even when we really understand its commandments, is as it were an obstacle between us and Poland's poetic reality of *Pan Tadeusz* and *Forefathers' Eve*. It is as if that charm begins to replace, for us, the real Poland. It is not just that Mickiewicz loses his essential nature in his inept imitators and glossers. He himself, partly because he is so great an artist and is capable of transporting us into the world of unreality, seems to become the great luller of the nation — despite the meaning and content of his poetry. And so, at the beginning of our century, a voice with another ring but with a force almost equal to Mickiewicz's appears in Polish verse. It appears in order to bring before the nation the problem of that puissant skeleton laid to rest in the Wawel crypt — that skeleton which had bewitched the nation with the beauty of its living voice. By its spellbinding words it had so enchanted the nation with the past that — in spite of itself — it transferred the struggle which it was evoking into a sphere of dreams and unreality from which the nation could no longer tear its gaze.

Stanisław Wyspiański, with dazzling dialectics and in scenic metaphor which enraptures with its wealth of poetic fantasy, grasps the paradox in an unusual way. He brings Mickiewicz's Konrad — who embodies Mickiewicz's true purpose and his will to action — onto the stage and compels him to defy the bronze Mickiewicz. He compels him to defy Mickiewicz's monument, the symbol of his false legend and at the same time the symbol of the ominous power of poetry — which, in arrogating to itself the function of a symbol, destroys at the same time all reality. Wyspiański's drama made us conscious of the fact that Mickiewicz himself, his work, and his poetic double, Konrad, had already become a part of the national mythology. He taught us that the life of that symbolic hero and Mickiewicz's posthumous vicissitudes are as vital for us as real historical events and the deeds of living heroes. The conflict involved in the battle between Konrad and the bronze Mickiewicz, although one that is so happily Polish and genuine, as I have already said — so genuine a phenomenon in the history of literature — permitted Wyspiański to wrestle with a problem of general significance. It enabled him, on the basis of a Polish example, to point to an eternal opposition between poetry and reality. It enabled him to solve the problem with not just mastery of the theater — with revelationally new artistic forms — but also with tragedy of the highest order: Wyspiański's Konrad banishes the bronze Mickiewicz from the stage, wishing thus to free the nation from the domination of poetry and open its eyes to reality. But in banishing the poetry from which he came, Konrad has committed the crime of Orestes and will henceforth be pursued by the Erinyes — for poetry is an enchanted circle from which no one can depart with impunity once he has gained entry. In touching upon his own drama in this fashion (for Wyspiański, like Mickiewicz, also wished to alter his nation's destiny with his art), Wyspiański reduced the problem of Mickiewicz's influence on the nation to its most essential element, the charm of his poetry. This element had been too often forgotten, owing to the attribution of a prophetic power to Mickiewicz and the extolling of his political leadership.

If one makes a critical survey of what is most generally termed Mickiewicz's influence on Polish poetry, one must come to the conclusion that that influence had to do above all with the selection of themes, literary forms, and ideology. But on the other hand, in what above all makes poetry poetry — that is, its musical qualities and its selection and use of words — Mickiewicz does not seem to have any followers. A whole Pleiade of major and minor romantics who came after him twinkled with the glitter of forms newly brought to them, such as the ballad. Many of our literary regionalisms developed out of his Lithuanianism. The stirring nostalgia and the Homeric objectivity of *Pan Tadeusz* degenerated into Pol's[3] petty-nobility sentimentalism and uncritical idolization of all things pertaining to the squirearchy. Słowacki took the Shakespearean fluctuation of time, place, and tone of *Forefathers' Eve* as a model in other works besides *Kordian.* Both he and Wyspiański modeled themselves on Mickiewicz by introducing contemporary figures into their works of art. Ujejski[4] strove for prophetic heights in Mickiewicz's footsteps. Konopnicka, undoubtedly with the intention of supplementing *Pan Tadeusz* with a peasant epos, accomplished her greatest poetic effort in *Pan Balcer w Brazylii.* Żeromski's novelistic mission was undoubtedly inspired by the spirit and example of Mickiewicz. Meanwhile, the metal of Mickiewicz's poetry, its flesh, its music (which escapes all investigations of the rhythm), its lexicon (the gift of speaking about the secrets of the Lithuanian cuisine and the mysteries of the Apocalypse with what seems to be a language

---

[3] Wincenty Pol (1807-1872). Lesser Romantic poet of Poland. He was also a geographer, and took part in the November Uprising of 1830.

[4] Kornel Ujejski (1823-1897). Polish nineteenth-century poet, associated with Lwów.

comprehensible to everyone), in a word the charm and suggestive strength of the *Sonnets, Forefathers' Eve,* and *Pan Tadeusz,* turned out to be an inimitable art. It was not to be equaled by anyone.

It was the gift of a single individuality. It was a mechanism which seemed obvious and simple to everybody, but from which Mickiewicz alone was able to draw forth celestial music. When one studies this marvelous instrument the thought occurs that, in reality, Mickiewicz had no recourse to art, that his poetic activity did not take place in the sphere of aesthetic effort at all. One has the feeling that it was a subconscious spiritual activity in which the process of finding the correct expression was an instinctive act and always infallible. One feels that Mickiewicz always found the unique simple word and always combined words in their indispensable quantity. It gives us the impression of everyday speech which, however, comes from some higher world (although always so human and simultaneously so Polish). None of his imitators could compare with him or be his pupil; for no one of them was Mickiewicz, no one could achieve his spiritual stature, no one had his genius for the simple word. And if, occasionally, there rang forth in our poetry a tone which by its purity and fullness was reminiscent of Mickiewicz, it only happened when a poet could achieve a like simplicity as, now and then, Syrokomla and Gomulicki[5] managed to do.

But in spite of everything which has been said up to this point concerning Mickiewicz's ideological influence and spiritual tyranny not only in Polish poetry but also in the entire life of our people, Słowacki, the patron of "Young Poland" and of several prewar formalistic movements, had more effect on the purely formal development of Polish verse. Słowacki worked always in a polishing and alchemical shop. It was possible and all too tempting to spy on him, to filch and imitate the prescriptions and sorceries. And many did just that. An interest

---

[5] Władysław Syrokomla (Ludwik Kondratowicz, 1823-1862). Polish poet and translator; Wiktor Gomulicki (1848-1919). Polish Parnassian poet, associated with Warsaw.

in Mickiewicz, on the contrary — an interest in him simply as a poet, a feeling that the most valuable part of his heritage is not the commandments and the prophecies but rather the poetry itself, the texts themselves, and a new placing of Mickiewicz in the Polish cultural consciousness — came after the acquisition of national independence. It came about as a result of freedom, which no longer needed prophecies and which governed itself with a normal national government rather than with a "rule of souls." It came about also as a reaction against the nebulousness and phrasemongering of "Young Poland." The Skamander group, poets affiliated with it, and its poetic mentor Leopold Staff[6] (whose age also made him a part of the preceding period), tried to concretize poetic language, which had been demoralized by the artificiality and pompousness of "Young Poland." Even if these poets did not entirely revert to Mickiewicz's lines, they often turned to them. And it so happened that, in poetry which seemed to be completely foreign to Mickiewicz's spirit (as, for instance, that of Tuwim), there often sounds that tone of simplicity, that gripping accuracy, that laconic quality which constituted the charm of Mickiewicz. It gives one the impression of a tightening of bonds between him and contemporary poetry.

The new catastrophe, which was to repeat, in gigantic proportions, for the Polish nation the tragedy which Mickiewicz lived through after the lost war of 1830, deepened and crystallized this as it were aesthetic influence into a genuine heritage which is spiritual and artistic in equal measure. Many of the leading Polish poets now found themselves in the emigration. They were to endure (first of all on that same "Parisian pavement" as Mickiewicz) the same feelings and experiences as he had. They were to endure, as events turned out, the same impulses of revolt, the same despair, the same impotence and, above all, the same painful nostalgia for their country as he had, even if not to that same matchless degree. *Pan Tadeusz* therefore

---

[6] Leopold Staff (1878-1957). One of the most important Polish poets of the early twentieth century; he had a large influence on Lechoń, Tuwim and the other Skamander poets.

became for them and for their kinsmen in Poland (again hurled into slavery) what it had been for Mickiewicz's contemporaries — a genuine "Book of the Polish Nation." For the nation, its poetic symbol replaces the freedom which has been lost; for the emigration, it replaces the distant native land. And so the first generation of Polish poets which seemed to be free from the curse against which Wyspiański's Konrad revolted, which seemed able, as it thought, to labor for the national artistic mission in a carefree manner, was compelled to write a new page in the history of Polish poetry. On this page it was not only to follow Mickiewicz's form, but also to fulfill, to the extent of its powers, that same task which Mickiewicz, in his own time, had placed before poetry. This is the page of the new Polish nostalgic poetry, war poetry, and journalistic poetry. From this page, amidst transitory poems — necessary for the moment but having, actually, only a temporary echo — the future will select, and forever preserve, a number of poems by Baliński, Broniewski,[7] Pawlikowska, Słonimski, Tuwim, Wierzyński, and others. They will be a testimony, in part, to Mickiewicz's artistic influence and, in part, to the eternal permanence of his myth. Despite the most unfavorable conditions for the penetration of Mickiewicz's spirit into the poetry of subjugated Poland, despite the system of falsification of its political and social values, we see both from academic projects and biographical fantasies that even in the present literature of our country there is discernible an instinctive return to Mickiewicz, and a spiritual refuge in him. In this jubilee year, Mickiewicz is not just on the lips of ceremonial speakers. He is an eternally young poetic myth which is eternally being reborn and eternally being enriched by new spiritual events.

Translated by Lawrence L. Thomas

---

[7] Władysław Broniewski (1897-1962). Polish twentieth-century poet. A Legionnaire with Piłsudski, he later adopted a Communist outlook.

In the Depths of Hell[1]

To write of German atrocities, of the persecution of the Jews, — in the fifth year of these atrocities, of atrocious war, — may seem useless and superfluous.

It may seem useless because during the course of these last four terrible years, we have not been able to find the means of retaliation or revenge which might have halted this infernal machine, whose horrible sounds reach our ears every day from martyred Europe and above all from Poland.

We who are free and safe have been living in a state of mortal sin — the sin of forgetting so many of our brothers. At every moment of our lives, whether we are peacefully sleeping or discussing politics and literature, our brothers are being massacred in Warsaw, in Belgrade, in Lille or the best of us are agonizing in the hell that is Dachau.

Certainly we might say to ourselves, in order to appease our conscience, that it is impossible for anyone, whoever he may be, whether he be Mr. Roosevelt or Mr. Churchill, to frighten the Germans by the menace of retaliation, because the Germans know very well that these retaliations cannot be achieved. But in our innermost conscience we know very well that we have not done our utmost because we have accepted too quickly and with a certain lightheartedness our impotence before so much woe.

It may seem superfluous to speak of these miseries because we pretend to ourselves that we are very well acquainted with them; and because after having read so many „black books" and so many terrifying accounts, after having seen so many horror films out of Hollywood, it seems to us that we know everything about martyred Europe.

And some of us even suspect that they have been taken in by exaggerated propaganda, and that after all European air must be more or less breathable as so many millions of people are still breathing there.

---

[1] First published first in *Tygodnik Polski*, 1944 no 19 (71) pp. 8-9.

I am Polish, born and brought up in Warsaw, that capital of Poland where for the last four years not a single issue of a Polish newspaper has been allowed (but where every day thousands of clandestine newspapers are printed). In that capital at this moment there exists not one school where Polish children can speak their native language, not one concert hall accessible to the citizens of that city, nor a single theatre where one word of Polish can be uttered. In that noble city it is not by hundreds but by tens of thousands — and in that unconquerable country by millions — that one counts the number of citizens who have disappeared during these four years, who were shot, hanged or kicked to death by the guards in concentration camps.

I have had the sad privilege for a long time of knowing very well to what lengths the Germans will go and of imagining what life might be under their heel.

Because I am a Pole and at the request of the editors of *Pour la Victoire*[2] I have made it my duty to speak of the tragedy of the Jewish people and of the massacres in the ghettos of Poland.

There are, alas! some further facts to be added to what the world thinks it knows of the martyrdom of Poland, of the fate of the most unfortunate of all unfortunate peoples, the Polish Jew. There are some scenes which have been acted out in reality and before which even the most audacious imagination would fail. Goya was not pessimist enough to paint such scenes and Dante did not surpass them in the most infernal visions of his *Inferno*. In order to depict the tragedy of the Polish Ghettos one would need the voice of the Biblical prophets.

Of the four hundred thousand Jews who were confined in the Warsaw Ghetto, only forty thousand are alive at this writing. This is a simple statement which should make even the most indifferent shudder.

Compared to the usual German cruelties, the idea of a Ghetto might not appear as frightful. But I must emphasize that

---

[2] A newspaper published by a group of French war exiles in New York City.

the walls of the Ghettos separate, completely and forever, the Jewish population from the Polish population; that they shut in, among others, the Jews who have worked diligently for the Polish cause, all the intellectuals and artists; that in order to fill up these Ghettos wives have been torn from their husbands and the children resulting from mixed marriages taken from their fathers. It was only by living like criminals in hiding and in exposing themselves to the constant dangers of discovery that some Jews were able to live outside of these shameful walls.

In fact, a few days ago I learned of the death of a family I knew, a journalist, his wife and their small baby who had all been shot because they had not registered to live in a Ghetto.

These gigantic prisons which forever deprive their inhabitants of the sight of green gardens, made them dream, as of a promised land, of the banks of the Vistula, of the streets and the monuments of Warsaw which were only a few steps outside of the Ghetto and yet out of reach. This immense prison might have appeared to its inhabitants as a purgatory, if not a paradise, when later they were passing through the circles of a Dantean inferno.

Condemned to a slow death, to famine or to the continuous contemplation of misery, one lives in spite of all. It is thus that one has lived the last three years in the Ghettos of Poland.

It was on the 27th of July 1942 that the suicide of Mr. Adam Czerniaków,[3] President of the Jewish Council (a sort of autonomous administration of the Warsaw Ghetto (revealed to the Polish Jews that they were already before the gates of Hell. On the eve of that day, the Gestapo asked Mr. Czerniaków to choose seventeen thousand inhabitants of the Ghetto to be transported to the East. Even though they gave him reassuring pretexts, Mr. Czerniaków understood that this was a simple

---

[3] Adam Czerniaków (1880-1942). Before the war, he was a Polish Senator. He also authored the invaluable *Dziennik getta warszawskiego* [Diary of the Warsaw Ghetto].

sentence of death and he killed himself rather than betray his people.

In the Ghetto the next day there began a manhunt, always under the pretext of drafting labor for the East and every day from that moment on, hundreds of thousands of Jews passed through the gates of the Ghetto and went off in trains whose true destination no one knew. For several months the families of some of these unfortunate people received letters which gave them the illusion that their relatives were still alive and actually working in some mysterious locality in the nebulous East.

But these letters became more and more infrequent and more and more people were being deported; and what at first was only a doubt, an obsessing suspicion, finally became a terrible reality, — the Ghettos were being gradually emptied by murder.

Thanks to some courageous souls who made their way among the guards in order to learn the fate of these unhappy Jews, we know in what unspeakable conditions, by what terrifying procedures, by what new diabolical inventions the Germans succeeded in liquidating the Polish Ghettos. They massacred three quarters of the Jewish population of Poland. We have learned with horror that thousands of these condemned people were forced to watch the mass executions of aged Jews, which was supposed to convince them that only the old and crippled were killed and that the others — that is to say themselves — would be reprieved. We now know to what use the railroad cars were put; that their floor-boards were covered with lime which burned the feet and whose fumes caused death. We now know that thousands of men were deprived of life simply by herding them in masses on the floorboards which very quickly became the base of a pyramid of corpses.

And we open our eyes to see humanity as it is, in the light of a great tragedy. We hear the sublime Judaic lamentations and the divine words which show us the way to salvation and which we have forgotten. What verses from Dante, what scenes from Shakespeare can surpass in grandeur

336

the last eight hours in the life of Samuel Zygielbom,[4] a Jewish member of the Polish National Council in London, A few hours ago a courageous Polish messenger brought him an appeal from the Jewish community in Poland, to attempt the impossible to save his people. He killed himself the next day, hoping his suicide would move people to help. And what could be more inspiring than the pathetic and naive drawing in a Jewish clandestine newspaper showing the hand of a Polish Jew holding the hand of a Polish Christian over the Ghetto wall?

The highest and best traditions of our nation, which welcomed the Jews after they had been expelled everywhere else and whose greatest writers defended their cause, have been affirmed during the course of these last few years in thousands of daily heroic acts.

We swear, we must all swear, that this first symptom of criminal madness which is devouring our world, that the sacrilegious division of humanity into master peoples and slave peoples, that the folly of the "superior" races, the humiliating distinctions between nations shall not only be condemned by fine words but that this horrible madness shall be forever erased form the earth. There is no place here for explanations, comparisons and diplomacy. There is here only one reasonable course: the application to the letter of the teachings of the Saviour.

---

[4] Samuel Zygelbom (Samuel Zygielbojm, 1895-1943). By trade a glovemaker. Leader of the Jewish Bund in Poland, member of the city council of Warsaw, member of the Polish Government in Exile in London during the war.

What Really Happened in Yalta[1]

Among those persons who are indifferent to what is happening to Poland, there are, besides those, who favor Russia, many who are fully conscious of realities, but who believe they result from political exigencies to which all human considerations should yield.

We do not believe such people constitute the majority in America and that their standpoint decides the prevailing insensibility to the crime committed against us. These conscious assenters to the partitioning of Poland could not bring a community of millions to such hardening of heart. It is rather the ignorance of the average American, in that it is impossible for him to picture our fate in the terms of what it would mean to him were he in our shoes.

If the Bolsheviks are able to represent the most downright, outrageous lies in such a way that many not only believe them but even come to their defense, the conclusion to be drawn is that the only road to the masses is that which leads not to the uncomprehending consciousness, but to the live imagination, to the emotions.

Figures, dates, facts — these are symbols, which often decide material and tactical calculations. That which directs the movements of the masses are impulses of imagination, eruptions of feelings, when they can see in the fate of others their own fate.

Even those who know how many square miles of territory have been taken from Poland are not aware that they make up half of the country; that cutting us with the Curzon-Hitler-Stalin[2] line is the same as the seizure of half of the United States would be to Americans.

---

[1] First published in the *Tygodnik Polski*, 1945 no 14 (119) p. 12.

[2] The Curzon Line was a proposed eastern boundary for the resurrected state of Poland, drawn up by British diplomat George Nathaniel Curzon (1859-1925) following World War I. As a result of Poland's victory over the Soviet Union in the Polish-Soviet war of 1920-1921, the

Eastern Poland that had to be incorporated into the USSR — is not a territorial scrap. It equals the territories of Belgium, Holland, Denmark and Hungary, taken together, and its population equals that of Argentina.

Would those who believe that for Mr. Churchill's peace of mind, the Poles should give away Lwów and Wilno, feel the same if Boston and Philadelphia were the cities involved? Yet these cities are of the same, or lesser importance to the United States that Lwów and Wilno are to Poland.

Could any honest American, in full possession of his wits, think that after the war now being won, half of the United States should be taken away and given to England because Montgomery, Wavell and Alexander had successes in the battle?[3] Yet what is being done to us is from our standpoint the same as if half of the United States were given, not to England, but to Japan.

Could one imagine that after this war Mr. Churchill and Mr. Stalin would decide who should be president of the United States and select for that post Ezra Pound?[4] Yet that is exactly what was done with us at Yalta.

Polish border was pushed farther to the East, and the Polish state between the two world wars thus possessed more of its traditional territory, including Wilno and Lwów, than the Entente powers had foreseen for her. Lechoń ironically refers to the boundary as the Curzon-Hitler-Stalin line, as this boundary was imposed upon Poland following the Second World War, as a result of German and Soviet aggression, and in despite of Anglo-American guarantees, early in the war, that Poland would not be made to suffer territorial loss.

[3] Bernard Law Montgomery, Lord of Alamein (1887-1976), Sir Archibald Percival Wavell (1883-1950), and Harold Rupert Alexander (1891-1969) were all British Generals, who played a large role in the Allied victory during World War Two.

[4] Ezra Weston Loomis Pound (1885-1972). American expatriate poet, one of the moving spirits behind Modernism. One of the most accomplished poets of the modern era, Pound lived most of his adult life in Italy — although he never renounced his American citizenship, or accepted the citizenship of any other country. Fascinated by

Those who try to persuade us that the Crimea pact has not taken away Poland's independence — could they admit the thought that after this war the Russian army should supervise elections for the followers of Roosevelt, and, in order to facilitate operations, the American army should be murdered or jailed, and its commanders called traitors?

Would not a person be acknowledged a fool if he would suggest that Russia be permitted to prevent Americans from taking part in the peace conference until they have elected a president named for them by Stalin and Churchill? Would he not be a criminal who would recognize such a conception as an act of democracy and justice?

Yet the Yalta pact established just such a fate for Poland, and when Poland protested, she was told that the decision must stand.

If 5,000,000 American soldiers had fallen in this war, and 2,000,000 civilians had been murdered — among them hundreds of educators from the universities of Columbia, Yale and Harvard — and then the sentence pronounced that Russia and England must supervise the United States to prevent the country from attacking in conspiracy with Japan, would not the whole of America regard such a decision as the greatest crime in history?

Mussolini and Italian Fascism, and rabidly inimical to Roosevelt, his radio broadcasts from Rome were used as grounds for treason when he was apprehended by the American Army in the closing days of the war. He was tried for giving aid and comfort to the enemy, and was only saved from execution by the fact that government psychiatrists found him to be mentally incompetent. After several years in St Elizabeth's Hospital for the criminally insane in Washington, D.C., Pound was released, and returned to Italy. His *Pisan Cantos,* written during the first stage of his incarceration by the U.S. Army in Italy, are considered by many to be the best poetic work in English of the latter twentieth century. By many Americans, especially in the 1950s, he was considered a traitor.

Suppose all the inhabitants of New York, women, old men and children, had been cut off from the American army, and they defended their city for two months from the Japanese. And suppose that as a result of this defense and because the English Army in New Jersey had stopped fighting the Japanese, New York was razed to the ground, and three millions of its inhabitants killed. Then, if England refused to permit the United States to participate in a common conference, stating that the Americans were collaborators with the enemy — would that not be a crime which would shake the conscience of the world?

Yet all this is exactly what has happened to us. And it is only a part of the awful truth about the martyrdom of the Polish nation, about the sufferings which cannot be compared to anything in this war except the fate of the Jews, about the heroism no other nation has equaled, about the voluntary sacrifices for freedom, about the wrong which calls to heaven for vengeance, and which, if reparation is not made, is the end of civilization, the end of democracy, the twilight of Christianity, and the beginning of centuries of tyranny, the horrors of which no American can comprehend because such a crime has never been perpetrated against his country.

President Roosevelt[1]

The death of President Roosevelt on the eve of Victory and of the American army's entry into Berlin gives a truly Shakespearean touch to the great drama of history through which we are living. No man capable of sensing greatness, grasping historical perspective, measuring the distance between intention and destiny can be indifferent to the passing of this great man who, by dint of thought and will, did so much to further the immortal work now culminating in Victory!

The tragedy and pathos of President Roosevelt's death is enhanced by the exceptional destiny that fate decreed for him. Because of his sudden and untimely death his unique life becomes an heroic legend to point the lesson that toil, suffering and disappointment are inseparable from all human endeavor.

No matter how deep and vital the differences of opinion in America and abroad on Franklin Delano Roosevelt's achievements for the United States and his role in world politics, their very vehemence betokens the unusual stature and spiritual strength of the figure that has departed from us not into the shade but into the light of history. No one doubts that President Roosevelt will live forever in the history of the United States and in that of the world, not only because in the most crucial hour he stood at the helm of the nation whose might decided the outcome of the greatest of world wars. No one can deny that the momentous decision reached by the United States in this war, was first and foremost his decision, and that it was he who made it the common will of the American people.

It is a truism to say that history is written by the human masses and by extraordinary persons. But at times the greatness, the genius of these individuals lay only in their ability to sense the will of the people and to follow it. Among such great interpreters of the will of the people were Louis XIVth and Queen Victoria.

---

[1] First published in the *Tygodnik Polski*, 1945 no 16 (121) pp. 3-4.

What better evidence of the greatness of President Roosevelt is there than this: that always remaining within the scope of the law, always appealing to the will of the people, during the twelve years of his Presidency, he wrought his will, his thought, his conception of the common good, and that in this most democratic of countries he never failed to win the consent of the masses and often aroused their enthusiasm for his will.

In a country where the commonplace and the average is the ideal, where the opinion of the majority is always right, where the best taste is that of the common man, Franklin Delano Roosevelt remained in power longer than any of his predecessors, ruled more independently than any other President, and won the love of all the people. All this because he was different, because relying upon democracy and serving it successfully he was the antithesis of the average and the commonplace, because he impressed the people as being different and above the common man.

The love that the common man — especially the poor and the underprivileged — gave to President Roosevelt was born of gratitude for the way he defended the interest of the masses in directing the internal policy of America from the day, thirteen years ago, when by unprecedented and almost revolutionary methods he mastered the crisis that was bringing ruin to the wealthy, but above all starvation to the poor.

The poor and underprivileged, too weak to make their way in the young and hard American life, with its adoration for strength and success, found something more than relief and financial succor in the Roosevelt reforms, they found what was more important: hope and comfort. They had a mystic feeling that they were no longer alone and helpless, that someone was thinking about them, someone who radiated a force more potent than strength, more important than success.

No political misgivings, no arguments however sound, no errors of Roosevelt's administration, ever lessened in the hearts of the underprivileged masses their instinctive faith in his greatness, their gratitude for what he had done for the common people. All political polls and election forecasts, no matter how mathematically perfect, were smashed to pieces by this emotional gratitude and beautiful legend.

That this defense of the poor and underprivileged was not dictated by his own reminiscences nor by his own experience; that he understood misery without ever having tasted of it; that he was a true democrat although born to the purple, added to popular gratitude an imponderable element, a fairy mysticism, something like the naive feeling the English have for their sovereigns.

Despite the manifest differences, Franklin Delano Roosevelt resembled the creators of Polish democracy who likewise were scions of wealthy families. His accessibility excluded familiarity, it had a trace of royal condescension. The masses, who thirst for legend as they hunger for bread, appreciate these gestures and this attitude.

While moving consciously and consistently, with the mastery of a great tactician in internal politics, towards America's participation in the war against the Germans, Roosevelt acted in the name of the same idealism that had dictated his internal reforms. Neither economic conflict nor imperial interest inspired Roosevelt's genius of persuasion, his undaunted will, his incomparable knowledge of the American people, to prepare them for the decision so dramatically hastened by the Japanese attack on Pearl Harbor. It was the ideological abyss between American freedom and Nazi bondage.

Attacked by Japan and Germany, President Roosevelt in three years created the most powerful army, air force, navy and war industry in history, achieved the immortal feat of invading two continents, liberated half of Europe from the direst oppression. In doing so he was guided by his love of humanity, by the same high ideals served by Washington, Lincoln, Wilson.

Who can doubt today, a few hours before American troops enter Berlin, that President Franklin Delano Roosevelt will live in history as one of the greatest conquerors of all times, the man who crushed the godless power that had risen to challenge all things human and divine.

We realize that this work undertaken with true American straightforwardness and ruthless idealism has been warped in contact and compromise with forces over which President Roosevelt, so independent in his internal policy — had no power. To these forces he made great, although probably only tactical concessions after a dramatic struggle the full details of which are as yet unknown to the public.

The resistance his allies opposed to Roosevelt's ideals, could not be overcome by the infallible instinct and knowledge of his opponent that so often had led him to triumph in internal difficulties. Here other methods were needed; suited to another kind of mentality. Roosevelt was no doubt the most European of all Americans, but this did not help him fully to understand Russia.

Among the arguments leveled against the President by his opponents, arguments which now seem so insignificant, was the inhuman charge that could only enhance his fame, that after so many years of heroic fight against his physical disability, he no longer had the strength to continue fighting. No one said he did not have the spirit.

In trying to embrace the whole of his life, one is impressed by its unmistakable grandeur. And if we add that Roosevelt's true legacy to his successor and to all American people was the command to fight to the end for the freedom of man and of the peoples, we shall have emphasized that which was most important in his life's work.

Rising above understandable passion, what Poles want to remember above all at this moment is the voice full of deep concern in which Roosevelt spoke of the concessions he had had to make at Yalta, and that his last act in the Polish matter was to refuse recognition to the Lublin impostor.[2]

---

[2] The *Tymczasowy Rząd Rzeczypospolitej Polskiej* [Provisional Government of the Republic of Poland], created under Soviet auspices from Communist and left-leaning Poles in the Soviet Union on 31

The victory we celebrate today — the paean of triumph mingling with the funeral dirge — will be genuine only if it places the world on a new road, if the United States in the realization of its strength and its stupendous war effort will build peace on those same principles in defense of which President Roosevelt led it into war and gave his own life.

Then only then will President Roosevelt's work gain the highest reward to which man can aspire: the blessing of posterity.

December 1944. It moved west with the Soviet troops, eventually installing itself in Lublin, before the complete liberation of the country. Later, the Western powers, headed by Churchill's Great Britain, induced Stanisław Mikołajczyk to lend his countenance to the pro-Soviet puppet government, which he had eventually to flee for his life once it ensconced itself in power.

Caviar and Machine Guns[1]

In their reports on the arrival of the Russian delegation in San Francisco some papers included an information of no mean interest to the gourmets of this country. They stated that Mr. Molotoff's[2] coming will soon be followed by the arrival of a boat loaded with vodka and caviar which are synonymous, in American opinion, with the splendor and exquisite taste of the Russian cuisine. The report appears to us incomplete. The cargo of said boat was surely not limited to vodka and caviar. It included, most probably, all kinds of "pyeroshkis", griddle-cakes (bliny), innumerable smoked fish, and possibly that legendary "labardan" mentioned by Gogol.

Not even the fiercest enemies of Russia will refuse to recognize the subtle qualities of her cuisine. We know of refined people who, though impervious to the charms of Chekoff, delight in "blinys" (Griddle-cakes) with caviar and sour cream. We have American friends who, though insensible to Prokofyeffs compositions, have not enough words of praise for smoked sturgeon. Many noisy admirers of Dostoyefski value a Russian borshch higher than the *Karamazoff Brothers*. Not a few noted New York journalists prefer, as a matter of fact, a "koolebyak" with cabbage to Stravinsky's *Pietroushka*.

Mr. Molotoff chose propaganda methods which, though less refined, are apt to serve Russian interests in America better

---

[1] First published in the *Tygodnik Polski*, 1945 no 19 (124) pp. 10-11. Article occasioned by the founding congress of the United Nations, held in San Francisco, 25 April—26 June 1945, to which no Polish representatives were invited.

[2] Vyacheslav Molotoff (Molotov, actually W.M. Skriabin, (1890-1986). Longtime Soviet diplomat, Foreign Minister of the USSR 1939-1949, 1953-1957. Especially hated by Poles for the Ribbentrop-Molotov Pact, which foresaw the fourth partition of Poland between Nazi Germany and the USSR, a fact accomplished by the German invasion of Poland on September 1, 1939, and the subsequent Soviet invasion from the East sixteen days later.

than new Shostakovich symphonies to which State Department officials (having no ear for music), and distinguished ladies, secretly in love with Sinatra' s crooning, had to listen for the few past years, with a feigned pious interest.

It goes without saying that this sort of propaganda is bound to be more efficacious in view of the fact that Russia has actually but one Shostakowich, while her supply of sturgeons is almost unlimited. It also would be hard for her to produce another Prokofyeff, while there is no limit to the number of "koolebyaks" her chefs may concoct to satisfy the demand of Russia's foreign policies.

The methods which Mr. Molotoff proposes to apply at San Francisco are not new. Not unlike all Russian policies, they have been inherited by the Bolsheviks from Tsarist days as reflected in Lubitch's[3] recent production, *The Royal Scandal*. Mr. Molotoff wants to dazzle and win over Messrs. Stettinius and Eden[4] by the same means that were used by the Tsars of old: by appeals to the palate of his guests. At such occasions Peter the Great addressed his butlers, most probably, exactly as premier Stalin does today. The lamented major Cazalet[5] reported that at a banquet offered to General Sikorski[6] at the Kreml, the latter had, after sixteen courses, declared that he could not eat any more.

---

[3] Ernst Lubitsch (1892-1947).   German film director based in Hollywood.   His films include *Lady Windermere's Fan* and *Ninotschka*, the latter starring Greta Garbo.   Illness forced Lubitsch to withdraw from *A Royal Scandal* [*sic*], which was then finished by Otto Preminger.

[4] Edward R. Stettinius (1900-1949).   Secretary of State 1944-1945, first US delegate to the UN 1945-1946.   Anthony Eden, first Earl of Avon (1897-1977).   Foreign Secretary 1935-1938, 1940-1945, 1951-1955, Prime Minister 1955-1957.

[5] Colonel Victor Cazalet (1896-1943), British liaison officer to General Sikorski.   He perished with Sikorski in the aircraft accident off Gibraltar on July 4, 1943.

[6] Władysław Sikorski (1881–1943), Polish general and statesman, head of Polish government-in-exile in London until his untimely death in an airplane crash off Gibraltar.

Hereupon the "little sun of the people" turned towards the serving comrade, and said: "Ubieraj astalnoje k'czortu".[7]

The barrels of caviar, the smoked fish, the "koolebyaks," "siomgas," "sigis," "pyeroshkis" etc., were brought over to San Francisco for the purpose to attest to Russia's willingness to collaborate with the United Nations, to bear witness to her spirit of cooperation and the sincerity of her friendly feelings. These savoury titbits have also to convince foreigners that all the inhabitants of Russia are rich and happy. Perhaps not all of them have as high living standards as Messrs. Stalin and Molotoff, yet, all citizens of the sixteen Soviet Republics enjoy at least as much freedom and happiness as the citizens of America — while their cuisine is by far superior. In the present political situation the "delicatessen" brought to San Francisco by Mr. Molotoff will serve as samples of that prosperity and affluence which is in store for Mr. Beneš's Czech followers, for the Yugoslavs who renounced King Peter, and for those Poles who believe that Mr. Osubka[8] is a true democrat.

But there is a rub: there are foreigners who know more of Russia than those Allied ambassadors whose acquaintance with Russian conditions has, as its only source, propaganda pictures, and banquets at the Kreml. There are nations who, by destiny's order, have been for centuries Russia's neighbors, and who are well informed of what was going on in the past in that land of liberty; nations knowing full well what is actually going on in Russian homes while Red Army marshals smash their glasses in honor of foreign guests; there are people who know the exact number of Soviet slaves, Poles, Ukrainians White-Ruthenians and Russians starving to death at that very hour

---

[7] "Go to Hell with the rest" (Lechoń's translation).

[8] Eduard Beneš (1884-1948). Czech politician. Unwilling to sign the imposed Soviet-style constitution, he resigned the presidency of Czechoslovakia in 1948. King Peter II Karađorđević, (reg. 1934-1945), Edward Osóbka-Morawski (1909-1997). Served as premier of the Soviet-supported postwar Polish government from 1944-1947.

when Mr. Molotoff treats Mr. Stettinius to caviar, just as he did treat five years ago Mr. Ribbentrop.[9]

Can an average simple-minded American who looks at the brilliant stars and epaulets of Russian generals, and peruses the fabulous menus of the banquets Mr. Molotoff offers the American delegation to persuade them to recognize Mr. Bierut's[10] "government" — can such an American, we repeat, realize that the government which displays such a splendor of jewelry, and such culinary luxuries, — that this is the same government which in 1932-33 had for political ends, starved to death six million Ukrainians?

How can a good-hearted New York or Philadelphia citizen who had been told by newspapers that Poland was a country of feudal landowners, that her socialist Prime-minister Arciszewski[11] used to beat up "his" peasants, and that President Raczkiewicz[12] (who has always been a poor man) maintained great racing stables, — how can such an American citizen after reading reports on the splendid receptions given by Soviet diplomats, believe that Russia is the only country in the world, which has restored ancient slavery in its most cruel form, a country whose war production is mostly the work of slaves, a country where no man can move from one place to another

---

[9] Joachim von Ribbentrop (1893-1946). Foreign Minister of the Third Reich from 1938, co-signer of the Ribbentrop-Molotov Pact in August 1939.

[10] Bolesław Bierut (1982-1956). Polish Communist, head of the puppet government installed by the USSR at the conclusion of World War II. He ruled Poland during its brief night of Stalinism.

[11] Tomasz Arciszewski (1877-1955). Legionnaire, deputy President and Prime Minister of the Polish Government-in-Exile (London) 1944-1947.

[12] Władysław Raczkiewicz (1885-1947). The Presidency of Poland was transferred to him on September 27, 1939, by President Ignacy Mościcki (who had been President during the catastrophe of September 1939). He thus became the first President of the Polish Government in Exile.

without an official permit; that no individual in the USSR is allowed to occupy an apartment of more than two rooms?!

Doing his best to convince ignorant and naive people that Soviet Russia is a country of freedom and happiness, Mr. Molotoff involuntarily contradicted himself when he asked the American authorities to place at his disposal an armored limousine and another car equipped with a machine gun, to serve as an escort. Mr. Molotoff obviously considers Americans as well as the representatives of the free nations assembled in San Francisco, an ignorant and servile mob. For how could he otherwise fail to see that in a free country armored limousines and machine guns are not synonymous with freedom? How could he delude himself, asking for such a Hitler or Mussolini-like protection, that he could be mistaken by citizens of a free country for a conqueror of totalitarianism and an apostle of democracy?

It appears most probable that the cautious Soviet commissar has tried to persuade American authorities that his demand was justified by "Polish fascism raging in the United States," and apt to arrange some public manifestations in order to make it impossible to Polish masses to enjoy the blessings of Soviet freedom. He was undoubtedly aware that Polish "fascists" or their foreign sympathizers had frequently hindered in the past the expansion of Russian democracy. He had, perhaps, in mind Floquet's[13] memorable words of welcome addressed to the „Tsar Liberator" in Paris: "Vive la Pologne, Monsieur!"

Mr. Molotoff seems to be afraid to receive a similar welcome in this country. And his fear is rather justified, for he is too well informed as to what happened to two million Polish citizens deported by his government to Siberia. He, unquestionably, knows how many prominent and kind-hearted Polish citizens have died there of starvation and because of mental tortures. Mr. Molotoff cannot be ignorant of what has happened to several thousands Polish army officers whose

---

[13] Charles-Thomas Floquet (1828-1896). French lawyer, journalist and senator.

murdered bodies were found in the Katyń forest.[14] He surely knows how many Polish fighters for freedom, how many underground heroes who for years had opposed the Germans, are being daily deported from Poland to northern Russia, and by what means the Soviets try to compel Polish leaders to agree to their country's perdition!. . .

Nor has Mr. Molotoff forgotten that the partitioning line of martyrized heroic Poland had been drawn by him and his associate, Mr. Ribbentrop, in the very moment when Poland, alone in Europe, was fighting German totalitarianism. He surely remembers too, that while Germany was ravaging Poland, he was treating Ribbentrop to Russian delicacies, and openly repeating Mussolini's declaration: "Poland has ceased to exist."

Having all that in mind and having no fear for his personal safety, Mr. Molotoff must feel astonished that none of the representatives of free nations has protested against the wrongs that are being done to the most courageous, the most indomitable fighters for the World's freedom — that no such voice was raised at San Francisco while national anthems of the great democracies were welcoming him who, but a few years ago, was eulogizing Russia's Alliance with Germany, and uttering little flattering words about British "imperialism."

Mr. Molotoff has been eavesdropping such a protest, and, perhaps, also the outcry of those Russian slaves who in 1941 bade a desperate farewell to their liberated Polish companions of misery: "Do not forget us!"

Mr. Molotoff knows what many most generous Americans have never been told — and Mr. Eden pretends to

---

[14] Until the 1990s, the official Russian version of the Katyń massacre of some 10,000 Polish officers, prisoners of war, was that this had been a Nazi crime. Forensics have proven since the very discovery of the mass graves that, on the contrary, these men had been murdered by the Soviet NKVD, upon their having been taken prisoner by the Soviets after the September 17, 1939 invasion of Poland. Only recently have the Russians admitted culpability — although they still refuse to cooperate fully in the ongoing investigation of the crime.

have forgotten — that Suvoroff had crossed the Alps, that Aleksandr's I Army had been billeted in Paris, and yet that Nicholas I was afterwards beaten by the Turks, Kuropatkin by the Japs. Grand Duke Nicholas by the Germans and Budienny by the Poles; that consequently no Russian victory has proved that Russia is a country which may with impunity blackmail the world.[15]

Mr. Molotoff is also fully aware of what would have happened to Russia were it not for America's help, for American war-materials, for American Lend-Lease, for American military assistance, for American's second, third, and forth fronts.

And this is why Mr. Molotoff carries to San Francisco so much vodka and caviar to convince gullible democracies that Russia does not ask the world for anything, that, on the contrary, she is willing to present them with some of her liberties and of her caviar. But at the same time Mr. Molotoff asks for an armored limousine, not just that he would fear for his life, but just because he does not want to hear that outcry which must resound sooner or later, if the world has to enjoy freedom, if the San Francisco Conference shall not be the burial place of our civilization: "Long live Poland, Mr. Molotoff!"

---

[15] Lechoń provides a catalogue of Russian military defeats from the Napoléonic years to the recent Polish-Soviet War of 1920-1921.

General Bór-Komorowski in New York[1]

General Bór-Komorowski is a symbol, the symbol of Warsaw, the symbol of the underground struggle, he is the commander-in-chief of the Polish Armed Forces, and thus the voice of all those Polish soldiers who from the first day of the War until the last fought stubbornly for your and our liberty, who achieved freedom for others, but who themselves cannot today return to their homeland.

That which General Bór-Komorowski symbolizes, that with which he linked his name and life forever, is all that which is dearest to the heart of every Pole, without which he cannot live and for which he is always ready to lay down his life: Country, Honor, Freedom, Justice.

Therefore, when the General is among us today, when we welcome him in New York, there appears before our eyes, evoked by his figure, the picture of Polish heroism in this war, of all the struggles, sacrifice, suffering, hope and terrible disappointments of the Polish nation: the Picture of Warsaw, indomitable as no other city of the world and perishing by treason unparalleled in world history.

He who would have even for a moment forgotten what befell Poland, who even for a moment of deceptive security and selfish comfort would have forgotten the services rendered by the Polish nation to the cause of freedom, the terrible injustice done to it, he whose personal cares or successes would have obscured even for a moment the picture of Warsaw perishing in flames because the Red Army did not want to cross a few miles separating it from the Polish capital — upon learning that General Bór-Komorowski is among us experiences, as it were, a dazzling of his imagination, a shock of conscience, and if he is truly a Pole, if he is a free spirit and a just man, he feels that he has only one thought, one desire — to do everything in his

---

[1] First published in the *Tygodnik Polski*, 1946 no 21 (178) p. 3, for the occasion of the General's tour of the U.S. in May of that year.

power to gladden the souls of those who died and to console those who remained in Poland.

General Bór-Komorowski has come to remind us of our duty. By the very sound of his name he penetrated the depth of our souls and caused everyone of us to take the solemn pledge that he would not rest, would not indulge in his deceptive personal happiness until Poland will be free again, complete, independent.

General Bór-Komorowski does not only speak to us, he has not only come to visit the America of Polish descent and the Poles residing in the United States. He is also greeted by representatives of the authorities, mayors, United States military leaders, therefore he is also a guest of America and addresses her and speaks to her as well.

His visit here is a reminder of the obligations that the United States has taken upon itself in the face of the world when entering the war for its liberation from totalitarian bondage, obligations confirmed in the Atlantic Charter and resulting from the entire history of this great country, from its very structure, the very nature of American democracy.

The United States has not yet fulfilled this obligation and by the pacts of Teheran and Yalta consented to a new bondage of Europe, a new partition and martyrdom of the Polish nation. What is taking place in Poland today is not only a result of the Soviet invasion, but also a consequence of the fact that the United States and Great Britain have broken their pledge given to the world, given to Poland, given to their own sons, their own soldiers.

Sooner than the greatest pessimists could foresee it became evident that the ominous world to which the United States and Great Britain have given their consent turns against themselves, that the godless and inhuman tyranny which plunged half of Europe into the darkness of a new slavery did not wait even a moment to turn against England and America, and the enemy who was permitted a year ago to seize and loot. Poland stands today at the gates of the British Empire and inside America.

If therefore by his visit General Bór-Komorowski awakens the conscience of this country, when he reminds it of the abandonment of Poland, the fate of the Polish Army, the misery of the Poles, he does not only speak in behalf of our cause, he does not only recall the injustice done to us, but becomes the spokesman of the truths to which all citizens of the United States owe their freedom, and this country its victory and power.

The cause of freedom is one: there is one freedom for all men and for all nations. The Polish Armed Forces, the Polish Home Army have fulfilled to the utmost limits of martyrdom, heroism and sacrifice the duties they had taken upon themselves to put these truths into effect. The Poles died for the freedom of France, Italy, Great Britain, Holland, the United States, convinced that freedom, integrity and independence would be restored to Poland.

General Bór-Komorowski is the voice of those soldiers, of the living and of those who died for Poland. He is among us, he is in the United States, to make this voice heard, to refer to the pledge given to Poland by the great American nation, to demand that this pledge be kept, to demand a free, complete and independent Poland.

A "Polish" Epilogue
BEATA DOROSZ

In August 1941, as a mature man and a well-known and acclaimed poet, Jan Lechoń arrived in New York. At that time he already had ten years of diplomatic experience in France, and a year in Brazil spent on various patriotic endeavors seeking support for Poland in its war with Nazi Germany. Almost from the very first day of his stay in the US he became one of the most important figures in Polish immigrant circles, continuing the fight against the Nazis politically as an exile in the U.S. He engaged in many patriotic political actions that surpassed his usual literary and cultural activity.

Already in September 1941 he presented a paper entitled "Przyszłość kultury polskiej" [The Future of Polish Culture] which was included in a program of the celebration of the 25th anniversary of the Polish Department at Columbia University in New York. In November of the same year appeared the first issue of the *Tygodniowy Serwis Literackiego Koła Pisarzy z Polski* [The Weekly Literary Service of the Writers' Circle of Poland], which was soon transformed into the *Tygodniowy Przegląd Literacki Koła Pisarzy z Polski* [The Weekly Literary Review of the Polish Writers' Circle]. Despite its name, the journal contained not only literary articles, but also information concerning the current political situation, and patriotic writings.

In May 1942, Lechoń was among the founding members of the Polish Institute of Arts and Sciences of America (PIASA), which was created at the moment when Polish art and sciences were facing complete destruction at the hands of the Germans. The Institute was founded by intellectuals, researchers, and writers — many of them members of the Polish Academy of Arts and Sciences [Polska Akademia Umiejętności] in order to facilitate the unobstructed development of Polish arts and sciences and enable Polish immigrant scientists and artists to continue their work in the time of raging European totalitarianism. The group of writers and literary critics chose

361

Lechoń as the vice president of the History of Literature and Art Committee of PIASA. The archival documents concerning the creation and the first years of PIASA activity make it clear beyond any doubt that it was Lechoń who, more than any other outstanding Polish writer in America, helped to write many petitions and stood behind many patriotic actions organized by PIASA in 1942-1943 which at that time (apart from pure research) consisted the core of the Institute's activities. Among many events organized by PIASA was a series of lectures devoted to the history of Polish literature during which Lechoń presented two papers: one, *Powieść od Młodej Polski do czasów ostatnich* [The History of the Novel from the Young Poland Period to the Present] and the second *O poezji polskiej XVIII wieku* [Polish Poetry in the Eighteenth Century]. Even though he had no university degree, he was among many literary Polish and foreign scholars invited to participate in a series dealing with several national literatures. In the introduction to his lecture about Polish literature, in March 1943, Prof. Wacław Lednicki, the head of History of Literature and Art Committee, called him a "Polish poetic genius" lending legitimacy to Lechoń's lectures on the historical and moral interpretation of the Polish literary heritage.

Need one say how much Lechoń's lectures deviated from university standards? Of course, nobody expected him to observe such standards, and the lectures naturally expressed his literary tastes. At the same time he stressed values that mattered to him personally, such as patriotism. For both audience and poet, the lectures meant a nostalgic return to the longed-for homeland. Such too was the moving talk he delivered at a special session devoted to Warsaw, organized in October 1944 in New York after the news about the tragedy of the Warsaw Uprising had reached the US. That extremely emotional talk titled "The Charm of Warsaw," inspired Prof. Lednicki to refer to it as "a child of Warsaw."

It seems that the 1945 PIASA Convention, organized on May 3, the Polish national holiday and entirely devoted to Adam

Mickiewicz, was of special political and patriotic significance. We can surmise that Lechoń's formulation of the convention's theme — *Mickiewicz wczoraj i dziś* [Mickiewicz Yesterday and Today], was not lacking in extra-literary meanings, given the political context of that time.

Further, in 1953, PIASA initiated the creation of the Polish-American Committee for the celebration of Mickiewicz's approaching centenary. This initiative was crowned with a special collection of essays dealing with the leading Polish Romantic poet, published in 1955. Lechoń's participation in these endeavors was not coincidental since his admiration for Mickiewicz was well known, and he often expressed it publicly in his lectures and *Journal* entries.

In July 1943, a year after PIASA's creation, Lechoń became one of the founding members of The Józef Piłsudski Institute in America, also located in New York, which was planned as a scholarly institution with a focus on contemporary Polish history.

It seems natural that during World War II, and later during the Communist régime's reign in Poland, the Institute not only encouraged free scholarly research projects, but also, and perhaps primarily, concentrated on the struggle for a free and independent Poland. Many of its members belonged to the pre-war "Sanacja" circles with which Lechoń shared political sympathies and the immigrant ethos. He had many personal contacts with them and was really dedicated to the Institute's work.

The political situation and Lechoń's strong patriotism meant that he did not limit himself to the narrow group of new immigrants to the US. He also became an important figure for the Kongres Narodowy Amerykanów Polskiego Pochodzenia [KNAPP, The National Congress of American Citizens of Polish Origin]. Not only did he write his own texts for the Congress' bulletin, but also often authored speeches for various members of the Congress delivered during official celebrations. The most interesting and significant fact is that he wrote two important

363

documents: one was the *Deklaracja ideowa* [Ideological Declaration] accepted at the Opening Session of the Congress in June 1942 which stressed the non-acceptance of the imposed territorial changes of the Polish borders after September 1939, and the rejection of the new world order which was instituted against Polish interest and without Polish consent. The second document *An Appeal to Franklin Delano Roosevelt, President of The United States of America on Behalf of Poland, Prepared in Commemoration of the Death of Joseph Piłsudski. Presented by the Delegation of American Citizens of Polish Origin at the White House*, dated May 21, 1942 in commemoration of the seventh anniversary of Józef Piłsudski's death, was written in the spirit of his thought. It showed the tragic history of independent Poland, and in the name of "History, Law, and Blood" called for justice and the maintenance of the "sacred borders from before1939." In 1947, the Congress presented another dramatic appeal to President Harry Truman, also authored by Lechoń, demanding justice for Poland. This happened after Truman's statement in defense of Greece and Turkey against Communism. Similarly, the well-known Polish-American Congress, founded in 1944 as an organization representing the interests of American Polonia to American authorities during and after the war, focused to a great extent on the political situation of Poland at that time. In 1945 Lechoń proposed the project of a *Ślubowanie* — an Oath of Allegiance for this organization, and also drafted an *Odezwa do Polonii* [An Appeal to Polonia] in which the Congress asked for financial and moral support for Poland, and especially for "the constant spreading of truth about the Polish nation's martyrdom" and enslavement by the Soviet régime. He also wrote "the emotional and patriotic" section for Congress President Karol Rozmarek's speech for the Congress Convention.

All these organizations were welcome to publish in the *Tygodnik Polski* [Polish Weekly], a journal published by Lechoń in New York during 1943-1947. As the magazine's editor, the poet stressed not only the necessity of integration of the Polish literary community in the United States, but also the need to integrate American Polonia with the war Diaspora. Equally important for him was the issue of Polish-American cultural dialogue. Lechoń propagated the ethos of patriotism both among the old Polonia and the new wave of Polish immigrants. Emphasizing the necessity of struggle for free Poland, he instigated the reaction against the enslavement of the Polish minds by the Communist régime; he demanded freedom for the arts and sciences, and at the same time stressed how the Polish intellectual tradition always emphasized actual political action.

The end of World War II and the stabilization of the new political order in post-war Europe changed Lechoń's status from war refugee to political immigrant. Separated by thousands of kilometers from his homeland, he had been dedicating all his efforts and poems to Poland. "Unbending and uncompromising" towards the post-war Communist régime in Poland, he worked as an editor of the *Tygodnik Polski* and, after its demise, for the Voice of America. Later he was one of the best-known voices at the Polish Desk of Radio Free Europe in New York. His activity gained full approval of the American political establishment, which appreciated Lechoń's personality and his position in the Polish Diaspora.

It is worth remembering that Radio Free Europe was founded by the National Committee for a Free Europe, established in June 1949 under the auspices of the Department of State, with the future president Dwight Eisenhower and Allen Dulles as its leaders. Formally the Committee was registered in New York as a not-for-profit organization, but in reality it was financed by the government. Its goal was to support "non-Communist" and non-fascist" immigration leaders from Central/Eastern Europe whose activity in the "free world" (including the radio) was directed to the people behind the Iron Curtain.

Formally, Lechoń was not employed by the National Committee for a Free Europe, but even before the creation of the Radio Free Europe he freelanced for the committee. Later, as a radio journalist, Lechoń participated in numerous discussions about culture, literature, and art — Polish, European and American — in a popular program called *The Voice of Free Writers*. He was the author of many propaganda texts and political commentaries. It may be interesting to many people, (and Lechoń's radio colleagues may have forgotten about it) that he was first to adapt George Orwell's *1984* for radio performance. For many years this novel was surrounded by a special fame (today we might call it a "cult" novel) in the countries of the Soviet bloc. In Lechoń's adaptation *1984* was on the air as a series beginning in November 1949. In this way Lechoń preceded by thirty years the book's underground editions in Poland.

Volumes have been written about the role of Radio Free Europe in instigating political changes in Eastern Europe — therefore it is important to note that our Polish poet was one link in that unusual organization.

When support from the Polish government-in-exile in London dried up, and after the *Tygodnik Polski* ceased publication, work in the radio was the only source of a stable (even if not so regular) income for Lechoń. In light of the difficulties encountered by thousands of Polish immigrants in America, Lechoń's situation was a bit privileged. Aware of the living conditions among the Polish community, in March 1955 the poet appealed for the creation of a support organization designed to help new Polish immigrants in the United States, who at that time numbered around ten thousand people. In this manner, as the documents put it, he became "the main initiator, founder, and spiritual creator" of the organization Polska Bratnia Pomoc [Polish Assistance]. Paradoxically, the first action of the PBP was the organization of the poet's funeral in June 1956. According to Prof. Jerzy Krzywicki, one of the poet's friends and the executor of his estate, the funding was unofficially granted by Radio Free Europe.

The memorial celebrations held at St. Stanislaus Bishop and Martyr Church on 7th Street in Manhattan and the funeral at the First Calvary Cemetery in Queens were not only a farewell to a great poet, but also a huge patriotic manifestation. At that time, PIASA performed a very important task for the deceased poet, namely, it took custody of Lechoń's papers, which remain one of the most precious treasures of Polish culture in the Diaspora. The "Lechoń Archives" at the PIASA headquarters in the Murray Hill section of Manhattan constitute at the present moment the largest and the most significant collection of papers documenting Lechoń's life and work. It is composed of a "life portion," which includes objects from his last apartment in New York (such as furniture, paintings, books, official and personal documents), and a literary portion.

Lechoń's library contains a priceless collection of book dedications that can serve as the foundation for many research projects dealing with Lechoń's reading preferences and the traces of other authors in his work.

The collection of private correspondence contains 2200 items and represents a practically bottomless source of biographical information. A rich collection of business cards and his "Guest Book," kept from his days in Paris, is an interesting addition to his private correspondence.

On the other hand, his official correspondence shows the presence of Lechoń's engagement in the political life of the Polish immigrant community (such as the Polish National Congress, or the Józef Piłsudski Institute). It also contains the *Tygodnik Polski* and sections relating to his other employments (for instance in the National Committee for a Free Europe and Radio Free Europe).

The personal documents (among them his passport, ID cards from various institutions, medical and financial statements), when meticulously examined, unveil seminal and often new facts about the poet's life.

Most fascinating is always the encounter with Lechoń's manuscripts. It was among these piles of paper that the author of this essay discovered the unknown one act play *Ksiądz i Bolszewicy* [The Priest and the Bolsheviks] and eight previously

367

unknown poems. The analysis of loose pieces of paper and thick copybooks covered with tiny, difficult to read handwriting, discloses a new face of Lechoń as a political writer, the author of film treatments, a parodist and the radio journalist adapting other texts for radio. The collection also enriches our image of Lechoń as playwright and novelist. These materials, however, have to be properly organized and researched for publication so that we can compare them with the already published dramatic and prose fragments.

Other archival materials about Lechoń are still in the possession of private individuals and institutions in America such as The Józef Piłsudski Institute in New York, The Central Archives of Polonia in Orchard Lake, Michigan, the Hoover Institution on War, Revolution and Peace at Stanford University in California, the Rare Books and Manuscripts Library at Columbia University in New York, and the Houghton Library at Harvard University in Cambridge, Massachusetts.

The full picture of Lechoń's life and creative activity can be achieved by collecting the information from all these sources dispersed in the United States. It has to be stressed, however, that PIASA in New York, due to its Lechoń archives and other collections of archival documents, is the unquestionable center of all research about the poet. The creation of a serious, scholarly work embracing the totality of Lechoń's life and work cannot be achieved without the thorough examination of the PIASA archives.

Here, I would like to express my gratitude to The Kościuszko Foundation in New York whose support (a 1998 grant and a fellowship in 2000) enabled me to undertake research of the Lechoń's archives in PIASA. I am extremely thankful to Mr. Joseph Gore, Kościuszko Foundation President, to Prof. Felix Gross, the President of PIASA at the time of my research, to Prof. Piotr Wandycz, his successor, and to Prof. Thaddeus Gromada, the Executive Director of PIASA. I am also grateful to all employees of the Institute who were always eager to advise and help me.

The publication of the present book in the "PIASA Books" series is partly an outcome of the cooperation between PIASA and myself — a scholar from Poland. It also contributes to the celebrations of the 50th anniversary of Lechoń's death in New York. In 1999, PIASA celebrated the centenary of Lechoń's birth with a special exhibit of Lechoń's souvenirs and a session during its yearly conference. New York celebrations of Lechoń's anniversaries prove that the special connection between the Institute and the poet lives on and reminds us that he was not only one of its most eminent members, but also that his memory in the Institute community is still vivid. His memory manifests itself not only in the special care afforded the documentation of his literary estate, but especially in the way that it preserves the legacy of his status as the leading poet (*wieszcz*) of the "second Polish immigration."

—- Translated by Krystyna Iłłakowicz

Chronicle of Major Events
in Jan lechoń's Life

1899 March 13	Leszek Serafinowicz, later known as Jan Lechoń, is born.
1912	First collection of poems, *Na złotym polu* [On a Golden Field] published.
1916	Passes the *Matura* (the baccalaureate, or final high school exam).
1916 –1918	Begins courses in the Polish Department at Warsaw University (He did not finish his studies).
1917 - 1918	Becomes a member of the editorial board of the student magazine "Pro Arte et Studio."
1918	Publishes a volume of poetic satires *Królewsko-Polski Kabaret 1917- 1918* [The Royal Polish Cabaret 1917-1918]; is one of the organizers of the famous poets' cafe "Under the Picador."
1918	Together with Antoni Słonimski, publishes *Facecje republikańskie* [Republican Follies], a collection of satires in prose and verse. Co-founds the poetic group "Skamander," and later the journal *Skamander*.
1920	Publishes a collection of poems *Karmazynowy poemat* [Crimson Poem] and a collection of satires in prose and verse *Rzeczpospolita babińska, Śpiewy historyczne* [The Babińska Republic: Historical Songs]
1921 March	Lechoń's first suicide attempt.
1924	*Srebrne i czarne* [Silver and Black], a collection of poems.
1924	Receives Polish Book Publishers' literary prize.

1926	Participates in the session of the League of Nations as a correspondent of the journal *Głos Prawdy* [The Voice of Truth].
1926 - 1928	Works as an editor of the major satirical weekly *Cyrulik Warszawski* [The Warsaw Barber].
1928 - 1929	Elected secretary-general of the Polish PEN Club.
1930	Receives the "Krzyż Oficerski Orderu Odrodzenia Polski" [Officer's Cross of Polonia Restituta] medal. In April, leaves for Paris.
1935	Receives "Złoty Wawrzyn" [The Golden Laurel], an award presented by The Polish Academy of Literature.
1940 January -March	Lectures about Polish literature in the Polish Library in Paris, as a part of the Polish University Abroad. The lectures were published as *O literaturze polskiej* [About Polish Literature].
1940 June - August	Leaves France through Spain and Portugal, finally arrives in Brazil.
1941 August	Arrives in New York.
1941 - 1942	Together with Kazimierz Wierzyński and Józef Wittlin co-edits the "Tygodniowy Serwis Literacki Koła Pisarzy z Polski" [The Weekly Literary Service of the Writers' Circle of Poland], later transformed into the "Tygodniowy Przegląd Literacki Koła Pisarzy z Polski" [The Weekly Literary Review of the Polish Writers' Circle].
1942 May	Acts as a founding member of PIASA and the Vice-president of the Committee of History of Literature of PIASA.

1942	Publishes a collection of poems *Lutnia po Bekwarku* [Bekwark's Lute].
1943 July	Founding member of The Józef Piłsudski Institute of America.
1943 - 1947	Publishes and edits *Tygodnik Polski* [Polish Weekly] in New York.
1945	Publishes a collection of poems *Aria z kurantem* [Aria with a Currant]
1946	Publishes a children's story *Historia o jednym chłopczyku i o jednym lotniku* [A Story of the Little Boy and the Pilot].
1948	Collaborates with Mieczysław Grydzewski's *Wiadomości*, London.
1949 August	Begins writing his *Journal*, which he will continue until the last days of his life.
1949	Participates in the programs of The Voice of America and, from 1952, collaborates with Radio Free Europe. One of his programs was a series entitled *Głos wolnych pisarzy* [The Voice of Free Writers].
1952	Receives the Award of the Polish Writers' Union in London.
1954	Publishes *Collected Poems 1916-1953*.
1955	Publishes a literary essay *Mickiewicz* and an essay about American culture *Aut Caesar aut nihil*. (In 1959 it appeared in English translation as *American Transformations*).
1956, June 8	Commits suicide by jumping from the fourteenth floor of the Henry Hudson Hotel in New York. Buried on June 12 in Calvary Cemetery in the borough of Queens.
1991	Lechoń's ashes deposited in the family tomb in the Laski Cemetery near Warsaw, Poland.

Editor's Note

The title of the present volume comes from an entry in Jan Lechoń's *Dziennik* [Journal] dated October 14, 1953.

The main intention of this volume is to present the reader with the poems written during Lechoń's years in the United States (1940-1956). There are three exceptions to this general rule: the first is the poem "Easter" written in the Spring of 1940 in Paris, printed in the journal *Polska Walcząca* [Fighting Poland, 7/8, 1940], one of the first Polish periodicals published during World War II outside Poland. The poems "To, w co tak trudno nam uwierzyć..." ["It may be hard to fathom now"] and "Od żalu nie uciekniesz" ["There's no escape from sorrow. . ."] were composed in the Spring 1941 in Rio de Janeiro, and first appeared in the London journal *Wiadomości polskie polityczne i literackie* [Polish Political and Literary News, 1941, nos. 16 and 20]. I decided to include these three poems in the present selection because they are representative of Lechoń's inability to accept Poland's defeat and his immigrant suffering, first in France and then in Brazil. These poems were included in Lechoń's first collection of poems published outside of Poland, *Bekwark's Lute*, printed in London by M.I. Kolin in 1942 and prepared for publication in the U.S. This collection is the basis for the present edition.

In general, the poems follow each other in chronological order. However, I have used two symbolic "frames" which break this scheme. "Bzy w Pennsylvania" [A Lilac-bush in Pennsylvania], the most "American" in spirit and content, opens the collection although, chronologically, it is Lechoń's last poem, published posthumously in *Wiadomości* [no. 270, London, 1956]. Secondly, in the poet's archives in PIASA, I found in 1998 a fragment of a poem "Weroniko nie myj plamy" ["Veronica, wash not the stains"] that Lechoń was working on since 1951 and never finished. It was previously unknown and was published for the first time in my book *Lechoń Nowojorski* [Lechoń of New York, co-edited with Maciej Patkowski; New

York, Warszawa: Oficyna Wydawnicza "Piast," 1999]. It was also published in "Pamiętnik Literacki", the quarterly of the Institute of Literary Research of the Polish Academy of Sciences [Instytut Badań Literackich Polskiej Akademii Nauk, 1999 no. 3].

All other poems appear in chronological order as in other anthologies of Lechoń's poetry. From the very start of the project I declined to resort to a tempting and attractive thematic organization of the volume (such as is explored in many contemporary anthologies) because Lechoń himself was against such an approach. Thus, I follow the order of the *Collected Poems 1916-1953* which he prepared with Mieczysław Grydzewski.

Most poems in the present collection appear in completely new translation, only one having been previously published: "Our Lady of Częstochowa" [Matka Boska Częstochowska], which was previously published in the anthology *Contemporary Polish Marian Poetry* (London: Poets & Painters Press 1974, translator unknown).

The second part of the book follows Lechoń's American themes from his *Dziennik* [Journal]. Obviously, I was unable to include all the "Americana" found in the *Journal*. The selections show different aspects of Lechoń's observations and familiarize the reader with the poet's intellectual and emotional being. The *Journal*, in three volumes, was first published in London many years after the poet's death: *Volume I, 1949-1950* (Wiadomości, 1967), *Volume II, 1951-1952*, (Wiadomości, Polska Fundacja Kulturalna 1970), *Volume III, 1953-1956* (Polska Fundacja Kulturalna 1973). The Polish edition (ed. Roman Loth, Warsaw: PIW 1992-1993) is the basis for the present collection.

Part III presents the essay *Aut Caesar aut nihil*, that Lechoń was working on during 1953 and 1954, was published for the first time in London in *Wiadomości* (1954 nos. 45-47). It appeared separately in London in 1955, printed by Poets & Painters Press. The American translation of this text, entitled *American Transformations*, with Kazimierz Wierzyński's introduction, was published posthumously in New York (1955) and it is this version that appears in our volume. Due to contradictory evidence, it has proved impossible to solve the mystery of the translator's identity. The poet's best friend, Prof. Jerzy Krzywicki, who knew Lechoń's life and work very well, points to Clark Mills. However, Lechoń's notes mention Franciszek Bauer-Czarnomski. In the New York publication, the translation was not signed.

Part IV, titled *Essays and Articles,* contains shorter texts published in English during Lechoń's life. Since the poet's command of English was inadequate, it is impossible to assume that he translated them himself; unfortunately, it is equally impossible to determine the names of the translators. The reader will find information regarding their provenance in notes to the articles themselves.

— Translated by Krystyna Iłłakowicz

INDEX OF PERSONS AND TITLES
Assembled by Beata Dorosz

Numbers in bold indicate pages containing short biographical notes of selected entries.

Dewey John 79, 125
Diagilev Sergei P. 68
Dickens Charles 301
DiMaggio Joe 72
Disney Walt 84, 116
Długosz Jan **136**
Dostoevsky Fyodor N. (also: Dostoyefski; Dostoyevsky) **103**,
129, 149, 189, 248, 250, 257, 298, 309, 351
    The Brothers Karamazow [or: *Karamazoff Brothers*] 129,
247, 351
Draper Ruth **164**
Dreiser Theodore 170
Dreyfus Alfred 175
Drucki-Lubecki Franciszek Ksawery **273**
Duhamel Georges **163**
Dulles Allen 197, 369
Dumas Alexander 251
Dybowski Benedykt **302**
Dziewanowski Marian Kamil 137

E

Eakins Thomas 77, 90
Edgar Allan *see* Poe Edgar Allan
Eden Anthony **352**
Einstein Albert 147
Eisenhower Dwight David XIII, 72, 90, 123, 128, 131, 132, 134,
135, 141, 142, 147, 162, 197, 199, 203, 369
Eliot Thomas Stearns 103, 175, **189**
    The Coctail Party 103
Elizabeth I (Queen of England) 289
Eluard Paul [i.e.: Eugène Grindel] **220**
Emerson Ralph Waldo 70, 256
Estreicher Karol Józef **136**

F

G

Iwaszkiewicz Jarosław IX

J

K

Krzemiński Stanisław **302**
Krzesińska Matylda Maria 228
Krzywicki Jerzy 42, 43, 370, 383
Kuncewiczowa Maria **163**
Kuropatkin Aleksei N. 357
Kuszelewska Stanisława 24, 25

L

La Fontanie Jean de 266, 288
Lagneau Jules **191**
Lane Bliss Arthur *see* Bliss-Lane Arthur
Layton Jim 74
    The Battleground 74
Le Roy Mervin VII
Lean David VII
Lednicki Wacław **83**, 137, 255, 321, 366
    Adam Mickiewicz in World Literature [ed.] 321
Léger Alexis Saint-Léger *see* Saint-John Perse
Lehár Ferenc 208
Lehman Cora 76
Leigh Vivien 85
Lelewel Joachim **239**
Lenin Vladimir I. [i.e.: V.I. Uljanov] 315
Leonardo da Vinci 158
Lewis Harry Sinclair
    Babbitt 164
Lewis John L. 198
Li Sygman *see* Rhee Sygman
Lifar Serge [i.e.: Sergei M. Lifarenko] X
Lilpop Felicja *see* Kranc Felicja
Lincoln Abraham 103, 108, 109, 162, 203, 204, 213, 220, 231, 322, 347
Lindbergh Charles Augustus 162
Lipton Elżbieta *see* Wittlin Lipton Elżbieta
Lokhvitskaya Mirra [i.e.: Maria A. Zhyber] **146**

N

O

P

Rej Mikołaj 259, **260**
Rejment Władysław Stanisław *see* Reymont Władysław
Stanisław
Renan Ernest **199**, 202
Renoir Auguste 100
Reszke Edward **95**
Reuter Walter **198**
Reymont Władysław Stanisław VII, **245**, 251, 255, 272, 274,
275
    Chłopi [The Peasants] VII, 245, 251, 255, 272, 274, 275
Rhee Sygman [i.e.: Li Sygman] **98**
Rhodes Dusty 162
Ribbentrop Joachim 351, **354**, 356
Ridgway Matthew B. 199
Ripka Hubert **122**
Rittner Tadeusz **208**
Rodziński Artur **85**
Romains Jules [i.e.: Louis Farigoule] 69
Ronsard Pierre de 246, 259, 260
Roosevelt Archibald 168
Roosevelt Franklin Delano 75, 92, 114, 115, 136, 142, 185, 194,
196, 197, 201, 335, 343, 345-349, 368
Roosevelt Theodore 168, 196
Rosen Maria *see* Wszelaki Maria
Rosenberg Ethel **219**
Rosenberg Julius **219**
Rostworowski Emanuel 313
Rostworowski Jan **313**
Rostworowski Karol Hubert 313
Rostworowski Marek 313
Rousseau Jean Jacques 202
Roussin André **188**
Rozmarek Karol 368
Różyczka *see* Bailly Rosa
Rubens Peter Paul 158, 282
Rubinstein Aniela (Nela) **85**

T

U

Forthcoming from PIASA Books:

Fifty Years of The Polish Review, 1955-2005

Edited by Charles S. Kraszewski, and introduced by Joseph W. Wieczerzak.

PIASA Books marks the first fifty years of **The Polish Review,** *the preeminent English-language quarterly devoted to Poland and Polish culture. A generous sampling of important articles originally printed in volumes I-L, from the pens of Czesław Miłosz, Stanisław Barańczak, Oskar Halecki, Józef Wittlin, Kazimierz Wierzyński, Zbigniew Brzezinski and others. Articles chosen represent all fields of scholarly endeavor, from musicology and art history, through history, sociology, literary studies, etc.*

To be available in April, 2006

Forthcoming from PIASA Books:

Grzegorz Szelwach

Listy Adama Mickiewicza (Lata 1817-1833)

An insightful study into the life and thought of Adam Mickiewicz in the formative period of his life (in Polish).

To be available in January, 2006

Forthcoming from PIASA Books:

His Holiness Pope John Paul II: a Commemmorative Volume of Essays Offered by the Polish Institute of Arts and Sciences of America

Including articles by Archbishop Józef Życiński, Prof. Harold Segel, Prof. Piotr Wandycz, Prof. Richard Hunter, Bolesław Taborski, Rev. Janusz Ihnatowicz and others.

To be available in December, 2005

Poland: a Transitional Analysis
Richard J. Hunter, Jr., Leo V. Ryan, C.S.V.
Robert E. Shapiro

Poland:
a Transitional Analysis

Richard J. Hunter, Jr.
Leo V. Ryan, C.S.V.
Robert E. Shapiro

ISBN: 0-940962-63-2

$15.00 ($12.75 for PIASA members), plus shipping and handling: $2.50 per first book (plus .50 for each additional, USPS book rate); $3.50 per first book (plus .50 for each additional, USPS priority).

The authors follow up their 1998 work with an exploration of what has happened to Poland and its Economic Transformation Program almost 15 years after the transition. In this project, Professor Hunter and Brother Ryan are joined by Professor Robert Shapiro to evaluate the impact of foreign direct investment and international trade on the development of Poland's post-communist market system, to assess the evolution of the Polish taxation system, and to appraise Poland's readiness for accession into the EU.

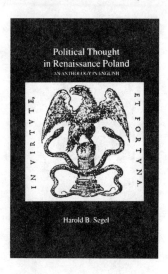